# Contents

**Introduction:** 5 Steps to Your New Car ... 7

**STEP 1: Get the Right Information**

CHAPTER 1: Determine Your Needs & Budget ... 15
CHAPTER 2: Gather the Facts ... 39
CHAPTER 3: Safety Issues & Answers ... 53
CHAPTER 4: Features to Look For ... 79

**STEP 2: Check Out the Cars**

CHAPTER 5: Get the Most From Your Test Drive ... 107
CHAPTER 6: How to Evaluate a Used Car ... 125

**STEP 3: Crunch the Numbers**

CHAPTER 7: Set a Target Price ... 145
CHAPTER 8: Get Top Dollar for Your Trade-In ... 157
CHAPTER 9: Understand Your Insurance Options ... 175

**STEP 4: Arrange Financing**

CHAPTER 10: Find the Best Financing ... 195
CHAPTER 11: Is Leasing for You? ... 213

**STEP 5: Get the Best Deal**

CHAPTER 12: Avoid Dealer Tricks ... 237
CHAPTER 13: Size Up the Dealerships ... 253
CHAPTER 14: Pros & Cons of Buying Online ... 271
CHAPTER 15: Negotiate the Best Price ... 289
CHAPTER 16: Close the Deal ... 305

**After the Sale**

CHAPTER 17: What to Watch for When Taking Delivery ... 325
CHAPTER 18: Save Money on Vehicle Maintenance ... 337
CHAPTER 19: Recalls & Service Problems ... 357

**Appendices**

APPENDIX A: Online Resources ... 373
APPENDIX B: Same Cars, Different Names ... 375
APPENDIX C: Other Car-Buying Resources from CONSUMER REPORTS ... 379

First Printing, August 2005
Copyright © by Consumers Union of United States Inc., Yonkers, N.Y. 10703
Published by the Consumers Union of United States, Inc. Yonkers, N.Y. 10703
All rights reserved, including the right to reproduction in whole or in part in any form.
ISBN: 0-89043-996-6
Manufactured in the United States of America

# Consumer Reports

## SMART BUYER'S GUIDE TO

# BUYING
# OR LEASING
# A CAR

# Consumer Reports®

## SMART BUYER'S GUIDE TO

# BUYING
# OR LEASING
# A CAR

### By Rik Paul & David Champion

Consumer Reports Automotive Experts

CONSUMERS UNION, YONKERS, NEW YORK

# A Special Publication from Consumer Reports

**Editor-in-Chief, Print Products/Senior Director:** Margot Slade
**Editor, Books and Special Publications:** David Schiff
**Group Managing Editor:** Nancy Crowfoot
**Automotive Editor:** Rik Paul
**Coordinating Editor:** Robin Melén
**Coordinating Editor, Autos:** Jonathan Linkov
**Senior Automotive Writer:** Gordon Hard
**Contributing Editors:** Christine Arrington, Lou Richman,
Michael Urban, Dave Van Sickle
**Director, Editorial Operations:** David Fox
**Design Manager:** Rosemary Simmons
**Art Director:** Joseph Ulatowski
**Contributing Art Director:** Wendy Palitz
**Contributing Production Designer:** Vicky Vaughn
**Production Associate:** William Breglio
**Associate Copy Editor:** Wendy Greenfield
**Research:** Margaret Keresey
**Editorial Associate:** Joan Daviet

**AUTO TEST**
**Senior Director:** David Champion
**Facilities Manager:** Alan Hanks
**Senior Engineers:** Jake Fisher, Eugene Petersen, Gabriel Shenhar,
Richard Small, Jennifer Stockburger
**Engineer:** Thomas Mutchler
**Data Program Manager:** Anita Lam
**Data Analyst:** Michael Leung
**Auto Content Specialist:** Michael Quincy
**Support Staff:** Michael Bloch, Frank Chamberlain, Erik Dill, John Ibbotson, Mary Reed,
Shawn Sinclair, Edward Smith, David Van Cedarfield, Joe Veselak

**CONSUMERS UNION**
**President:** James A. Guest
**Executive Vice President:** Joel Gurin
**Vice President and Technical Director:** Jeffrey A. Asher

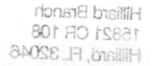

# Introduction

## 5 Steps to Your New Car

**Your mission:** Get the right car … at the best price … with minimum hassle. We can help.

Buying a new car can evoke mixed emotions. It's exciting to picture yourself driving an updated vehicle, perhaps with more features, better performance, or greater versatility than your current car. Maybe a specific model has caught your eye. Or maybe you're looking forward to trying out the many new choices that have become available since the last car you bought.

On the other hand, you might be intimidated by the dealership experience, including the high-pressure sales tactics. Maybe you don't like having to sort through a lot of confusing numbers, and perhaps you fear being manipulated into spending more than you need to.

Or you may be confused by the bewildering range of models in today's automotive market. Every year, many new models are introuced, familiar ones are discontinued, and many others receive major redesigns. With new safety and convenience features being introduced each year, it can be hard to know what's important and what's a waste of money.

## How We Can Help

The automotive experts at CONSUMER REPORTS anonymously buy more than 60 new vehicles each year. We repeatedly go through the process of finding the right vehicle, negotiating the best price, and closing the deal. This book draws on our experience to help you effectively navigate the entire car-buying process, with the sole intent of helping you get the right car for your needs at the best price while minimizing the confusion, intimidation, and frustration.

In this book you'll find in-depth information on every aspect of the car-buying and leasing experience. To ensure that you get the right vehicle at the best price, you do have to invest some time in research and preparation. The entire process can be boiled down to five basic steps that you can tackle at your own pace:

- Narrow your choices by getting the right information.
- Do a thorough test drive.
- Crunch the numbers: Set a target price, learn the value of your trade-in.
- Arrange your financing.
- Contact dealerships and compare offers to get the best price.

If you have time, a reasonable schedule would be to tackle one step per weekend. This would give you ample time to familiarize yourself with the buying landscape and dig into the details that are most important to you. In about five weeks, you'd be ready to buy with the assurance that you had done your homework and know which vehicle is best for your needs, how it should be equipped, and what your target price should be.

If you're in a hurry to get a new car, you can accelerate the process by tackling one step per day and have a new car at the end of a week without compromising on the vehicle or price.

Here's a quick breakdown of each step:

## Step 1: Narrow your choices by getting the right information.

This includes assessing your needs and gathering all the facts to make a good vehicle decision. Chapters 1 through 4 provide detailed information on:

- Assessing which vehicles best fit your lifestyle and budget.
- Where to find critical information on vehicle ratings, reliability, fuel economy, and more.
- How to compare vehicles in terms of overall safety. For instance, did you know that electronic stability control is more important for safety than antilock brakes?
- Choosing features and options that make the most sense without over-inflating the vehicle price.

With the advice offered in these chapters and a few hours spent on the Internet or at home with some printed reference sources, you can hone in on the models, trim levels, and options you should seriously consider.

## Step 2: Get hands-on experience.

No matter how good a model looks on paper, there's no substitute for actually driving it and giving it a thorough walk-around. Once you know which models to concentrate on, you should get some experience with each of them by doing test drives. This is a critical step, yet many car shoppers either skip it or short-change themselves by not giving it sufficient time and attention. As a result, many people can experience buyer's remorse after the sale.

You don't want to find out too late that there's not enough headroom for everyone in the family or that the child safety seat doesn't fit.

Chapter 5 provides advice on how to get the most from your test drive and ensure that you thoroughly experience each vehicle you're considering. Often, it's this step that helps clear up any lingering indecision about which model to buy.

If you're buying a used car, Chapter 6 offers additional information about what to look for when assessing a used vehicle, questions you should ask the seller, and the best way to have it inspected for hidden problems or damage.

### Step 3: Crunch the numbers: Set a target price, learn the value of your trade-in, and select your insurance.

Once you know which model or models you really want to follow through on, you should prepare for the negotiating phase by determining what a good price would be for the vehicle configured the way you want it, and how much you should reasonably expect to receive for your trade-in vehicle, if appropriate.

Chapter 7 provides a road map through the auto-pricing maze, showing you how to:

- Use the Internet to see what different sources are asking for the same vehicle.
- Identify the amount of profit margin a dealer has to negotiate with.
- Take full advantage of rebates and hidden dealer incentives.
- Set a target price with which to begin your dealer negotiations. A reasonable price is 4 percent to 8 percent above the dealer's actual cost figure, which you can find by doing that research.

A good deal on your new car, however, can be easily negated by a bad deal on your trade-in. Chapter 8 walks you through the process of assessing the real value of your current vehicle so you don't get cheated. It also examines the option of selling it yourself, which typically gets you a higher price. Remember that every additional dollar you get for your current vehicle is a dollar less you have to finance on your new car.

Chapter 9 will help you size up how much insurance you will need to pay, which could also affect the models you choose to pursue.

## Step 4: Arrange your financing.

The interest you pay on your financing is one of the major expenses of buying a car, but many consumers let financing considerations go until they're at the dealership. Then they're at the mercy of the dealership and whatever interest rates the dealer can offer.

You can reduce the overall cost of your vehicle by hundreds—or thousands—of dollars over the term of your loan simply by shopping around for good financing terms in advance. What seems like a little can add up: On a typical loan, a 1 percent difference in the APR can save you nearly $300 over the life of the loan.

Chapter 10 explains the ins and outs of auto financing, including:

- How to assess competitive interest rates.
- Where to shop for an auto loan.
- The advantages of getting prequalified for a loan.

And Chapter 11 examines the pros and cons of leasing your new car.

## Step 5: Contact dealerships and compare offers to get the best price.

You often get the best price when you can get different dealerships bidding against each other for your business. By the time you've reached this final step, you should be fully prepared to deal with the dealerships.

Whether you're visiting dealerships in person, negotiating by phone, or buying through the Internet, you will eventually end up at a dealership to close the deal. This is where all of your preparation pays off.

Chapters 12 through 16 prepare you for the dealership experience, focusing on:

- How to negotiate effectively.
- Sales tricks and pitfalls you may encounter and how to avoid them.
- Unnecessary extras that could cost you money. Paint sealant, VIN etching, and rustproofing are three examples of extras you just don't need.
- The pros and cons of using the Internet to buy a car.
- How to work the pricing game to get the lowest price.

By following these five steps, paying attention to detail, and using the advice offered in the following chapters, you can come away from your buying experience not only with a great new vehicle that's right for your lifestyle, but also with the confidence that you went into the dealership prepared, controlled the negotiating process, and got the best deal and financing possible. That's a solid foundation for long-lasting satisfaction with your car.

# Step 1

# Get the Right Information

■ CHAPTER 1: Determine Your Needs & Budget      **15**

■ CHAPTER 2: Gather the Facts      **39**

■ CHAPTER 3: Safety Issues & Answers      **53**

■ CHAPTER 4: Features to Look For      **79**

# 1

# Determine Your Needs & Budget

**As a car buyer,** you're faced with what can be a bewildering array of choices. There are about 40 major brands on the market and about 250 different models. For each model, there are also typically several trim lines, which differ in their available features and often in the powertrains they offer. This expands the number of choices to well over a thousand.

Moreover, while most models don't change that much from year to year, there can be 30 or 40 models in any given model year that are either new or have received a major redesign. There could be well more than 100 models that have significantly changed since the last time you bought a car.

Automaker ads and TV commercials can add to the confusion because of their overstated claims and misleading comparisons. Ads can claim that model A, for instance, has quicker acceleration than model B, better handling than model C, and more interior room than model D. If you choose your comparisons carefully, you can pretty much make that kind of claim about any vehicle.

Likewise, some models (that we call "twins") are very similar to—or virtually the same as—models that have completely different names and styling. This is the case with the Ford Explorer and Mercury Mountaineer SUVs, Pontiac Vibe and Toyota Matrix wagons, and Dodge Grand Caravan and Chrysler Town & Country minivans (see Appendix B for more). Yet, ads and commercials often try to portray them as distinctly different vehicles.

The key to making a smart car-buying choice is to find the vehicle that best fills your personal or family needs. To do this, you need a systematic approach and up-to-date information sources that help you cut through the clutter.

This chapter will help guide you through your first steps: looking at your needs and desires. You'll find advice on:

- Knowing when the time is right to buy a new car
- Separating your "wants" from your "needs"
- Figuring out how much you can afford to spend
- Determining what type of vehicle is best for you
- What to look for in a family vehicle
- The best vehicles for teenagers and first-time drivers
- Deciding whether you should buy a new or used car

In following chapters, we'll help you focus on narrowing your choice of models through informed comparisons, choosing the right features, and comparing vehicles on the road during your test drives.

## Should You Be Thinking About a New Car?

Sometimes it's easy to decide when to buy a new car. Your family outgrows the current one. Your lease will soon be up. Or the transmission falls out of your 15-year-old clunker. Most of the time, however, there aren't such clear-cut signposts. If you've owned a vehicle for a while, your monthly payments may be done or close to an end, and the thought of not having to make monthly car payments is a strong incentive to stay with your current car, even if it's getting old. Many owners complain about a car "nickel-and-diming" them to death, but the cost of regular maintenance and small repairs rarely add up to the cost of a monthly payment on a newer vehicle. It's the big repairs that you need to watch for.

There are good reasons to jettison an older car in favor of a newer one, including better safety protection, increased ride comfort and handling capability, or more creature comforts.

Still, many people let their vehicle decide the old car vs. new car debate for them. Some owners tend to hang on to their car until it breaks down or needs a major repair. They may reluctantly shell out $1,000 or more for a new transmission or engine overhaul only to have something else fail two months, two weeks, or two hours later. Then they face the same question all over again: Junk it or keep it? There's no easy answer because so many variables come into play: Is the vehicle safe? Is it reliable? Is it cost-efficient? Is it spewing too much pollution?

Here are five checkpoints to help you determine whether you and your old car have come to the end of your road together:

## Checkpoint 1: Is it safe?

Older vehicles lack much of the safety equipment now widely available on newer models. Dual front air bags did not become mandatory on all vehicles until 1998. Advanced safety systems such as electronic stability control (ESC), side- and head-protection air bags, and advanced air-bag systems have only become widely available in the past few years. Moreover, newer vehicles are designed to better protect occupants during a crash.

Because there's no effective way to retrofit up-to-date safety features in older cars, one of your primary considerations in determining whether to keep a car should be how safe it is. Often parents hand down their old car to a teenager, but that's not necessarily a good idea. Teen drivers, less experienced on the road, have the highest rate of fatal crashes of any group on the highway. If you can afford it, a teen driver—possibly more than any other age group—should have the benefit of as many modern safety features as possible. Elderly drivers also have a higher-than-average fatal-crash rate, based on miles driven, partly because they are more vulnerable to injury. So they, too, should choose a vehicle with as much safety equipment as they can afford.

We'll cover safety features in more depth in Chapter 3.

## Checkpoint 2: What's it worth?

Most cars drop 15 to 20 percent in value after their first year on the road, and an average of about 45 percent over three years, often the time when the basic warranty expires. After that, depreciation generally becomes less steep, averaging about 25 percent over the next three years. Once a car reaches about 100,000 miles, the value hits a floor that slopes downward at a gentler rate. Still, at any time, a vehicle's true value is largely dependent on its mileage and condition.

Unless you want to wring every last mile out of your car, it's advisable to look for the sweet spot in your car's life, where you've gotten the most out of it relatively trouble-free, but it hasn't yet sideswiped you with big repair bills and still has enough value to provide a decent down payment on new wheels.

To find out how much your current vehicle is worth, see Chapter 8.

## Checkpoint 3: How's it running?

You may want to start thinking about an end-of-life strategy for your vehicle by the time it has between 75,000 and 80,000 miles on the odometer. An inspection from a trusted mechanic should tell you what work, if any, your car needs immediately and reveal the status of its major mechanical systems—helpful in determining whether the old cruiser can go the distance.

Ask for a complete physical whenever your mechanic prescribes an

## Making choices

A thorough inspection of her 11-year-old Volkswagen Golf with 116,000 miles on it helped one owner make her keep-or-trade decision. The examination turned up 14 problems needing repairs totaling about $1,300, about what the car itself was worth.

Determining that she could defer making some of them, she decided it was worth paying the $670 it would cost to replace brake rotors, joint boots, and a valve-cover gasket. Her rationale for holding on to her old car was to avoid having to make car payments. Instead, she would put the money that would otherwise go to a car payment into a mutual fund and keep her old car going.

expensive repair. You don't want to spend $1,200 on a major engine repair only to learn a month later that the radiator needs replacing, too.

Where can you take your car for a good look-see? The garage that normally services your vehicle should be monitoring its overall condition. But for a second opinion, you may want an assessment from a mechanic who doesn't have a financial stake in doing the repairs or in selling you a new car. For the same reason, it's not a good idea to accept the "free" inspection some repair shops offer—often as a pretext for finding costly "problems." Mechanics qualified by the National Institute of Automotive Service Excellence (they carry an ASE medallion on their windows and in advertising) can give your car the same inspection they offer to buyers of used cars; it usually costs about $100. If you're a AAA member, you can access a list of approved shops on the club's Web site.

For more tips on finding a good repair shop, see Chapter 18.

## Checkpoint 4: Fatal flaws?

The inspection could uncover problems that ring a death knell for your car. When we took a 15-year-old Nissan Stanza with 161,000 miles to a mechanic for a thorough inspection, for instance, his initial inspection revealed cracked bumpers, a passenger door that didn't completely close, a dysfunctional oil gauge, exhaust problems, and corrosion in the radiator. Based on this, if somebody had intended to buy it, he would have advised taking a pass. But he felt someone who already owned it could keep driving it, despite these problems.

After he hoisted the car on a hydraulic lift and found a rust-eaten frame, however, he declared the car a goner. Frame-rail rust and major collision damage are deficits that cannot be easily overcome—even with thick applications of money. If your car has them, it is most likely doomed.

As a general rule, any repair that costs more than the vehicle's trade-in value isn't worth making. Short of those problems, cars today can be restored to health even if their engine and transmission are shot. Auto parts for all but the rarest models are readily available, and factories churn out rebuilt engines and transmissions—many with three-year, 75,000-mile warranties.

People used to think that it wouldn't pay to put a $2,000 engine into a $4,000 car. But now if you can keep your car going two or three years longer, it could make sense. As a guideline, mechanics we've consulted suggest adding up the value of the car and the cost of the repairs, then asking yourself if you want to own that car for that amount of money.

## Checkpoint 5: How reliable?

Just as important as the money you might spend to fix your older car is the time it will potentially spend in the garage. That depends on a car's overall reliability.

In CONSUMER REPORTS' annual subscriber surveys, we see that the older a car gets, the more problems it has. According to our 2004 survey, for instance, new cars (2004 models that had been on the road for about six months) had only about 16 problems for every 100 vehicles. Vehicles that are 3 years old averaged about 51 problems per 100 vehicles, and by age 5, the average problem rate jumped to 79 per 100. Of course, these are average problem rates; some models hold up much better than others.

Because problems in older versions of your model can give you an indication of what might go wrong with your vehicle, it can help to check CR's
reliability history charts, which are available in our automotive print publications or to ConsumerReports.org subscribers (see Appendix C). Our reliability history charts show how models from 1 to 8 years old have held up in
14 different areas. By looking at the chart for the model you own, you can see
immediately which of its systems have been the most troublesome. If you see
that older versions have had below-average reliability, especially in the engine
or transmission, it's possible that yours might too as it ages. In this case, you
may want to cash it in sooner rather than later. (See Chapter 2 for information on accessing CONSUMER REPORTS' latest Ratings and recommendations.)

Beyond money, an unreliable vehicle can affect your peace of mind. If it
begins to have problems, it erodes your confidence that it will be there when
you need it and that you can depend on it to get you where you want to go.

## How Much Can You Afford to Spend?

Once you've decided to buy a new car, you need to know what price range
to focus on. Take a look at your budget and assess the costs of buying and
maintaining a vehicle. To get a sense of what price vehicle you can afford,
you need two basic pieces of information:

- **Down payment.** How much can you pay up front, either in cash or with
  a trade-in, or both? If available, a cash rebate can also be used toward
  your down payment.
- **Monthly payment.** If you plan to borrow money or lease a vehicle, what
  is the maximum car payment you can afford every month?

To get a ballpark figure for the monthly payment, CONSUMER REPORTS'
financial experts recommend that your total debt payment should be no
more than 36 percent of your gross income. Going by this rule, you can use

## When is it time to buy a new car?

There are two rules of thumb that can help you decide when it's time to replace your car: One, if you're facing a major repair that will cost half the retail value of your existing vehicle, or two, if your monthly repair bills average close to what a new car payment will be.

the following steps to calculate how much of your monthly income you can comfortably afford to put toward your auto payments.

- Calculate what 36 percent of your gross monthly income is.
- Itemize and total all your monthly payments, including mortgage, credit cards and other installment loans.
- Subtract this total from the 36-percent figure

If your pretax income is $75,000, total debt payments should not exceed $27,000 a year. If you other debt payments equal, say, $20,000 a year, you can afford to pay $7,000 annually, or $583 a month, for car payments.

By knowing your down payment and monthly payment, along with a typical interest rate and the number of years you're willing to be making car payments (the term of the loan), you can calculate the price of the vehicle that you can afford and the loan amount for which you'll need to qualify. Go to *www.ConsumerReports.org/smartcar* and look in the Calculators and Worksheets section for a calculator labeled, "What vehicle can I afford?" You can also check this with any lending institution. (See Chapter 10 for more information on auto financing.)

In addition to the vehicle price, however, you also need to consider other costs associated with a new car:

- Sales tax
- Registration fees
- Higher insurance premiums

Taxes and registration fees can increase your out-of-pocket cost by as much as 10 percent or more, and driving a car that's worth more will certainly cost more to insure. Be sure to check with your insurance agent so you understand what you're getting into (see Chapter 9 for more information on auto insurance).

# Your Wants vs. Your Needs

Once you know what price range to concentrate on, you need to shrink that long list of models in the marketplace to a short list of choices that best fit your needs. That means taking an honest look at your priorities. You don't need to set your sights on only one vehicle at this time, but you should narrow the list down to a manageable few. Further research and your all-important test drives will help you decide which models on the short list deserve serious consideration.

Buying a new car is often filled with emotion. But to do an accurate assessment of the vehicle that's best for you, you should set emotion aside for now and focus on more practical concerns.

If you're unsure about what type of vehicle you want, begin by asking yourself some basic questions. To determine which models excel in the areas that are important to you, see Chapter 4. Add this point, you may also find it helpful to use Consumer Reports' New Car Buying Kit. Among its many features, the kit includes an interactive vehicle selector that helps you choose models based on your priorities. See page Appendix C for more information.

### How many people will you be transporting?

Most vehicles will accommodate five people (although the center rear position can be too uncomfortable in some vehicles to be considered a reasonable seating position). If you need to carry more people, you should look for a vehicle with a third-row seat. This includes all minivans, a growing number of SUVs, and a few wagons. Depending on the design, these vehi-cles can carry seven or eight people.

Keep in mind that the third-row seats in some SUVs and wagons are small and cramped and appropriate only for children. In addition, the third-row seats in most wagons face the rear.

A few vehicles offer a three-person front bench seat that increases pas-senger capacity to six. But the center position is small and typically equipped with only a lap belt, which doesn't provide adequate protection in a frontal crash. A vehicle with a third-row seat is a better choice.

Many coupes provide seating for four or five people, but the rear seat is often very tight and uncomfortable. Anyone who has owned such a coupe will tell you that rear-seat passengers don't appreciate having to bend and twist just to get into a cramped and confined seating area. Folding the front seat forward so you can load groceries or a child safety seat into the back seat gets old fast.

## How much cargo space do you need?

Most passenger cars include a trunk that can accommodate some luggage and other relatively small items. If you need to carry more cargo or longer items, many have a rear seat that folds down, which effectively enlarges the trunk area. Some sedans also have a front passenger seat that can fold for-ward flat so you can carry extra long items.

If you regularly carry large items, such building or nursery supplies, or camping or sports equipment, you may find a minivan, SUV, or wagon is better suited to your needs. These typically have a sizable cargo area that can be enlarged by folding down or removing the rear seat(s). Keep in mind that a third-row seat, when in use, significantly reduces the available cargo space.

If you prefer a smaller car but want to maximize its cargo-carrying abil-ity, a hatchback may be a good option for you. They typically have more interior space than a similar-sized car with a trunk, and the rear hatch makes it easier to get large items in and out.

## What type of driving experience do you prefer?

In addition to practical concerns, it's important to think about the driving experiences of different models. Good acceleration, crisp handling, and responsive steering are important in any vehicle. If you are an automotive enthusiast who enjoys driving, wants to feel the road and sense every aspect of the driving experience, however, then these aspects will likely be high on your priority list, so you'll want a vehicle that excels in these areas. Most sports cars and many coupes, of course, fit that bill, but some make you sacrifice space for passengers and cargo.

Many car buyers used to face a dilemma when considering this question, because they wanted a sporty, fun-to-drive car but needed the practicality of a four-door sedan or wagon. Today, there are a number of sedans and wagons that provide a good balance between the two. A common trade-off for sportier cars, however, is a firm, sometimes uncomfortable ride.

On the other hand, many drivers place more importance on a comfortable driving experience. They like a softer ride, luxurious seats, plenty of convenience features, and isolation from the outside world. With a proliferation of luxury vehicles in recent years, you can now find a wide range of models that fit this mold, from family sedans to SUVs.

Perhaps you really only need basic transportation—a reliable, economical, fuel-efficient car for commuting or simply to get you from point A to point B as comfortably as possible. While on paper there are a number of models that could fill this need, it's still important to do your research. Within a given price range, there are big differences in reliability, fuel economy, comfort, and overall value.

The best way to size up the type of driving experience that a vehicle provides is to read reviews to narrow your list, then do a thorough test drive.

## Is performance or fuel economy more important?

Many automakers offer several engine choices in each model, but which is best for you depends on what your priorities are. Do you want a high-

## Love is blind. Or needs a strong prescription

"Love at first sight" is not necessarily the best way to approach the car-buying process. Many people see a striking new model go by on the highway and decide that's the one they've got to have—no questions asked. To get too infatuated with a car—especially one that you haven't driven yet—is to invite buyer's remorse. Some new cars with sexy styling or loads of pre-intro hype haven't been able to live up to the high expectations.

The latest version of the Ford Thunderbird is a good example. Enthusiasts were eagerly anticipating the stylish two-seat roadster a year before it hit the showrooms. When it was introduced, it caused such a stir that dealers had long waiting lists of buyers. Six months after its release, the car was still commanding as much as $10,000 over the sticker price. But when we tested it for the June 2002 issue of CONSUMER REPORTS, we found that it wasn't very sporty to drive, was too cramped for taller drivers, drank a lot of fuel, and couldn't measure up overall in our tests to comparably-priced roadsters.

Moreover, after the initial sales rush, the Thunderbird's affair with buyers ended quickly. Enthusiasm for the Thunderbird began to wane rapidly, and within about two years, sales were down to only about half of what they had been. It was discontinued after the 2005 model year. In the end, attention-getting styling may turn heads, but it doesn't guarantee that the car underneath will be all that special.

er performance vehicle? Or is fuel economy more important to you? Or is quiet, smooth operation at the top of your list?

Smaller vehicles and many midsized models provide four-cylinder engines, which typically provide the best fuel economy but may lack power or smoothness. Some manufacturers are getting better at squeezing more performance out of their smaller engines, so family sedans such as the Honda Accord and Toyota Camry have perfectly adequate four-cylinder engines. Some automakers offer turbocharged versions that deliver more power than you might expect from a small package. Turbocharging gives you the advantage of good fuel economy when driving under normal conditions, with extra power in reserve when you need to accelerate quickly.

Six-cylinder engines typically provide the best balance between performance and fuel economy, and are usually quieter and smoother than four-cylinders. These are available in most midsized and some larger models. The majority of these are V6s, but a few imports and some SUVs use an  inline six-cylinder design similar to that of most four-cylinder engines.

V8 engines deliver the most power but, as you might expect, the lowest gas mileage. These are available in a few midsized vehicles, as well as most larger cars, SUVs, pickups, and luxury vehicles. Some models offer a V10 or V12 engine that can provide even more power. A V8 or larger engine is essential if you plan on towing heavier loads (see Chapter 4).

If fuel economy is a high priority, you might want to consider a gasoline/electric hybrid or diesel model. These tend to provide better fuel economy than a similar-sized conventional vehicle. Some hybrids even provide quicker acceleration than their conventional counterparts. On the other hand, hybrids typically cost more to buy (about $2,000 to $3,000 or more) and diesel engines produce more nitrous oxide and particulate (soot) emissions.

## Automatic or manual transmission?

Most models are only available with an automatic transmission. Many automatics, however, now provide a manual-shift mode that works similar to a manual transmission but without a clutch. Selecting the gears yourself can make a car more fun to drive and can be handy when driving in hilly or mountainous areas, where you might want to shift down when making long descents to ease the burden on your brakes. A few automatics have what's called a winter mode, where the transmission starts in second gear to improve traction on slippery surfaces.

Manual transmissions, which are often available in inexpensive or sporty models, provide better performance and fuel economy than automatics. Many drivers also find them more fun to drive. However, if you spend a lot of time in stop-and-go traffic, working the clutch a lot can become a real chore.

## 2WD or AWD or 4WD: How much traction do you need?

Most vehicles use two-wheel drive (2WD), where engine power is sent to either the front or rear wheels only. Front-wheel drive is used in most cars, wagons, and minivans because it's space efficient. It allows a smaller engine compartment, leaving more room inside for passengers and cargo. It's also better than rear-wheel drive in slippery conditions because there's more weight on the front drive wheels and the wheels pull rather than push the car along the road. This helps prevent the vehicle's rear end from sliding sideways.

Rear-wheel drive places less demand on the front wheels, allowing them to be used primarily for steering. It's commonly used on pickups and traditional, truck-based SUVs that are designed to handle heavy-duty chores such as towing. But rear-wheel drive is also very popular on sports cars and high-performance sedans because of its contribution to good handling.

Traction control, available on many two-wheel-drive vehicles, helps maximize traction at the drive wheels by preventing wheel spin. It's particularly useful when accelerating on a wet, snowy, or icy surface. If neither drive wheel has grip, however, traction control won't help. In wintry conditions, we've found that a vehicle with traction control can have more difficulty getting up a slippery slope than one with all- or four-wheel drive.

All-wheel drive (AWD) feeds power to all four wheels. It provides maximum forward traction and is especially helpful in wintry conditions and when driving over moderate off-road terrain. AWD systems are helpful in

## You need to know

One of the reasons many people buy a traditional sport-utility vehicle is for the extra security of four-wheel drive. But for most drivers, 4WD may be overkill. The type of vehicle that's best for you depends on the types of conditions you typically face. For rain and light snow, two-wheel drive will likely work fine. Front-wheel drive with traction control is preferred. AWD is fine for normal snow conditions or for traveling on packed sand or dirt roads. For more severe conditions, you should opt for 4WD.

In addition, a common misconception is that 4WD and AWD systems help in all driving situations. In fact, these systems provide added traction only when accelerating. They do not help in braking or cornering.

Drivers often make the mistake of using less caution when driving in slippery conditions with a 4WD vehicle, and pay the consequences by sliding off the road and sometimes rolling over. Because the added traction of 4WD can allow a vehicle to accelerate more quickly in slippery conditions, drivers need to be more vigilant, not less. For extra help in braking, get a vehicle with antilock brakes. For a cornering aid, look for an electronic stability control (ESC) system. But neither of these systems can overcome the laws of physics. Slippery conditions demand extra caution, no matter what you drive.

rapidly changing conditions or when driving on a road with intermittent snow and ice. Its lightness and compactness makes AWD the system of choice for wagons, some minivans and pickups, and most car-based SUVs.

Although four-wheel drive (4WD) and AWD are designations that are often used interchangeably in advertising and sales literature, the key difference between the two is that 4WD incorporates low-range gearing which, when selected, helps in more challenging off-road conditions, such as traversing rocks or deeper water, or tackling steep off-pavement hills. The vast majority of 4WD-vehicle owners, however, never come close to needing this capability. In addition, 4WD systems add a lot of weight, compromising fuel economy.

Modern 4WD systems are either full-time, which means they can stay engaged all the time, or automatic, where the vehicle automatically switches between two- and four-wheel drive mode, depending on the driving conditions. Many pickups and some truck-based SUVs, however, have only part-time 4WD systems. These require the driver to manually shift between two- and four-wheel drive, which limits the vehicle's ability to provide optimum traction when the road surface suddenly becomes slippery. In addition, a vehicle with a part-time system can't be driven on dry pavement when in 4WD mode without running the risk of severe damage to the vehicle's drivetrain.

## Looking for a Kid-Friendly Vehicle?

Transporting kids on a regular basis adds a whole new dimension to your vehicle needs. In addition to your own needs, you have to be concerned with your kids' comfort, convenience, and safety as well. The more comfortable they are, for instance, the less distracting they will be to the driver.

The size and makeup of your family and the types of activities in which you participate will certainly influence the type of vehicle that's best for you. Try to imagine how you'll be using your vehicle, what type of cargo you intend to carry, and how your needs will change during the years you own it.

Even if you have only two or three kids, for instance, you may want a vehicle that can seat seven or eight so you can accommodate friends or car pooling. Are your kids active in sports, scouts, or other activities that require carrying a lot of equipment or gear? If so, cargo capacity should be a priority. In either case, a minivan, SUV, or wagon could fill the bill. Will your vehicle be comfortable for both short trips and long road vacations? Most sedans can hold a five-person family, but will three kids be happy seated tightly in one rear seat?

Other aspects you should focus on include:

## They're only going to get bigger ...

Small children might not need a lot of room now, but if you intend to keep a vehicle for a number of years, their space needs will change as they grow. Also, if you have kids who will reach driving age while you own the vehicle, keep in mind that they probably will be using the vehicle themselves.

**Access.** How easy is it for your kids to climb in an out of the vehicle? Taller vehicles, such as large SUVs and pickups, require a higher step up, which can be difficult for kids.

**Child-seat compatibility.** If your kid needs a child seat, make sure it fits well and can be easily secured. Take the child seat along when you do your test drive and initial inspection. If it's a hassle to install it securely, focus on other vehicles. (See Chapter 5 for more information on evaluating test drives.)

**Rear-seat comfort and convenience.** Since your kids will be spending a lot of time in the rear seat, it needs to be as kid-friendly as possible. If the window line is so high that children can't see out the window, for instance, kids can get bored or antsy. There should be adequate storage cubbies, such as pockets in the seat backs and doors that can keep toys and books within easy reach. Cup holders in the back seat are another plus; some models even have ones that can accommodate juice boxes.

Uncomfortable safety belts can also cause a child to fidget and affect your kid's willingness to wear a safety belt. Comfort guides, which pull the chest strap away from the child's neck and position it more appropriately on the shoulder, are available on some models. They're not only a safety aid, but they can also make belts much more comfortable.

Many vehicles now offer rear-seat entertainment systems, which can be especially handy on longer trips. These systems allow rear passengers to watch videos, play video games, or listen to a different audio source (through headsets) than the front-seat passengers. Kids can use this latter function to listen to books on tape, which can keep them occupied for hours.

See Chapter 3 for more information on child safety and Chapter 4 for more on features and options.

# Cars for Teenagers

When buying any vehicle, safety and reliability are always important. But those considerations are even more significant for young drivers, since they usually do not have a lot of driving experience or money. Following are some of the things you should consider before buying:

**Safety.** Look for vehicles with advanced safety features and good crash-test results. CONSUMER REPORTS' used-car profiles (available in CR's used-car publications and to subscribers of ConsumerReports.org) note the availability of key safety equipment, such as air bags and ABS on specific models. The profiles also give offset, frontal, and side-impact crash-test results when available. (For more information on safety equipment and crash tests, see Chapter 3.)

Generally, bigger and heavier vehicles perform better in crash tests. But larger vehicles tend to have unwieldy handling and offer poor fuel economy. Large pickups and SUVs are not recommended for young, inexperienced drivers because the high centers of gravity on those vehicles make them more prone to rollover than other vehicles.

Sports cars are also often a poor choice for young drivers. They beg to be driven too fast and have a higher rate of accidents than other cars.

Newer models generally offer more safety features and better crash protection. Try to buy the most safety that your budget can afford; no one needs these safety advantages more than a teenage driver.

**Reliability.** An inexpensive car isn't so inexpensive if you end up paying for major repairs later. Even vehicles deemed reliable in our profiles could be lemons if they were poorly maintained, so it's very important that you thoroughly examine the condition and look into the history of any car you're considering. (See Chapter 6 for advice on evaluating used cars.)

## Recommended cars for teenage drivers

In the following list, which was prepared in mid-2005, we've identified vehicles that CONSUMER REPORTS has tested that we feel are appropriate for young drivers. The list is based on our test results, and government and insurance-industry crash-test results. These vehicles also showed average or better reliability, according to our 2004 subscriber survey.

We did not consider autos with 0-to-60-mph acceleration times faster than 8 seconds or slower than 11 seconds, or those with lower emergency-handling scores. Note: All vehicles that have been tested in the Insurance Institute for Highway Safety (IIHS) side-crash test without side air bags, including several in this list, have been rated Poor—the lowest rating. Therefore, we recommend that you look for a vehicle with head-protecting side air bags, when possible. You can see all IIHS crash-test ratings at *www.hwysafety.org.*

Ford Focus ('02 or later, except two-door models)

Honda Accord EX (4-cyl.) ('98 or later)

Honda Civic EX

Mazda3

Mazda Protegé EX ('99-'03)

Nissan Altima 2.5 S (4-cyl) ('03 or later)

Subaru Forester 2.5X

Toyota Camry LE (4-cyl.)

Toyota Camry XLE (V6)

Toyota Corolla LE ('99 or later)

Toyota RAV4 ('01 or later)

Volkswagen Passat (4-cyl) ('00)

If you have done a good job of maintaining your car over the years, you may consider handing it down to your teen, which will help ensure that the young driver inherits a car with a known history.

# New vs. Used: Risk vs. Value

If your budget starts at $15,000, you have the option of buying either a new or used vehicle. Deciding which is right for you depends on how you balance risk against expense. Both have their advantages. But you may find that buying a late-model used car is a better overall value than buying a new one.

It's not just that the initial price is lower—it also means that items tied to the car's value, such as collision insurance and taxes, will be lower. If the vehicle is less than three years old, it's probably still covered by the factory warranty. And buying used is often a great way to get a better-equipped vehicle than you'd be able to afford new.

## Reliability

One thing that has made used cars more appealing is their improved reliability. In a 20-year reliability analysis, based on 1980 through 2000 CONSUMER REPORTS annual subscriber surveys, we found that the reliability of vehicles has vastly improved. The reported problems per hundred vehicles has declined to a fraction of what it was in 1980. Rust and exhaust-system problems, once common, are now no longer of major concern. As a result, buying a late-model used vehicle is not as much of a risk as it used to be. When properly maintained, many vehicles can now reach 200,000 miles without a major breakdown.

## Warranties and repairs

Although used cars are proving more reliable than ever, maintenance and repair costs are important considerations. In the first two to three years of a new car's life, it has fewer problems and is typically covered by a comprehensive bumper-to-bumper warranty. A used car, on the other hand, is either close to coming off warranty or already off it.

This means that owners will have to pay for repairs out of pocket. However, most costs will still likely go to replace worn-out parts such as tires, brakes, and battery. The expense of replacing all of these items, if necessary, would still be a relatively modest considering the overall savings from buying used over new.

There is always the risk that you'll buy a lemon, of course. Even a car with a great reliability history can be a risky proposition if it was abused by a previous owner or had been seriously damaged and the impairments hidden. However, a thorough vehicle inspection by a qualified mechanic will usually reveal most problems. (See Chapter 6 for more information on evaluating a used car.)

Certified used cars are intended to take the worry out of buying a used vehicle by providing professional screening and a warranty. However, you'll pay a premium for one, and certified programs can vary substantially.

## Depreciation

A disadvantage to buying a new car is the rapid depreciation it undergoes in the first few years. Models typically lose about 45 percent of their value in the first three years, compared with 25 percent over the next three. But this rate varies greatly among models. The 2002 BMW 3 Series, for example, held its value relatively well (25 percent depreciation over its first three years), while the Hyundai Accent depreciated rapidly (65 percent over the same period).

Several factors determine depreciation, including the model's popularity, perceived quality, supply, and whether or not the vehicle is of the current design. Nevertheless, the average depreciation on a $27,500 new vehicle leaves little more than $15,000 after three years, a huge hit in residual value.

## Interest rates

Loans for new cars typically have a lower interest rate, but the difference usually is not enough to be a major concern. In March 2005 the bank rates for a 36-month new-car loan hovered at 5.9 percent; a 36-month used-car loan was about 6.8 percent. It is typical that these two rates are within just one percentage point of each other, and the additional 0.9 percent extra interest you pay on a used-car loan adds only about $3 to $6 on a typical monthly loan payment.

## Insurance

You'll typically pay less to insure a used vehicle than a new version of the same vehicle. Auto insurer USAA quoted a New York policyholder with a good driving record $441 for a six-month policy on a 2002 Honda CR-V EX and $483 for a 2005 CR-V, an $84 annual savings.

## Safety

One of the things you miss out on when buying a used car is having the latest safety features. Newer features such as electronic stability control (ESC), head-protecting side-curtain air bags, LATCH child-seat restraints, and advanced frontal air-bag systems are harder to find on older vehicles. On the other hand, a vehicle with more common safety features such as antilock brakes, traction control, and side air bags will be more affordable on a used car than on a similarly equipped new car.

If you can accept a reliable vehicle that is in less-than-mint condition and for which you're responsible for maintenance and repair costs, you may want to consider the cost difference in owning a used car instead of buying a new one.

## New vs. used: A cost comparison

This table was prepared for an article we published in 2004, but the figures still clearly show how a used car can save you money. The average new car in 2004 cost $27,500. New cars typically depreciate 45 percent of their value in the first three years, then another 25 percent in the next three years. In this comparison, we calculated the cost of taking out a 3-year loan on this car for these two distinct periods. We found that if you had bought the vehicle as a 3-year-old, as opposed to new, your overall ownership costs (not including maintenance and repair) would be about $9,400 less.

| | New car | 3-year-old car |
| --- | --- | --- |
| Price | $27,500 | $15,125 |
| Down payment | $2,000 | $2,000 |
| 36-month loan interest rate* | 5.03% | 5.77% |
| Auto-loan payments (per month/36-month total) | $764.60/27,525.60 | $397.92/14,325.12 |
| Gross ownership costs (down payment plus loan payments) | $29,525.60 | $16,325.12 |
| Residual value after 36 months of ownership | $15,125.00 | $11,343.75 |
| Net ownership costs after 36 months of ownership | $14,404.60 | $4,981.37 |
| Net ownership cost savings after 36 months of ownership | ———— | $9,423.23 |

* Bankrate.com's Overnight Average Auto-Loan Rates for 3/3/04

## Worksheet: Wants vs. Needs

The following worksheet will help you organize your thoughts about your vehicle priorities and how it will be used. Then using the resources in Chapter 2, you can research which vehicles best meet your priorities. The interactive vehicle selector in Consumer Reports' New Car Buying Kit (see Appendix C) can also help you pinpoint models that would be right for you.

Affordable price range       _____

Number of seats       _____

|  | Very important | Average | Not important |
|---|---|---|---|
| Cargo space | _____ | _____ | _____ |
| Acceleration | _____ | _____ | _____ |
| Fuel economy | _____ | _____ | _____ |
| Good handling and steering | _____ | _____ | _____ |
| All- or four-wheel drive | _____ | _____ | _____ |
| Manual shifting | _____ | _____ | _____ |
| Fun to drive | _____ | _____ | _____ |
| Off-road driving | _____ | _____ | _____ |

# 2

# Gather the Facts

**To get the right vehicle** at the best price, you need to be an informed shopper. That means getting as much information as you can before making your purchase decision. It used to mean trips to dealerships to pick up brochures and compare window stickers, to newsstands for magazine reviews and ratings, and to the library for harder-to-find information, such as crash-test and reliability ratings.

The Internet, however, has made research much easier. By going online, you can easily gather all the information you need in a matter of hours. You can look up anything from photos, features, and specifications to dealer-invoice prices and government and insurance-industry test results. In fact, rather than facing the prospect of too little information, today's car buyers often face the challenge of having to sift through too much. Moreover, just as cars can vary greatly in quality, so can sources of information. The key to doing your auto research quickly and efficiently is knowing where to go and how to evaluate the information you get.

In this chapter, we'll guide you through the auto-information maze by showing you:

- Where to find key auto information
- What to look for in car reviews
- The importance of accurate reliability information
- The limitations of some information sources
- How to access and interpret CONSUMER REPORTS' Ratings and test reports
- Where to find the opinions and experiences of other car owners

To help with your online research, we've included a list of major providers of auto information and services in Appendix A for quick access. While CONSUMER REPORTS has not rated and doesn't endorse the Web sites listed in this book, they are included for your convenience.

For sources of safety information, see Chapter 3. For pricing information, see Chapters 7 and 8, and for car-buying Web sites, see Chapter 14.

# General Model Information

### Auto manufacturers' Web sites

These sites are a good place to turn for basic information on a model. Here, you can quickly see which models and trim levels the manufacturer offers, assess the available features and options, and look up specifications, retail pricing, warranties, and the locations of dealerships.

The best sites also provide some handy tools. Some, for instance, let you take a 360-degree view of a vehicle, inside and out. They also let you "build your own car" by walking you through the process of choosing everything from the trim line and powertrain to the colors and options, and then giving you the retail price for your individual configuration. Some will calculate the monthly payment for you, but, in most cases, you should accept this only as a rough estimate; it's based on the manufacturer's suggested retail price (MSRP), which is a higher figure than what you will likely need to pay. A few manufacturer sites now post the dealer-invoice price, as well as the MSRP, but, as you'll see in Chapter 7, even that can be a misleading figure if you're trying to use it to determine how much to pay for a vehicle.

Some sites let you do side-by-side comparisons of the manufacturer's vehicles with those of other manufacturers. But these types of comparisons have limited value. They are designed to show a vehicle's strengths while casting a blind eye toward its shortcomings. Every automaker, after all, wants to sell its own vehicles, not its competitors'.

Manufacturer Web sites can be handy in gathering the basic information, but keep in mind that the main purpose of these sites is to promote their own products. Their vehicle descriptions are the same as advertising, so don't expect to find unbiased critiques.

## Vehicle Ratings

Ratings can help you hone your list of vehicles by giving you a quick look at how vehicles compare overall with their competitors and the strengths and weaknesses of individual aspects of a vehicle.

CONSUMER REPORTS maintains an easy-to-reference, continually updated Ratings chart of all vehicles we've tested, so you can quickly see which vehicles have done better or worse in a number of key areas, including performance, reliability, and safety. It's available in CR's April Annual Auto Issue and special auto publications, and to subscribers of ConsumerReports.org. To access them online, go to *www.ConsumerReports.org/smartcar*.

The CR Ratings chart includes several critical pieces of information:

**Overall test score.** This is based on the results of more than 50 individual tests and evaluations that gauge a vehicle's acceleration, braking, handling, comfort and convenience, safety, fuel economy, cargo capacity, and more. (CR also provides ratings for many of these individual evaluations.)

**Predicted reliability.** This is our forecast of how well a new car will likely hold up based on its recent history. This is based on information from our latest annual subscriber survey.

**Owner satisfaction.** This rating also comes from our latest subscriber survey, and is based on the responses to a question that asks owners and leasers if, considering everything, they would get the same vehicle if they had it to do over again. The scores are based on the percentage of respondents who reported that they would definitely buy the same car again.

**Accident avoidance.** This reflects how capable a vehicle is in helping you avoid an accident through braking, steering around an obstacle, or accelerating out of harm's way. The rating is based on our tests of braking, acceleration, emergency handling, and, to a lesser extent, driving position, visibility, and seat comfort.

**Crash protection.** This rating is based on our composite of the most recent frontal- and side-crash tests conducted by the Insurance Institute for Highway Safety (IIHS) and the National Highway Traffic Safety Administration (NHTSA). We weight the results according to our judgments of their importance and the percentage of time a passenger is likely to be sitting in a particular seat. (See Chapter 3 for more information on these important tests.)

**Fuel economy.** This is the overall fuel economy that a vehicle achieved in our real-world tests. The overall mpg figure is based on results from several fuel economy tests, reflecting a realistic mix of city, country road, and highway driving.

**Highs and lows.** These notes give a quick summary of a model's notable strengths and weaknesses.

## CR's recommended vehicles

CR has a two-tier system for recommending vehicles.

To earn a standard recommendation, identified by a check mark in our Ratings, a vehicle must:

- Perform well in CR's testing program.
- Have average or better reliability, according to CR's latest annual subscriber survey.
- Have good overall crash protection, if crash-tested by the IIHS or NHTSA.

SUVs and pickups must either have been included in the government's dynamic rollover test and not tipped up, or be equipped with electronic stability control (ESC). If the latter, then only ESC-equipped version is recommended.

Our more stringent top-tier recommendation, identified by a checkmark in a circle in our Ratings, is intended to provide an extra level of assurance for consumers who place the highest priority on crash protection. To earn this, a vehicle must:

- Meet all of the standard-recommendation requirements listed above.
- Have been tested in both the frontal-offset and side-crash tests conducted by the IIHS.
- Have very good or excellent overall crash protection.

Our requirements for recommending vehicles can change from time to time to accommodate new tests or other standards in our information or in the automotive market.

# Model Reviews

While vehicle ratings can tell you at a glance how different models compare, to get a more in-depth perspective, it's important to read vehicle reviews from sources you trust. Good reviews can tell you about a vehicle's driving character; how it handles, accelerates, and brakes; and how comfortable and user-friendly the interior is for everyday use. They can also give you insight into shortcomings and deficiencies that may not be apparent on a test drive.

There is no shortage of vehicle reviews, both in print and online. Because different sources have varying points of view, we recommend reading a variety. But keep in mind that most are in publications or on Web sites that are supported by automaker advertising, and no one wants to bite the hand that feeds them.

So, while you can get insight into a vehicle's performance and driving character from these reviews, you often won't find very much hard-hitting analysis or an in-depth exploration of safety or reliability aspects. Moreover, only a few do their own instrumented testing, which allows more accurate comparisons between different vehicles.

The key is to find reviews that are in-depth enough to give you a good, solid overview of the car and cover the aspects that are most important to you.

## Consumer Reports road-test reports

Consumer Reports conducts the most comprehensive auto-test program of any U.S. publication or Web site. It differs from those of other reviewers in several significant ways, including the fact that we don't accept advertising; we buy all of our test vehicles from dealers, just like you; and we conduct more than 50 individual tests and evaluations on each vehicle over several months.

The best way to test vehicles is as a competitive group, so that testers can go directly from one to another. This gives you a better perspective of a vehicle's strengths and shortcomings and makes it easier to assess even subtle differences that wouldn't be as noticeable when testing vehicles months or even weeks apart.

As a result, every month (except for the April Annual Auto Issue) Consumer Reports magazine and ConsumerReports.org publishes a road-test report on a group of competitive vehicles in a similar price range and category (such as sedans, coupes, SUVs, minivans, pickups, etc.).

Our summary reviews from these tests appear in our vehicle profiles, which are included in the April issue, in special auto publications, and to subscribers of ConsumerReports.org.

Subscribers to CR's New Car Buying Kit (see Appendix C) can also access the detailed engineers' technical report (called Expert Reports) that our auto-testing staff generates for each tested vehicle. Together, these give you one of the most comprehensive perspectives of a vehicle you'll find anywhere.

## Other sources of vehicle reviews

There is a wide range of publications and Web sites that regularly review new models of autos, but keep in mind that they typically borrow test vehicles from the auto manufacturers' specially maintained press fleets. Many types of problems that would show up in a car you bought from a dealership are addressed before the cars are delivered to auto reviewers. If a vehicle has major problems, it is often taken out of the press fleet so that reviewers don't experience it.

Auto-enthusiast magazines, such as Automobile, Car and Driver, Motor Trend, Road & Track, and others, test a wide variety of vehicles and can often give you an early look at a new model. These early looks, however, are often based on manufacturer vehicle introductions for the press. Typically, a single person from each publication will get to drive specially prepared vehicles for just a day or two—sometimes for only a few hours. These articles can give you an initial take on a model's general driving character and new features or technology, but take them with a grain of salt. You won't find the type of in-depth analysis and observations that come with spending more time with a vehicle.

The full tests are more in-depth, but as with most auto reviewers, they're based on driving a press vehicle for two weeks or less, with instrumented testing typically limited to acceleration, braking, skid pad, and slalom. Auto-enthusiast publications also tend to focus heavily on a vehicle's performance attributes, often at the expense of more everyday concerns like safety, reliability, and fuel economy.

Many newspapers print auto reviews that provide a perspective geared toward the everyday driver rather than the auto enthusiast. A word of caution, however: Many newspapers publish special auto sections that are intended to draw advertising from automakers and local dealerships. These sections can be filled with so-called "puff pieces" that don't offend the advertisers. They can make everything sound good and shy away from hard-hitting criticism or comparisons with competitive models. Some are written by reviewers who have limited automotive experience. As such, they're not very reliable sources of information when researching new cars.

Several dedicated auto Web sites, such as TheCarConnection.com, MSN autos, and New Car Test Drive (nctd.com), feature reviews written by some well-qualified auto writers. As with many outlets, though, these are supported with advertising from the automakers and none do their own instrumented testing.

Sites like Epinions are a bit different in that they publish reviews that have been submitted voluntarily by owners. It's always insightful to get the perspective of an actual owner, but keep in mind that the owners usually haven't experienced a wide range of vehicles with which to compare theirs and you don't know who is writing the reviews or whether they have conflicts of interest that would affect their impartiality.

Most car-buying Web sites provide reviews of many new vehicles, but such articles are often not written by automotive experts. Many just recycle what they pick up in automakers' press kits. They don't rely on "expert opinion" and don't review, judge, or test products and services themselves.

# Reliability Information

Reliability is an important concern for a new- or used-car buyer. Reliability ratings give you an idea of how well vehicles have held up, compared with competitive models, and how much you could be inconvenienced by problems and repairs.

A vehicle's reliability can have a huge impact on how satisfied you'll be with your car over the years, and it can significantly affect its resale value when you're ready to replace it. Important as it is, reliability is a difficult—and expensive—quality to evaluate, because the information has to come from vehicle owners; the more, the better.

CONSUMER REPORTS provides the most comprehensive reliability information available to consumers. It's based on CR's annual surveys of our approximately six million magazine and Web site subscribers. These surveys ask vehicle owners about any serious problems they've had with their vehicles in the preceding 12 months. They generate hundreds of thousands of responses—the 2005 survey, for instance, generated information on more than 900,000 vehicles—which give us a solid foundation for our reliability ratings.

We provide reliability information in several forms.

For new-car buyers we provide a Predicted Reliability rating that indicates how the vehicles that are currently on sale are likely to hold up. To create these ratings, CONSUMER REPORTS averages a model's overall reliability scores for the past three years, providing it wasn't significantly redesigned during that time. Scores are weighted to emphasize more serious problem areas, including the engine, transmission, cooling system, and drive system. Predictions are made for some new models if the manufacturer's track record has been consistently good.

For used-car buyers we provide reliability ratings for 14 different trouble areas over eight model years, so you can see a model's individual strengths and weaknesses. We also provide a Reliability Verdict for each model year that sums up a model's overall reliability. All of these ratings are included in our Reliability History charts, which are available in CR's April Annual Auto Issue, special auto publications, and to subscribers of ConsumerReports.org.

We also provide a list of the Best and Worst Used Cars, in terms of reliability. It lists all models, by model year, that have had either above average or below average reliability, so you know which models to look for and which to avoid.

## Other sources of reliability information

Other sources of reliability ratings are available online. Even if they lack the comprehensive reach of CR's data, they provide a supplemental source of information.

The most widely known of these services is J.D. Power and Associates (*www.jdpower.com*). The Power survey that is most useful to new-car shoppers is the Initial Quality Survey (IQS). It is based on about 60,000 responses to J.D. Power's annual IQS survey, which asks owners and lessees about their new model-year vehicles based on their first three months of ownership. The survey was designed to help automakers gauge the initial quality of the vehicles they're producing, but it can be useful to car shoppers, despite the short ownership period it covers. One limitation with J.D. Power's information is that the company only releases the names of makes that have above-average ratings, so you can't compare models that are in the lower half of the scale.

Used-car shoppers will find J.D. Power's Vehicle Dependability Study (VDS) most useful. The VDS looks at problems related to three-year-old models. It's easy to find a list of the top three models in 17 different vehicle segments, but you have to dig out the rest with individual searches that may or may not yield information. You can choose up to four cars at a time and get comparative ratings on them, but you can't see all the surveyed models arranged top to bottom.

J.D. Power surveys are also the source for reliability data on some other sites, such as Kelley Blue Book (*www.kbb.com*), Edmunds.com (*www.edmunds.com*), and CarFax (*www.carfax.com*).

Some Web sites, such as Autobytel Inc. (*www.autobytel.com*), Epinions (*www.epinions.com*), and MSN Autos (*www.autos.msn.com*) provide reliability scores based on information supplied by consumers who visit the site and fill out questionnaires. The number of reviews for a particular model, however, can range from only a handful to hundreds.

MSN Autos also provides service data based on input from master service technicians. This lets you get details about common problems and estimated repair costs for a particular model.

You can also post and read messages using the Google search service. Go to *www.google.com* and click on the "groups" tab. Be aware that gathering individual anecdotes about particular vehicles is not the same as consulting a scientifically designed survey.

## Ownership Costs

The costs of owning and operating a vehicle once you've bought it can vary by hundreds of dollars, depending on its insurance premiums, fuel economy, maintenance and repair costs, and more. To get an idea of how much a vehicle will cost you on a regular basis, you'll want to take a look at its estimated cost of ownership.

Perhaps the best-known source of ownership costs is IntelliChoice *(www.intellichoice.com)*. The company provides five-year projections of ownership costs in several areas, based on depreciation, financing, insurance, state fees and taxes, fuel, maintenance, and repairs. If you prefer working with a book, IntelliChoice annually publishes "The Complete Car Cost Guide" and "The Complete Small Truck Cost Guide," which you can often find in libraries.

Keep in mind, though, that future ownership costs are projections and can change dramatically as conditions in the market change.

## Fuel Economy

The fuel-economy figures printed on a vehicle's window sticker and in automaker advertising and brochures are estimates that are calculated based

## Warranties: Compare the after-sale support

When comparing vehicles, don't forget to factor in their warranties and other after-sale support, such as free maintenance or roadside assistance. Over the long term, this can make a difference in both your satisfaction and financial outlay. Automakers usually provide several different warranties:

**Basic warranty.** This covers most parts of the vehicle. However, certain items, such as high-wear parts and audio systems, either are excluded or have separate coverage periods. As an extra sales incentive, some companies throw in free maintenance during the basic warranty period.

**Powertrain warranty.** The engine, transmission, and related components are covered by this warranty. It is often for a longer period than the basic warranty.

**Rust-through warranty.** Also called a corrosion or anti-perforation warranty, it covers damage resulting from rust and corrosion. This warranty can extend from 3 to 12 years, with mileage specifications from 50,000 miles to an unlimited number of miles.

**Roadside assistance.** Offered by most manufacturers, this provides emergency service during the basic warranty period. "Limited" roadside assistance only allows for service due to the failure of items still covered under warranty.

on a test created by the U.S. Environmental Protection Agency (EPA). For each vehicle, there are two figures:

- *City* represents urban driving, in which a vehicle is started in the morning and driven in stop-and-go rush hour traffic.
- *Highway* represents a mixture of rural and interstate highway driving in a warmed-up vehicle, typical of longer trips in free-flowing traffic.

Based on dynamometer testing, these figures provide a way of comparing the gas mileage of different models. All EPA fuel-economy estimates can be accessed at *www.fueleconomy.gov* or *www.epa.gov/greenvehicles.*

In CONSUMER REPORTS' real-world fuel-economy testing, however, we've found that the EPA estimates are often higher than you're likely to get in normal driving. That's why we conduct several different fuel-economy tests of our own, including separate city and highway driving loops, and a 150-mile mixed driving loop. Vehicle speeds and atmospheric conditions are carefully monitored throughout these tests to ensure consistency, and fuel is measured by splicing a fuel meter into the vehicle's fuel line.

The EPA has been reviewing its method of calculating fuel economy, and Consumers Union, the nonprofit publisher of CONSUMER REPORTS, has been one of several organizations with which the agency has consulted.

Regardless of where the original figure comes from, a vehicle's fuel economy is not a constant or fixed number; it varies among vehicles of the same make and model, and it will vary over time for an individual vehicle.

## Personal Experiences

Hearing about the problems and experiences of vehicle owners can give you insight into what it's like to live with a model, and there are plenty of Web sites on which you can either voice your opinion or read those of others. The sites can be very informative, but one must be careful—sometimes the reliability of the information can be questionable. You have no way of determining the source—it could be a qualified individual, a disgruntled automaker employee, a dealer, or a dealer's competitor.

Chat rooms and bulletin boards such as those on the Edmunds and Epinions Web sites are popular and can include a range of topics. You might find them informative and even entertaining.

ConsumerReports.org also publishes user reviews from its subscribers and provides ongoing Expert Forums that feature discussions on various subjects between CONSUMER REPORTS auto-testers/engineers and subscribers. You must be an online subscriber to participate; transcripts of previous conversations are available online.

# Time Well Spent

With so much auto information so readily available on the Internet, there's no reason why a car shopper shouldn't be thoroughly informed and prepared before buying or leasing. By spending some time comparing models in the key areas covered in this chapter, you can quickly narrow your list of choices, concentrating on those with the best ratings and reviews and bypassing models that don't compare as well.

In the next chapter, we'll take an in-depth look at auto-safety information and how to compare vehicles in various safety areas.

Knowledge is power when it comes to the car-buying process, and you'll want to be empowered when the time comes to select your new vehicle so you can negotiate the best deal possible. The more preliminary research and gathering of facts you do prior to selecting and buying your next car, the more likely you'll be satisfied with your purchase.

# 3

# Safety Issues & Answers

**Evaluating a vehicle's safety potential** brings to mind the story of the blind men who each try to describe an elephant by feeling different parts of its body. One man, feeling the leg, says the elephant is similar to a tree. Another, touching the tail, argues that the elephant is more like a rope. The remaining blind men, feeling only the elephant's side, trunk, tusk, and ear, each insist it's like a wall, a snake, a spear, or a fan, respectively.

So it can be with vehicle safety. Too often, buyers look at only one part of the safety picture, without getting the overall perspective. Automaker marketing can take advantage of this. A commercial or magazine ad, for instance, may tout a model's "five-star government crash-test rating," which could give you confidence that it's a pretty safe vehicle. But there's often much more to the overall safety picture.

- Many vehicles get a five-star rating in government crash tests; don't be overly swayed by this.
- That same car may not have performed as well in the more severe insurance-industry offset-frontal and side-crash tests.
- It may not handle well in emergency situations in which you're trying to avoid an accident.
- It may not have the latest safety features.
- It may be hard to properly secure child-safety seats in it, or it may have other risky designs for children.

You get the picture.

Similarly, some buyers think they need a large vehicle because of its perceived crash safety, without considering that it may handle clumsily or, in the case of SUVs and pickups, have a higher incidence of deadly rollover accidents.

As you can see, there are many variables that contribute to a vehicle's overall safety potential, and the challenge is to look at them in a systematic way that allows you to fairly compare one vehicle to another. In this chapter, we'll help you do that by:

- Covering the major safety issues of which you should be aware
- Telling you where to find key safety ratings
- Giving you a rundown of the safety features you should look for and why they're important
- Providing you with a worksheet that can help you compare all aspects of a vehicle's safety potential

# Key Safety Issues

There's an array of safety issues—from crash protection to safety features—that you should consider for any vehicle you're thinking of buying. To help you accurately compare vehicles in terms of overall safety, we'll take a look at each issue individually in the following pages.

## Crash protection

This is perhaps the vehicle safety issue that gets the most attention. Although vehicles, in general, are much safer in collisions than they used to be, about 30,000 people traveling in passenger vehicles die in highway accidents each year. As a driver, you want the confidence that your vehicle will be able to get you through a crash with as little injury as possible.

How well a vehicle protects its occupants from injury depends primarily on its structural design and safety systems. Safety belts are the single most important element. According to federal government statistics, safety belts saved 14,900 lives in the U.S. in 2004—and that's at an estimated 80 percent usage. Advanced safety-belt features such as pretensioners and force limiters (see page 75) can also help minimize injury.

Air-bag systems provide additional protection. There is now a variety of systems available, as described later in this chapter. All new vehicles come equipped with standard dual frontal air bags, and many now offer side air bags and head-protection side-curtain air bags to help in side impacts.

In addition, all vehicles have "crumple zones" in the front that are designed to collapse in a way that both helps to absorb the crash energy and to minimize any deformation of the cabin. The better the vehicle manages this energy, the less chance that occupants will suffer serious injury.

## Crash tests

How well a vehicle protects you in a crash varies, depending on the vehicle speed, angle of impact, size and positions of the driver and passengers, and other variables. No one can predict what will happen in a specific crash, but the best indicators come from independent crash-test programs conducted by the National Highway Traffic Safety Administration (NHTSA), a branch of the U.S. Department of Transportation, and the IIHS (Insurance Institute for Highway Safety), which is sponsored by the insurance industry.

Both organizations conduct frontal- and side-impact crash tests. NHTSA's tests, which are part of its New Car Assessment Program, are scored on a five-star scale, with fewer stars indicating a greater likelihood of injury or death. NHTSA conducts a full-frontal test in which the entire width of a vehicle's front end impacts a rigid barrier at 35 mph.

The test is equivalent to a head-on collision between two vehicles of the same weight, each traveling at 35 mph. Instrumented crash-test dummies in the two front seats record crash forces on the head, chest, and legs, and separate ratings are given for the driver and front passenger. The resulting information indicates a belted person's chances of incurring a serious injury in the event of a crash.

Some have criticized NHTSA's full-frontal rigid-barrier test as unrealistic because full-frontal crashes into a solid flat object are rare in real life. Safety experts say it's a good indication, though, of how well a vehicle's safety belts and air-bag systems protect the occupants in these circumstances.

NHTSA's side-impact test simulates a vehicle being hit on the side by a 3,000-pound car traveling at 38.5 mph. Such a scenario might be

## Key to government crash-test ratings

Vehicles that are tested in NHTSA crash tests are rated on a five-star scale, as defined by the following key. In these definitions, a serious injury is one requiring immediate hospitalization and may be life-threatening. The percentages show the chance of serious injury.

| Star rating | Frontal-crash test | Side-crash test |
|---|---|---|
| ★★★★★= | 10% or less | 5% or less |
| ★★★★= | 11% to 20% | 6% to 10% |
| ★★★= | 21% to 35% | 11% to 20% |
| ★★= | 36% to 45% | 21% to 25% |
| ★= | 46% or greater | 26% or greater |

likely if a driver ran a red light while you were easing out into an intersection after having waited for a green light. Scores that reflect the chance of a life-threatening chest injury are provided for the driver and left rear-seat passenger.

The IIHS tests vehicles in an offset-frontal crash. In this, a vehicle is crashed into a deformable barrier at 40 mph, but only the portion of the vehicle in front of the driver (40 percent of the width) impacts the barrier. This test challenges the car's structural integrity and restraint systems to assess a vehicle's ability to protect the area around the driver without collapsing. Vehicles are rated as Good, Acceptable, Marginal, or Poor.

The IIHS side-impact test is more severe than the government's side test. It simulates a car being hit in the side by a typical SUV or truck and measures head injury as well as chest injury. The test uses a 3,300-pound deformable barrier, shaped to simulate the typical front end of a pickup or SUV, that strikes the test vehicle with a perpendicular impact at 31 mph. In each tested vehicle are two instrumented test dummies representing a small female or a 12-year-old adolescent.

Except in the above IIHS side-impact test, NHTSA and IIHS test results apply best to average-sized adult males, since that's the size approximated by current crash-test dummies. The test results may not apply as well to smaller or larger men or to women or children.

## The effect of vehicle size and weight

The frontal- crash tests performed by NHTSA and IIHS simulate a collision between two vehicles of the same weight. Many real-world collisions, however, occur between vehicles that are different sizes and weights. As the IIHS states, "Everything else being equal, lighter vehicles have higher occupant death rates" in a crash. This is because larger, heavier vehicles project more of their energy into other vehicles, at the smaller vehicles' expense. This, in turn, helps to better protect the larger vehicles' occupants, but it will likely cause greater injuries to the occupants of smaller vehicles.

## Higher bumper heights

In a crash, the higher bumper on many taller vehicles, such as SUVs and trucks, hits a typical passenger car above the car's bumper line, exerting its force into weaker portions of the smaller vehicle and inflicting greater damage. To address this, many SUVs—especially car-based ones—are being designed with lower, more compatible bumpers. In 2003, 15 major automakers agreed to implement new specifications on all their light trucks (SUVs, pickups, and minivans) to help alleviate this problem, but those designs won't begin to be phased in on all vehicles until the 2010 model year.

## Behind the scenes: Carmaker tests

Vehicles must also pass government certification tests performed by the manufacturers before they can be sold. Those test results are not published. They are pass/fail, with unbelted crash dummies that determine how well a vehicle protects unbelted occupants—a crucial concern, since about 20 percent of drivers and passengers still don't buckle up.

At one time, carmakers conducted these tests, which are part of Federal Motor Vehicle Safety Standard 208, in a way that closely resembled NHTSA's full-frontal tests. Entire vehicles were rammed into a fixed barrier, though at a less-stringent 30 mph rather than 35 mph. Carmakers had to certify that unbelted dummies didn't sustain the human equivalent of serious or fatal injuries, and as with the NCAP tests conducted by NHTSA, data came solely from dummies approximating average-sized males.

## Where to find crash-test information online

Results of crash tests and other information can be found online at:

- NHTSA              *www.safercar.gov* or *www.NHTSA.dot.gov*
- IIHS               *www.hwysafety.org* or *www.IIHS.org*
- ConsumerReports.org  *www.ConsumerReports.org*

# When crash tests collide

Models with high NHTSA scores, poor IIHS scores in side tests. Sometimes a vehicle scores well in the government's annual New Car Assessment Program (NCAP) and not so well in side-crash tests conducted by the insurance industry. Those in the following chart are among the 50 or so 2005 models for which both sets of data are available. All were awarded four or five stars for their driver and driver's side rear passengers in the NCAP side-crash test, equating to a 10 percent or less chance of serious injury in a collision, NHTSA estimates. Yet their Poor ratings in tests conducted by the Insurance Institute for Highway Safety for a side-impact crash indicate that the driver would likely suffer serious injury.

| 2005 Vehicle | NHTSA side-crash scores | | IIHS side-crash scores |
| --- | --- | --- | --- |
| | Driver | Passenger | Combining driver and rear passenger |
| Hyundai Elantra | ★★★★★ | ★★★★ | Poor |
| Chevrolet Malibu* | ★★★★ | ★★★★★ | Poor |
| Kia Optima | ★★★★ | ★★★★ | Poor |
| Honda Element* | ★★★★★ | ★★★★★ | Poor |
| Saturn Vue* | ★★★★★ | ★★★★★ | Poor |
| Toyota RAV4* | ★★★★★ | ★★★★★ | Poor |
| Ford Escape | ★★★★★ | ★★★★★ | Poor |
| Mitsubishi Outlander* | ★★★★★ | ★★★★ | Poor |

* Models were tested without optional side airbags.

In 1997, to reduce deaths attributed to air bags that deployed too power-fully, the auto industry successfully argued that the test standards be lowered to allow for less powerful bags. NHTSA permitted the industry to use a sim-ulated crash test, with part of a vehicle mounted on a sled, rather than crash-ing real cars. The less severe sled test was one that vehicles could pass with less powerful bags, which were introduced on many 1998-model vehicles.

Analysis of crashes with depowered bags have not shown an increase in deaths, so we could surmise that they are giving adequate protection.

## Smarter air bags

To provide greater protection for a wider range of occupants, many vehi-cles are now coming equipped with advanced air-bag systems. These deploy at variable rates, depending on factors such as whether the front safety belts are buckled, the position of the driver's seat, the weight and/or position of the front passenger, and the severity of the crash. By varying the force of the bags' deployment—or in the case of front passenger air bags, whether they deploy at all—the systems can be designed to provide optimum protection for different-sized occupants while minimizing the risks. For instance, they could provide maximum protection for large, unbelted occupants while reducing the possibility of injuring smaller occupants during a relatively low-speed crash. These smart air-bag systems are currently available in a number of models and are showing up in more vehicles every year. They are required for all vehicles by the 2007 model year.

The move to smarter air bags has allowed NHTSA to revise the mini-mum performance standards required by Federal Motor Vehicle Safety Standard 208, starting with 2004 models. Tests now involve two crash dum-mies that simulate a medium-sized adult male and a small adult female.

- Dummies are tested belted and unbelted, in full-frontal and offset crashes. That puts added emphasis on protecting belted occupants while still evaluating protection for unbelted ones.

- Frontal air bags are tested with crash dummies seated close to them. Vehicles pass only if they protect belted and unbelted crash dummies from severe injury.
- Vehicles are statically tested with child-sized dummies in the front passenger seat to test that the air bag is suppressed, as designed.
- Crash-test data includes expanded neck- and chest-injury results.

In addition, automakers are again crash-testing actual vehicles, instead of using just sleds that simulate vehicles. The rules specify a maximum unbelted-test speed of only 25 mph, however, which automakers feel is best for overall protection.

# Accident Avoidance

A vehicle's ability to help you avoid an accident is just as important as its ability to protect you in a crash. For every accident there are numerous near misses that statistics don't reflect. Several factors contribute to a vehicle's accident-avoidance capability, with the two most important being braking and emergency handling. A good way to gauge a vehicle's performance in those areas is CONSUMER REPORTS' vehicle test Ratings.

- **Braking.** A vehicle's braking system has to stop the vehicle in as short a distance as possible and keep the vehicle under control and on its intended path. CONSUMER REPORTS' tests measure braking performance on both dry and wet pavement, and evaluate the effectiveness of a vehicle's antilock brake system (ABS). We'll talk about antilock brakes and other braking aids later in this chapter.
- **Emergency handling.** The more controllable and secure a vehicle is when pressed to its handling limits, the better you'll be able to avoid an accident by, for example, steering around an obstacle without losing control. CR rates emergency handling on the basis of three tests. The first is a double-lane-change avoidance maneuver to evaluate a vehicle's

handling in a situation where a driver needs to suddenly steer around an obstacle on the road. In the other tests, vehicles are pushed to their cornering limits around our handling course and skid pad.

- **Other accident-avoidance factors.** Acceleration, driving position, visibility, and even seat comfort can also affect accident avoidance. Quick acceleration can make it easier to merge safely into highway traffic or to avoid an accident. A driver's seating position can affect outward visibility; the ease of operating the controls such as the radio, lights, or heater; and comfort. The better drivers can see out of their car, the more aware they'll be of other vehicles and conditions. Seat comfort also plays a role because a driver who is fatigued or uncomfortable may concentrate less on the road.

Braking, handling, acceleration, driving position, seat comfort, and much more are evaluated on every vehicle tested by CONSUMER REPORTS. The test results and ratings are published regularly in CONSUMER REPORTS magazine, CR's special auto publications, and on ConsumerReports.org. (See Appendix C.)

## Rollover Resistance

Rollover accidents may be relatively rare—occurring in fewer than 3 percent of serious crashes—but they have a high fatality rate, accounting for about 33 percent of all vehicle-occupant deaths. According to government statistics, in 2003, 52 percent of occupants involved in rollover accidents died, compared with 35 percent in other types of accidents. Those who survive a rollover often suffer an incapacitating injury.

Rollovers are of particular concern with taller vehicles, such as SUVs and pickups. Government statistics for 2003 show that about 37 percent of the SUVs involved in fatal crashes had rolled over, compared with 16 percent of the passenger cars involved in fatal crashes.

It's mostly a matter of physics. A taller vehicle has a higher center of gravity, which makes it more top-heavy than one that sits lower. In a situation where a vehicle is subjected to strong sideways forces, it's easier for a taller vehicle to roll over. During normal circumstances, drivers typically don't encounter such strong forces, but an emergency can happen without warning. A rollover becomes a danger in several types of situations:

- **An accident-avoidance maneuver.** If a driver swerves sharply to avoid an obstacle or person in the road, the hard-cornering forces can cause the vehicle to tip onto two wheels or roll over. Alternately, the vehicle can strike a curb, guardrail, or other low obstacle and "trip" over it, causing the vehicle to roll.
- **Taking a corner too fast for the conditions.** This can cause a vehicle to slide or skid to the outside of the turn, where it could go off the pavement or, as above, trip over a low obstacle.
- **Tire failure.** At least some of the accidents that initiated the massive Firestone tire recall in 2000 took place when a sudden tire blowout caused the driver to lose control, causing the vehicle to swerve sharply and roll over.

To give consumers a way of telling which vehicles have a higher rollover propensity than others, NHTSA has developed a five-star rating, called the Rollover Resistance Rating (RRR). One star signifies a more than 40 percent likelihood of rollover in a single-vehicle crash; five stars mean less than 10 percent.

The RRR is calculated from two factors: a vehicle's static stability factor (SSF) and a dynamic rollover test. The SSF, which is determined from measurements of a vehicle's track width and the height of its center of gravity, essentially indicates how top-heavy a vehicle is. The dynamic rollover test puts vehicles through an extreme handling maneuver called a fishhook, which simulates a driver having to make a series of sharp steering maneuvers, as can happen in an emergency. Vehicles are run through the test at progressively higher speeds, ranging from 35 to 50 mph. Vehicles that tip up at any speed fail the test. Among the 48 SUVs and pickups that NHTSA tested for the 2005 model year, 19 percent—almost one in five— had at least one version that tipped.

CONSUMER REPORTS believes a vehicle that tips up in this type of situation has serious stability problems, and we will not recommend it. The results of the dynamic test, however, have little effect on NHTSA's overall star rating. Several vehicles have a mid-level 3-star rating despite having tipped up in the dynamic test; some even have a 4-star rating.

**Where to find the information:** NHTSA's five-star rollover ratings are posted at their Web site, *www.safercar.gov*. To see if a vehicle tipped up in the dynamic test, however, you need to dig a little deeper than the five-star ratings. Click on the vehicle model's name or star ratings to get more information. Then scroll down to Rollover.

Also check out CONSUMER REPORTS' emergency-handling ratings, which can alert you to any stability problems that show up when a vehicle is pushed to its handling limits. See Appendix C for information on accessing CR ratings.

Because the dynamic test wasn't introduced until 2004, all NHTSA rollover ratings prior to 2004 models are based only on the SSF. Because it's a static measurement, the SSF doesn't account for vehicles' different suspen-

## What to do if you have a blowout

A blowout, or rapid loss of air from a tire, can severely limit your vehicle's ability to steer or brake. An over-reaction by the driver—rapid steering, hard braking, or abruptly taking your foot off the accelerator—can cause your vehicle to swerve or go into an uncontrollable skid. If your vehicle goes off the road or is tripped by a curb, a rollover crash can occur.

If you experience a blowout, gradually release the accelerator, steer in the direction you want the vehicle to go, and, once the vehicle has stabilized, slow down and safely pull off the road.

sion designs, tires, or the presence of safety systems such as electronic stability control (ESC)—factors that can make a significant difference in how a vehicle performs in the dynamic test and in real-world driving.

# Rear-Impact Protection

Although "rear enders" have a low fatality rate, they have a high injury rate, especially for whiplash neck injuries. The design of a car's head restraints and seats are critical factors in how severe a whiplash injury will be. Restraints need to be tall enough to cushion the head above the top of the spine. The top of the head restraint should be at least as high as the top of the person's ear. It should also be positioned as closely to the person's head as possible. Many cars' head restraints can be adjusted for height, although many people don't take the time to make the adjustment.

Look for head restraints that lock in the raised position. Those that don't can be forced down in a crash, losing effectiveness. Many cars' rear restraints are too low to do much good. Unfortunately, the higher the rear head restraint, the lower the visibility to the rear for the driver.

A vehicle's seat needs to work in conjunction with the head restraint. According to the IIHS, the seat shouldn't rotate backward in a rear impact because this would move the head restraint away from the head. It also can't be too stiff; the seat must "give" a bit so a person will sink into it, moving the head closer to the restraint. Some vehicles offer systems to prevent whiplash and according to the IIHS, they do work well to prevent the head from moving too far rearward.

**Where to find the information:** CONSUMER REPORTS evaluates head restraints for all seating positions in every tested vehicle. Any problems are noted in the road-test reports that are published in the magazine and on ConsumerReports.org.

Another good source for information on rear-impact protection is the IIHS Web site, *www.hwysafety.org*. Since 1995, the Institute has been conducting evaluations of head-restraint geometry and publishing ratings for different models. With 2004 models, it also began conducting dynamic rear-impact tests that measure how well different seat/head restraint combinations protect against whiplash. Tested models are rated Good, Acceptable, Marginal, or Poor, just as in the crash tests.

# Child Safety Issues

If you're in the market for a family car, child safety is likely one of your top priorities. There are a number of issues, features, and options that you should know about when evaluating and selecting the right vehicle for your family needs.

### Blind zones

Every year, children are injured and killed because drivers don't see them while backing up. According to Kids and Cars, a nonprofit group whose mission is to improve child safety in and around cars, back-over incidents in 2004 killed at least 100 children. A contributing factor is that some larger vehicles, such as SUVs, pickups, and minivans, have larger blind spots— the area behind a vehicle that the driver can't see.

To check a vehicle's blind spot, sit in the driver's seat of the parked vehicle while someone stands in back and holds out a hand at about waist level. Have the person walk back slowly until you can see the hand through the rear window. This will give you an idea of how big that vehicle's blind spot is.

Some vehicles are now available with an optional rear-view video camera that gives the driver a wide-angle view of much of the area that's usually hidden in the blind spot. The scene appears in an in-dash display. When used regularly, this system can be an effective aid in reducing back-over accidents, but these camera systems are typically expensive and usually offered as part of a navigation package that can run well over $2,000.

There are also aftermarket camera systems costing between $400 and $800 that can be installed on any vehicle.

Many vehicles are also available with a parking-assist system that uses sensors in the vehicle's rear to alert the driver to solid objects behind the vehicle. Such systems are also available as aftermarket add-ons, priced around $300 to $400. In CONSUMER REPORTS tests, we've found that these systems work well as parking aids but aren't reliable enough to be used as safety aids.

## Child safety seats

Child safety seats save lives and should be used until a child is big enough to use the vehicle's regular safety belt. The traditional method of attaching a child seat called for using the vehicle's safety belts. Still, incompatibilities between the car's safety belts, the car seats, and the child safety seats often have made a good, tight fit difficult and sometimes impossible to achieve.

2001 and later vehicles are required to have the Lower Anchors and Tethers for Children (LATCH) system. The LATCH system features built-in lower anchors and ready-to-use tether attachment points allowing compatible child safety seats to be installed without using the vehicle's safety-belt system. The LATCH system simplifies child safety seat installation when an owner installs a LATCH-compatible child seat.

This system doesn't work equally well in all vehicles, however. In many cars the new attachment points are obscured or difficult to access, so that it's not easy to use them even with some of the newest child seats. In other models the LATCH anchors are positioned too far out from the vehicle's seat, making it difficult to secure the child seat tightly against the rear seat's back cushion. The key is to try your child seat in the vehicle before you buy.

## Power-window switches

At least 33 children have died during the past decade from injuries involving power windows in cars, according to Kids and Cars. Typically, the child is left in the car with the engine running or keys in the ignition. The child leans his or her head out the window of a parked car and then accidentally leans or kneels on the window switch. The glass moves up forcefully, choking the child. Because the window can quickly crush the windpipe, the child cannot scream for help.

Two types of switches are inherently riskier than others if they're mounted horizontally on the door's armrest:

**Rocker** switches move the glass up when you press one end of the switch, down when you press the other.

**Toggle** switches work when pushed forward or pulled back.

A third type, the **lever** switch, is safer because it makes it almost impossible to raise the window accidentally. Lever switches must be pulled up to raise the glass. Switches of any design mounted vertically or on an upswept armrest are also harder to activate by accident.

Lever switches and autoreverse sensors are common in Europe. But autoreverse is required in the U.S. only in vehicles with auto/one-touch-up windows and remotely controlled windows. A safety regulation enacted by NHTSA in late 2004 mandates that all new vehicles be equipped with safer window switches. Automakers, however, have until late 2008, meaning the 2009 model year, to comply fully.

In the meantime, there are plenty of vehicles that still have the riskier designs. You definitely should look for cars with lever switches when shopping for a family vehicle, particularly if you have younger children.

**Where to find the information:** Every road test report for each vehicle that is published in CONSUMER REPORTS or online at ConsumerReports.org has a section called Safety Notes, where issues such as LATCH problems, safety-belt troubles, head-restraint shortcomings, and child comfort are discussed.

# Load Capacity

It's natural to assume that if a vehicle has a large cargo area, you should be able to fill it without worrying about overloading the vehicle, but that's not always the case. Some vehicles have a large cargo area but a relatively low load-carrying capacity—the maximum combined weight of people and cargo that the vehicle is designed to handle safely. Surprisingly, it's easy to overload just about any vehicle.

Overloading a vehicle can compromise its safety by degrading its handling, stressing its brakes, and possibly overheating its tires, increasing the risk of tire failure. Prior to September 1, 2004, however, most auto manufacturers didn't provide load-capacity specifications in a form that's easily accessible to the consumer. Exceptions included Honda, Jeep, Mercedes-Benz, Nissan, and Toyota. All vehicles manufactured after that date are now required to have a load label attached to the driver's door pillar.

**Where to find the information:** In addition to a vehicle's load label, CONSUMER REPORTS calculates the load capacity on every vehicle it tests and includes those figures in the road test reports.

# A Guide to Safety Features

Today's vehicles offer an array of advanced safety features. But many buyers don't know what to look for or which are most important.

Antilock brake systems (ABS) and electronic stability control (ESC), for instance, are effective and well worth the money. Buyers who don't know the advantage of these systems, however, may not know to look for them when comparing vehicles. You also can't always depend on a dealership's salespeople to give you accurate information about these features. Many are less knowledgeable than they should be.

In the following pages, you'll learn about all the major safety features and why they're important.

Remember, the most important thing you can do to protect your life is to buckle your safety belt. Belts save lives on their own, but many of the more advanced safety features, such as safety-belt pretensioners and air bags, work best for people who are buckled up to start with.

## Air bags

Air bags are part of what automakers call a "supplementary restraint system," or SRS. That means they are intended for use as supplements to your safety belts. By law every new passenger vehicle comes equipped with dual frontal air bags, but the sophistication of the systems can vary. It's worth checking what type of air-bag systems a vehicle has, both in the front and the rear.

### Frontal air bags

Depending on the severity of the crash, frontal air bags inflate to prevent occupants from hitting the steering wheel, dashboard, and windshield. Frontal air bags for both drivers and passengers have been standard equipment in all passenger vehicles since 1998. Frontal air bags do not eliminate the need for safety belts and do not offer protection in rollovers, or side-impact or rear-end crashes. Any new car you purchase will come with frontal air bags.

**How they work:** Crash sensors connected to an onboard computer detect a frontal collision, monitor its severity, and trigger the bags. Each bag inflates in the blink of an eye, then immediately starts deflating, cushioning the occupant as it deflates. Air-bag effectiveness depends upon the proper use of safety belts, which help keep you in place in the event of a collision. Occupants who are unbelted or out of position can end up being seriously injured or killed if they are too close to the air bag when it deploys.

A new generation of adaptive, or multistage, frontal air bags is appearing as standard equipment in many cars. Depending on the model, these adaptive systems can detect whether or not the safety belts are fastened, the presence and weight of a front passenger, and the position of the driver's seat, as well as the severity of the crash. In a low-level collision, the system inflates the frontal air bags less aggressively—with 70 to 80 percent of the force of a single-stage air bag. In a higher-speed collision they inflate with full force.

These advanced air-bag systems are becoming available in more cars each year and are mandated for all vehicles by the 2007 model year.

## Side air bags

The design of a side-air-bag system can vary greatly, depending on the model. When they first arrived, side air bags were fairly small cushions that popped out of the door trim or the side of the seatback. They helped protect the torso but weren't as effective in protecting an occupant's head. Many models still use a single bag per side, but most still don't provide effective head protection in a side impact.

On the other hand, many automakers have added a second side bag that deploys from overhead and is specifically designed for head protection. The most common design is a side-curtain air bag, which spreads across both front and rear side windows to prevent occupants from hitting their heads and to shield them from flying debris. A curtain bag, once deployed, stays inflated for about 6 seconds, which also can keep people from being ejected during a rollover. On some vehicles with third-row seats, the bag covers the windows of all three rows.

Each year more than 9,000 people die in side impacts, according to the IIHS, mainly from head injuries. The Institute also has found that side-air-bag systems that provide effective head protection are reducing deaths by about 45 percent among drivers of cars struck on the driver side. Side bags that protect the chest and abdomen, but not the head, also reduce deaths, but only by about 10 percent.

Fortunately, more vehicles are coming with head-protecting side bags as either standard or optional equipment, and we strongly recommend that you buy one with this feature.

**How they work:** Side-mounted crash sensors connected to an onboard computer detect a side collision and trigger the bags. The bags inflate in a few milliseconds, cushioning the impact. Some models—such as the Ford Explorer and Expedition, Mercury Mountaineer, Lincoln Navigator and Aviator, and Volvo XC90—automatically deploy the vehicle's side-curtain bags if the system detects that the vehicle is beginning to roll over. This can help prevent ejection and head injuries during a rollover.

### Knee air bags

Knee air bags, available in some high-end luxury vehicles, supplement the frontal air bags in protecting front occupants. They are designed to prevent what is called submarining in a frontal impact. This is when an occupant slides under the safety belt and into the footwell, where he or she can be crushed. All vehicles have solid structures called knee bolsters to help prevent this, but the bolsters themselves can cause injury. A knee air bag is better than a bolster at holding the occupant in the seat during a crash.

**How they work:** When not in use, knee bags are tucked away, out of sight under the dashboard. In a frontal impact, they are deployed by the same sensors that trigger the frontal air bags.

## Antilock brakes

An antilock brake system (ABS) is a safety feature that CONSUMER REPORTS highly recommends. It prevents a vehicle's wheels from locking up during "panic" braking. This, in turn, helps prevent the vehicle from sliding sideways and allows the driver to maintain steering control—a key factor in avoiding a collision. In many situations, ABS can also stop a vehicle in a shorter distance.

ABS, however, cannot overcome the laws of physics if you're driving too fast for the conditions. ABS is a standard feature on most vehicles, but a few automakers make it a $500 to $600 option to keep the vehicle's base price lower. This is a poor marketing tactic because it encourages buyers to eliminate a feature that has proven safety benefits.

**How they work:** Antilock brakes use wheel-speed sensors at each wheel and a computer that coordinates the braking action, regulating the brake-fluid pressure at each wheel to keep them from locking up. Most antilock brake systems monitor and control all four wheels of the vehicle. Some SUVs, trucks, and vans come with two-wheel ABS, which monitors and controls only a vehicle's rear wheels. This doesn't provide the full benefits of ABS, because the front wheels can still lock during hard braking, which can result in the loss of steering control.

## Brake assist

Some antilock brake systems also include brake assist. If this system determines that the driver is trying to make an emergency stop, it will automatically apply maximum braking from the ABS, even if the driver is too tentative while pressing the pedal. Under certain conditions, brake assist can potentially reduce overall stopping distance by activating the braking system more forcefully.

**How it works:** This feature monitors the speed or force at which the driver is pressing the brake pedal in order to determine whether the driver is intending to make an emergency stop. If so, it automatically applies maximum braking force through the ABS, reducing the stopping distance.

## Electronic stability control (ESC)

This is another safety system that CONSUMER REPORTS highly recommends, especially for SUVs. This system helps keep the vehicle on its intended path during a turn, to avoid sliding or skidding out of control. It is especially helpful in slippery conditions or when a driver swerves to avoid an accident or an object in the road. On an SUV it can help keep the vehicle from getting into a situation where it could roll over.

We believe that ESC is one of the best safety features to be introduced in years. Once you have experienced ESC in an emergency, its benefits become clear. An IIHS study found that equipping cars and SUVs with ESC can reduce single-vehicle fatal crashes by more than 50 percent. Similarly, NHTSA found that with ESC, single-vehicle crashes—fatal and nonfatal— were reduced by 35 percent in passenger cars and by 67 percent in SUVs.

We believe that this feature would be very beneficial for teenagers and other drivers with limited experience in dealing with an emergency driving situation and loss of vehicle control. As of this writing, no vehicle with ESC has tipped up in the government's rollover test.

One source of confusion with ESC is that automakers each have a proprietary name for their stability-control systems (see the table on page 77).

## You need to know

If you're a first-time ABS user, you need to forget everything you learned about conventional braking. ABS automatically pulses the brakes on and off during hard braking, many times faster and more accurately than any person could. As a result, you do not have to pump your brakes to avoid a skid. In fact, trying to pump them defeats the effect of the ABS and can make matters worse. With ABS, you simply need to "stomp and steer." You will feel a pulsing vibration in the pedal when the ABS is active, but don't let up until the car has come to a stop. If possible, try to take advantage of the ABS benefits by steering the vehicle where you want it to go.

If in doubt as to whether a car has it or not, find out before you buy. Stability control is usually an option and can add up to $1,000 to a vehicle's price, but it's well worth the extra money.

**How it works:** Stability control uses a computer linked to a series of sensors to detect wheel speed, steering angle, sideways motion, and yaw (spin). If the car starts to slide, the stability-control system momentarily brakes one or more wheels and, depending on the system, reduces engine power to keep the car on course.

Ford and Volvo use an ESC system called Roll Stability Control (RSC). It uses a gyroscopic sensor to monitor roll angle and roll speed and determine whether rollover is imminent. If so, it triggers the standard stability-control system and instantly reduces power and applies the brakes to the necessary wheels to bring the vehicle back under control.

## Safety-belt features

While the safety belt is arguably the single most important piece of safety equipment, enhanced belt features are helping safety belts do their job more effectively. Features vary from one automaker to another, so it pays to look carefully at what's available.

**Adjustable upper anchors** for the shoulder belts can make a meaningful safety difference. Adjustable anchors let you change the position of the shoulder belt so it can be positioned across the chest instead of across the neck to prevent neck injuries. They also can make a safety belt more comfortable to wear and can help keep the belt from pulling down on a tall person's shoulder.

**Safety-belt pretensioners** and **force limiters** work with the air bags to protect you in a crash.

**How they work:** Pretensioners automatically take up the slack in the safety belt during a frontal crash, helping to restrain people securely and to properly position them for the air bag. Force limiters relax the safety-belt tension slightly following the initial impact, so they can help absorb some of a person's forward thrust. That helps prevent chest and internal injuries caused by the belt.

## Other safety features

**Daytime running lights (DRLs).** This is a system that continually illuminates the headlights (although at a lower intensity than normal low-beams) in order to make a vehicle more visible to other drivers, even during daylight hours. This system is mandatory on all vehicles in Canada, and in the U.S. it is standard on all GM, Lexus, Mercedes-Benz, Saab, Subaru, Suzuki, Volkswagen, and Volvo models. According to the IIHS, studies conducted in various countries show that DRLs reduce daytime crashes by 3 to 11 percent, depending on the study.

**Tire-pressure monitoring system.** Underinflated tires can hurt handling and fuel economy, as well as cause premature wear—or a possible blowout—of the tire. Yet a tire can lose air so slowly that many drivers don't realize it's happening. Some models come with a tire-pressure monitoring system that automatically alerts the driver if a tire's air pressure drops below a specific point.

NHTSA has mandated that by the 2008 model year, all passenger cars will have a tire-pressure-monitoring system that can detect when one of more of the vehicle's tires are 25 percent or more below the recommended inflation pressure.

The type of tire-pressure monitor we favor measures tire pressure directly. A less-effective system gauges air loss indirectly by using sensors to count wheel revolutions and computing whether any wheel is turning at a slightly faster speed than the others—an indication that it is losing air pressure. If, however, all four tires are losing pressure at a similar rate, as our tests show can happen over time if a driver doesn't check the tire pressure regularly, this system would not necessarily see any difference and wouldn't issue a warning. In any case we suggest checking your tires with a conventional tire pressure gauge at least once a month (see Chapter 18).

**Accident-alert system.** This is a system that, among other functions, is automatically activated if an air bag goes off and can be used to bring emergency aid to a vehicle, even if the driver is unconscious. The best-known system is GM's OnStar, which is provided as standard equipment in a number of GM models (including Hummer and Saab), Acura, Audi, Isuzu, and Volkswagen models. Mercedes-Benz provides a similar system called Tele Aid. The system uses a cellular telephone system to allow a driver to contact a central dispatch center and a Global Positioning Satellite (GPS) receiver to let the center precisely locate the vehicle.

When an air bag is deployed, the system automatically notifies the center, which locates the vehicle and sends emergency aid if the driver does not respond to an inquiry. Other services are also available, including tracking a vehicle if it's been stolen or even opening a locked vehicle if the keys aren't available. Typically, after an initial year of free service on a new vehicle, you must pay a subscription fee to keep the service active. OnStar costs about $200 a year for a basic plan; Tele Aid about $240. Keep in mind that the system depends on cellular service; if no service is available, the system can't connect with the center and vice versa.

**Traction control.** This electronically controlled system limits wheel spin

# A spotter's guide for electronic stability control (ESC)

Consumer Reports strongly recommends getting a vehicle with electronic stability control. Because automakers give their ESC systems different names, however, it can be confusing to identify it on the features list. To help, here are the trademarked names for the ESC systems of various brands:

| Brand | Name of ESC system |
| --- | --- |
| Acura | Vehicle Stability Assist (VSA) |
| Audi | Electronic Stability Program (ESP) |
| BMW | Dynamic Stability Control (DSC) |
| Buick | StabiliTrak |
| Cadillac | StabiliTrak |
| Chevrolet | Active Handling, StabiliTrak |
| Chrysler | Electronic Stability Program (ESP) |
| Ford | AdvanceTrac |
| Infiniti | Vehicle Dynamic Control (VDC) |
| Jaguar | Dynamic Stability Control (DSC) |
| Land Rover | Dynamic Stability Control (DSC) |
| Lexus | Vehicle Stability Control (VSC) |
| Lincoln | AdvanceTrac |
| Mercedes-Benz | Electronic Stability Program (ESP) |
| Mercury | AdvanceTrac |
| Pontiac | StabiliTrak |
| Porsche | Porsche Stability Management (PSM) |
| Saab | Electronic Stability Program (ESP) |
| Scion | Vehicle Stability Control (VSC) |
| Subaru | Vehicle Dynamics Control System (VDCS) |
| Toyota | Vehicle Stability Control (VSC) |
| Volkswagen | Electronic Stabilization Program (ESP) |
| Volvo | Dynamic Stability and Traction Control (DSTC) |

during acceleration so the drive wheels have maximum traction. It's particularly useful when starting off in wet, snowy, or icy conditions. Some traction-control systems operate only at low speeds, while others work at all speeds. Traction control is frequently bundled with other options, but when available as a stand-alone option, it can cost from $300 to $500.

Most low-speed traction-control systems use the same components as the car's antilock brake system. If the system detects wheel spin while accelerating on a slippery surface, it momentarily applies the brakes to the slipping wheel. This stops the slipping and automatically routes power to the opposite drive wheel. All-speed traction control uses a combination of ABS and powertrain control. In slick conditions and at higher speeds, a system of sensors and computers may upshift the transmission, reduce engine power, or apply brakes—or a combination of these—to prevent wheel spin.

## Not All Safety Systems Are Created Equal

More models are coming with advanced safety features that make a profound improvement in both crash survival and accident avoidance. Still, just because every automaker has to comply with government regulations, you can't assume that all vehicles are the same when it comes to safety. Frequently, the devil is in the details; the effectiveness of safety systems depends on their design and how they're integrated into the vehicle. When choosing a vehicle, don't rely only on a checklist of safety features. Read CR's vehicle reviews and check test results and ratings to see how the vehicle performs overall.

# 4

# Features
## to Look For

**Deciding on the car model** is only the first step in picking the right vehicle. You also need to decide on the exact features you want. Today's vehicles offer a wide range of options and accessories—from more powerful engines to an array of comfort and convenience items—that allow you to personalize your car to better fit your needs and lifestyle.

Some features, like alloy wheels or rear spoilers, are primarily cosmetic. Others make a meaningful improvement. For instance, seats with height adjustment and a steering wheel with a telescopic (fore-aft) adjustment can make the difference between a good driving position and prolonged discomfort. Sometimes a more powerful engine can make a vehicle more fun to drive and make it easier to pass and merge into highway traffic. Other features, such as heated seats or a rear video-entertainment system, are not essential but certainly add to comfort or convenience.

Most models are available in two or more different trim levels, which are differentiated by their standard and optional features, price, and sometimes powertrain. To get the best value for your money, you need to select the trim level that provides the most features you want as standard, without getting one that makes you pay for a lot of features you don't care about.

Once you've decided on your trim level, you can add additional options, if necessary. Ordering optional equipment, however, can be a juggling act. While many options can be selected individually, others are available only as part of a large group or package. This can work for or against you. If a particular package consists of items that you would want anyway, you'll likely save money, since the package price is usually lower than if you'd bought the items separately. But sometimes you can't get an option you want without buying ones you don't. You need to weigh the price for the package against how much you want any given option.

In this chapter, we'll help you make your selections by describing many of the commonly available features and highlighting those that CONSUMER REPORTS recommends you look for. In the following pages, we'll cover:

- The difference between options and accessories
- Features that CONSUMER REPORTS strongly recommends
- Other features that are nice to have
- Features that need more time at the drawing board
- Tips on choosing a trim line
- How options can affect trade-in value
- The pros and cons of custom-ordering a vehicle

## Options vs. Accessories

Add-ons that are installed on the vehicle at the plant are commonly called factory options. When dealerships order vehicles, they typically specify different configurations of options so customers have a choice, from relatively inexpensive versions with few options to fully loaded versions.

In addition to factory options, there is usually a selection of dealer-installed accessories, such as floor mats, car covers, and so on. Only specific factory options are available for any given model and trim level, whereas many dealer accessories can be ordered for any vehicle.

In addition, there is a wide range of aftermarket accessories available for many models. Those are add-ons that are sold by independent companies and can be installed on the vehicle after you buy it. They range from high-performance engine modifications and custom wheels to audio and DVD entertainment systems. Take care when choosing aftermarket accessories, though. Some performance modifications can void your manufacturer warranty or even make your vehicle less reliable or less safe. In addition, you shouldn't install aftermarket accessories that require any vehicle modifications to a leased car. In this chapter, we'll talk only about factory options and dealer accessories that have been approved by the automaker.

## What Are Your Priorities?

Before perusing the many features available for a given model, we recommend that you spend some time thinking about the ones that are most important to you and those that you don't want to spend money on. Perhaps a strong engine is important because you live in a mountainous area or you want a navigation system because you drive in a lot in unfamiliar areas. On the other hand, things like a sunroof, leather upholstery, or wood interior trim may not be worth the price to you.

As you go through the car-buying process, your list of features will likely change as you become more familiar with the benefits of different features or decide that some on your "want" list are unnecessary or cost too much. To help tailor your list, in this chapter we describe the advantages and disadvantages of some common features, and we list some of those options we recommend you consider.

# Shopping for Features

A manufacturer's Web site or a model brochure are often good places to start reviewing what features are available for a given model and trim level. Lists of standard and optional features are also available in Consumer Reports' New Car Price Reports (see Appendix C) or on auto-pricing Web sites (see Appendix A).

When you look up a model through any of these sources, check which trim lines are available. For example, the Honda Accord is available in DX, LX, EX, or Hybrid trims, with each priced progressively higher. The Ford Explorer is available as an XLS, XLT, Eddie Bauer, or Limited edition. Sometimes the engine defines a particular trim level, as with the Jaguar S-Type, where the 3.0 and 4.2 refer to the displacements of the V6 and V8 engines that are offered.

Sometimes the lowest-priced version of a model doesn't have a specific trim designation. For example, the lower-priced version of the Pontiac Vibe is simply called the model name, whereas the upgraded version is called the Vibe GT. In these cases, the trim line is generically referred to as the base model.

For each trim level, it's important to check the price, the list of standard features, and the available options. If you're lucky, you may find the lowest-priced version includes most of the features you want as standard features, and you can get any others you desire as options.

Many buyers, however, find that they need to get a higher trim level that includes more standard features and a greater choice of options. In order to get some features, such as a rear-entertainment or navigation system, you may find that you have to opt for the highest trim line.

The trick to getting the most value in features is to choose the trim level that offers the most features on your "want" list as standard equipment while adding as few optional features as possible.

Often you'll find that some features you want are only bundled in an option package, which makes you buy other features that you may not care about. This can make it tricky to equip a model exactly the way you want it while minimizing your expense. You have to decide how much a particular feature is worth to you and whether the other packaged features are worthwhile or a waste of money. When you run into conflicts like this, you may find that one of your alternative model choices, even if it has a similar base price, will save you money when you compare models feature for feature.

Even after you've decided on paper which features you want, it may be hard to locate that exact configuration in a dealership's inventory. Many models are readily available only in certain option configurations. For instance, it may be hard to find a vehicle with a sunroof that isn't also equipped with leather seats.

Unless you decide to special-order a vehicle, which can take weeks, you may have to compromise on your features list—and the price you pay for the vehicle. This is why it's important to check the inventory of local dealers before you go to buy the car. You'll find more information on checking dealer inventories in Chapter 13.

# Features that CR Recommends

Many times, buyers overlook important features because they aren't aware of them or don't understand the benefit they provide. The following list includes those features that we typically look for when buying test cars and recommend that you consider for your vehicle:

## Safety features

- Electronic stability control (ESC)
- Antilock brake system (ABS)
- Side-curtain air bags (for head protection)
- Side air bags
- All-wheel drive (in a snowy climate)
- Traction control

Studies have shown that electronic stability control (ESC), side air bags, and head-protecting side-curtain air bags have a dramatic impact on saving lives. Antilock brakes are also an important feature for avoiding accidents.

## The dilemma of option packages

You may find that the only way to get certain desirable options is as part of a package that includes features that you don't want nor need. This is because automakers can boost profits by bundling less desirable options with ones that many people want.

For instance, to get side- and head-protection air bags for the Toyota RAV4, you have to buy "option combination C," which costs $3,315 and adds features you don't necessarily need, such as a rear spoiler, mud-guards, and upgraded interior trim.

Similarly, side-curtain air bags and traction control, safety features that we highly recommend, aren't available for the 2005 Nissan Altima 3.5 SE with a manual transmission, which retails for $23,880 (with des-tination charge). To get them, you must opt for the automatic transmis-sion , which pushes the vehicle's retail price to $24,530.

We strongly recommend that you look for all of these on your vehicle. Traction control or all- or four-wheel drive can significantly improve trac-tion in slippery conditions. (For a detailed description of these and other safety features, see Chapter 3.)

## Comfort and convenience features

The following features are commonly available and can make a big differ-ence in your comfort and convenience over the years.

- Power adjustable seats
- Keyless entry
- Power door locks
- Power outside mirrors

**Power seat adjustments** make it easier to find a comfortable driving position and to adjust your position, if necessary, on long drives. The basic adjustments to look for include seat height, forward/backward, and lumbar support. Higher-priced models may offer many more adjustments, including multiple lumbar adjustments, side cushions for lateral support, and the ability to tilt the seat cushion.

**Power door locks** aren't just for convenience anymore, even though that's the primary reason they're so popular. They can enhance your personal safety by making it easy to ensure that all doors are locked to keep intruders out and passengers safely in. Some power door-lock systems lock all doors automatically when the transmission shifter is moved to "Drive," while others lock when the vehicle starts to move. And an increasing number of lock systems can be programmed to operate in a number of ways, such as to unlock one or more doors when the shifter is moved to "Park." Most vehicles come standard with power door locks these days.

**Keyless entry** is one of those options that once you've gotten used to having it, you'll wonder how you ever got along without it. Available on vehicles with power door locks, it allows you to unlock the car from a distance—and often turn on the interior lights—which is a convenience if your arms are full of packages or you are approaching your car in a dark place. With a panic button on the remote, you can also honk your car's horn and flash its lights, potentially scaring off an intruder. Keyless entry is standard on many mid- and higher-priced vehicles, but it may be part of an option package on lower-priced cars.

Most systems appear to work pretty much the same, but more-expensive vehicles tend to use much more sophisticated technology to thwart thieves. And many of those high-end systems have the operating buttons incorporated into the key, making it very handy to use—and very expensive to replace if lost. In the rare cases where keyless entry is not standard equipment, expect to pay $100 or more for it.

**Power outside mirrors** are especially handy because they allow each driver of a vehicle to adjust the mirrors properly—and in the process, avoid the temptation to leave the mirrors as they are because they are difficult to adjust. Correctly adjusted side-view mirrors enhance safety by allowing the driver to see what's beside the vehicle at all times, which can be critical when changing lanes or in an emergency situation.

Some models provide a memory system for individual adjustments. This allows two or three different drivers set the mirrors to their preferences and save those settings in the system's memory. When necessary, these adjustments can be recalled by simply pressing a button. Some power mirrors are heated—a handy feature if you live where condensation or ice frequently cover the mirrors. Power side-view mirrors with all of the bells and whistles mentioned above can run up to $400.

## Nice Options to Have

These are features that aren't necessities, but they contribute greatly to the quality of life in your vehicle, especially for those who spend many hours behind the wheel.

- Cruise control
- CD or cassette player
- Navigation system
- One-touch power windows
- Automatic climate control
- Heated seats
- Rear-seat video/DVD system
- Sunroof
- Full-sized spare tire
- Self-tinting rear-view mirror

**Cruise control** may be considered either a convenience or safety feature. It takes some of the stress out of driving, especially on long trips, and makes it easy to cruise along the highway at a safe, legal speed. Systems can cost as little as $100 or up to $1,400 as part of a package.

A more sophisticated but fussier type of system is adaptive cruise control. With this, an electronic sensor mounted on the front of the vehicle determines the speed and distance of the vehicle ahead and automatically adjusts your vehicle's speed to maintain a safe distance. Some systems can even apply the brakes on your car if the following distance decreases rapidly. This type of system can be handy for long drives on highways that aren't very crowded. But when there are more cars on the road, the system's sensitivity can make it cumbersome to use. These systems can run about $500.

**Heated seats** are usually available only on leather power seats, but they're a popular option in cold climates where it takes a long time for non-fabric seats to warm up. The heat level can usually be adjusted in two or three steps to cover a range of outside temperatures. Combined with leather, heated seats cost from $1,500 to $3,000.

A related feature on some seats is ventilation, where air is forced through perforations in the seat cushion and seatback to cool the driver in hot weather. A few more expensive cars offer a feature where either chilled or warmed air is pumped through the seat cushions. This is truly a luxury item, and you can expect it to be priced accordingly.

**Upgraded audio system.** If you spend endless hours commuting or you travel long distances frequently, a good sound system that provides high-quality audio is a nice benefit. There are plenty of great choices for audio components when shopping for almost any new car.

Most standard audio systems provide good sound quality and integrated theft protection. Most cars now also come with CD players standard; you can sometimes upgrade to a system with both a CD and cassette player for as little as $100 to $630. In-dash changers are usually included in a package of options, but if available separately, they can add at least $300 to a vehicle's price. In-dash changers are easier to access than rear-mounted changers, which is something to consider when selecting an audio system.

Most automakers are offering satellite digital radio services from two subscription services, XM and Sirius. For a monthly fee, these services provide high-quality sound, coast-to-coast reception, and a wide array of music formats and other programming choices. If you spend a lot of time in your vehicle, such services can come in handy. Expect to pay an additional $325 or so for a digital audio system that can deliver satellite programming.

The sky's the limit on what you can expect to pay for the latest high-tech audio gear. Small upgrades can run less than $200, but sophisticated systems can easily escalate to several thousand dollars.

## Portable video players belong in the back seat

Driver distraction is a well-documented cause of highway mishaps. Placing a video screen where it can be seen by front-seat occupants is not only illegal, it presents the potential for a huge driver distraction, one that could have disastrous results.

**Rear-seat entertainment systems** can be helpful for entertaining kids on long drives. These allow rear-seat passengers to watch videos, play video games, or use headsets to listen to a different audio source than what's playing over the car's speaker system. Earlier systems played only video cassettes; the latest systems play DVDs.

Built-in factory systems offered by the automaker typically cost between $1,300 and $1,400 and are nicely integrated into the vehicle's interior. Aftermarket systems that can be used in any vehicle are available at electronics stores and car-audio specialty shops. Portable units are less expensive (about $400 to $600) and can be easily removed from the vehicle when not needed, but they're less attractive. Keep in mind that portable units can be removed just as easily by thieves.

You can also buy aftermarket built-in systems at a car-stereo installer. These can be individually tailored to your needs, but the installation isn't always as neat as factory systems. Depending on the components used, the system cost is anywhere from $1,000 to several thousand dollars for a complete custom theater with surround sound and multiple screens that fold down from the roof or are built into head restraints.

**Navigation systems** track your vehicle's location, plot routes, provide turn-by-turn directions, and include an extensive database of easily searchable locations, from ATMs to hospitals, gas stations, restaurants, and more. A navigation system typically costs about $2,000, whether you buy it as an automaker option or an aftermarket system. Built-in systems work best because they're integrated into the car, they're difficult to steal, they frequently have convenient touch-screen controls, and they're generally easier to use than less expensive portable systems.

The best systems we have used have been in Acura, Honda, Lexus, and Toyota vehicles. We've found them intuitive to use, and they include a touch-screen display. Some car brands, such as Acura, BMW, Infiniti, Jaguar, and Lexus, offer navigation systems with voice control—an important feature that allows you to perform common functions by simply speaking commands, while keeping your eyes on the road and your hands on the wheel. Voice-control systems, however, can take a while to get used to and can be finicky in their ability to understand all commands.

**Sunroofs** are popular with those who want lots of fresh air but don't want a convertible. Most sunroofs are power-operated and will open two ways, either by sliding all the way back or by tilting up. When parking on hot days, leaving a sunroof in the tilt position allows hot air to vent out of the vehicle, without seriously compromising the vehicle's security. The best ones are those installed at the factory as original equipment. Aftermarket products and their installation can be plagued with leaks and overall poor quality. Either way, prices range from $1,000 to $2,000.

**Performance tires** provide more grip than standard all-season tires, which improves handling and braking performance. However, they also tend to deliver a firmer ride and worse winter traction, and they tend to wear more quickly. Subscribers to Consumer Reports.org can access all of CR's tests of performance and other tires (see Appendix C). They can range from $500 to $3,000.

**A full-sized spare tire** may be more convenient than a limited-service "space-saver" spare. While a limited-service space is useful for flat-tire emergencies, it's designed as a temporary replacement that shouldn't be left on the car any longer than necessary. A full-sized spare, in contrast, can be left on the car indefinitely. It may also help you extend the life of the original tires by including the spare in your tire rotation maintenance regimen. If the car has alloy wheels, you want the spare to have an alloy rim as well.

A full-sized spare mounted on an alloy wheel can be pretty expensive—perhaps $150 to $500. Be careful, though. In some vehicles, there isn't room for a full-sized spare. So before purchasing a full-sized spare, check to make sure it will fit in the vehicle you're considering.

**Automatic climate control** is a standard feature on almost all upscale vehicles. It's available on many midpriced cars but is seldom found at the entry level. It allows you to dial in the desired temperature, push the automatic button, and let the system do the rest. Dual-zone systems allow the driver and front passenger to input different temperatures. A few models offer a tri-zone system that allows rear passengers to choose their own temperature, as well.

Systems incorporate a sun sensor to compensate for the solar-heating effect on sunny days. Some systems work better than others, so a trial run during your test drive is a good idea. Most automatic systems are part of a trim package and can seldom be purchased separately. That said, the additional cost that's rolled into the package ranges from $300 to $600.

**Self-tinting rear-view mirror.** More-expensive vehicles have a photochromic, or self-tinting, interior mirror that helps prevent glare from the headlights of following vehicles.

**One-touch power windows.** One-touch operation is popular because it permits the window to be opened (and closed in some cases) with just one touch of the window switch. One-touch closing capability is almost always accompanied by pinch protection that prevents serious injury from a closing window. One-touch power windows are almost never offered as a stand-alone option and are usually incorporated into a trim package.

# Other Considerations

## Towing packages

Towing can put a heavy strain on a vehicle, and it's important that your vehicle be set up for the load you'll be pulling. Don't be misled by a model's

## Plus-size wheels and tires: When is it too much?

A trendy option these days are what's called plus-size wheel-and-tire packages. Though largely a cosmetic customization for some, it can provide improved handling and grip. Plus-sizing involves replacing the vehicle's stock wheels with ones with a larger diameter. If the wheels have a one-inch larger diameter, it's called plus-one conversion, two-inch larger wheels is called plus-two, and so on.

To keep the overall diameter of the wheel-and-tire combination the same as stock, when a larger-diameter wheel is used, it must be matched with a tire with a shorter sidewall, or narrow profile, to compensate.

Because the tires also tend to be wider, a vehicle does gain some performance advantage, improving its tire grip and cornering capability.

The tradeoffs, however, are a stiffer ride (because of the shorter tire sidewall) and decreased hydroplaning resistance and snow traction (because of the wider tire). Because of the shorter tire sidewall, the wheels are also more vulnerable to damage from potholes and curbs—a major consideration since these plus-size conversions can cost anywhere from $800 to $5,000 per set.

When CONSUMER REPORTS tested the performance capabilities of plus-one, plus-two, and plus-three conversions, we found that increasing the wheel diameter 1 inch (plus-one) yielded the greatest benefit with the fewest drawbacks. Beyond that, the trade-offs became great enough that they outweighed any performance gains.

CR is especially leery of putting plus-size tires on pickups and SUVs because it can make them more susceptible to rolling over when pushed to their handling limits. Wider tires could stick to the pavement more, increasing its chances of rolling over. This is a major reason some automakers warn against using tires of a different type or dimension from the ones the vehicle came with.

maximum-towing-capacity specification. Often a vehicle needs to be equipped with optional equipment or a special towing package before it can handle the maximum load.

If you plan to tow a trailer, choose an optional towing package when you're buying the vehicle. A towing package will likely include towing hardware such as the hitch receiver, a heavy-duty radiator for the engine, and wiring for the trailer's brakes and brake lights. A transmission oil cooler is often included to help keep the transmission from overheating.

In the case of full-sized pickups and SUVs, the towing capacity also varies based on whether the vehicle is classified as a ¼-ton, ½-ton, or 1-ton model, and whether it uses rear- or four-wheel drive. For towing heavier loads, rear- or all-wheel-drive vehicles are better suited than front-drivers. That's because a trailer tends to weigh down the rear of your vehicle, which reduces traction at the front. Front-drive vehicles also tend to have unibody construction that's less appropriate for heavy towing.

In addition to the trailer weight, consider the added weight of fuel, water, gear, and people, and make sure that total doesn't exceed the vehicle's gross combined weight rating (GCWR). Look at a vehicle's window sticker or in its owner's manual to verify its towing capacity.

Make sure your vehicle is equipped with the right hitch. The types include Class I (up to 2,000 pounds), Class II (2,000 to 3,500 pounds), Class III (3,500 to 5,000 pounds), Class IV (5,000 to 10,000 pounds), and Class V (more than 10,000 pounds). Be sure the hitch ball is correct for the trailer you'll be towing. Typical sizes are 1⅞-, 2-, and 2 5/16-inch.

## Off-road packages

Many pickups and some SUVs offer optional equipment designed for off-road driving. These can include:

- Skid plates to protect vulnerable underbody components such as the oil pan and radiator

## You need to know

If towing is something you'll need to do, the load you'll be towing can influence which vehicle you need to buy. Use the following as a general guide:

| Load weight | Typical load | Tow vehicle |
|---|---|---|
| Light load up to 1,000 pounds | Two off-road motorcycles or an ATV, snowmobile, or personal watercraft | Most wagons and minivans; all pickups and SUVs |
| Small load up to 2,000 pounds | Small boat or camper, two ATVs, snowmobiles, or personal watercraft | Some wagons; most SUVs and minivans; all pickups |
| Medium load up to 3,500 pounds | Medium-sized boat (up to 20 feet), large camper, or small travel trailer | Most minivans, SUVs, and pickups |
| Large load up to 5,000 pounds | Car transport (up to 24 feet) or medium travel trailer | Many SUVs; a few minivans; all full-sized pickups |
| Heavy load of 7,000 pounds or more | Large travel trailer, larger boat trailer, or a two-horse trailer | Full-sized SUVs and pickups only |

- Tow hooks
- A limited-slip differential or locking rear differential for extra traction
- Special suspension components, such as stiffer springs and special shock absorbers (which can raise the ground clearance a little)
- All-terrain tires with aggressive tread designs for better grip in dirt and mud

Depending on what's included, off-road packages have a wide range of prices. Some also require you to get other equipment that has nothing to do with off-roading. The prices and content of these packages change, but a few examples available as this was being written illustrate the point.

## Trim level vs. load capacity

A vehicle's trim level, model year, amount of optional equipment, type of transmission, and even the amount of sound-deadening material can affect the maximum amount of load that a vehicle can safely carry. That's why a high trim level in a vehicle loaded with a lot of optional equipment often has a lower load capacity for cargo than a base model.

The GMC Yukon's $639 off-road package, for example, includes gas shocks and minor suspension modifications. But to get it, you also must opt for a minimum of $2,530 for other items, including special tires, skid plates, alloy wheels, leather seats, and a premium audio system.

The Jeep Grand Cherokee's $420 off-road group (primarily skid plates and tow hooks) requires adding a V8 engine and mostly cosmetic power-accessory packages, which adds an additional $1,760 to the bottom line.

The Ford Ranger FX4's off-road package is a little more reasonable, even though it costs $3,435 more than an entry-level 4WD model. It includes tow hooks, special shocks, a limited-slip rear axle, skid plates, and an array of power accessories, such as power locks, windows, and mirrors, that you would probably want anyway.

The Toyota Tacoma pickup has a whole trim line, TRD, that's designated as the off-road version. It adds about $3,000 to $4,400 to the price of the truck and includes a raised suspension, special tires and shocks, a locking rear differential, and some nice, but nonvital, power accessories.

There are downsides to buying off-road components. Special shocks and springs can significantly degrade on-road ride comfort by making the vehicle much stiffer. A raised suspension can make it more difficult to get into and out of the vehicle. Off-road tires can compromise steering feel when you're driving on the highway. And skid plates add weight to the vehicle, which can lower fuel economy slightly.

Do you need an off-road package? For the moderate type of conditions encountered by most drivers who venture off pavement—dirt roads, packed sand, or similar terrain—we've found that stock vehicles with all- or four-wheel drive and decent ground clearance are usually fine without additional equipment.

If you're going into rougher terrain, where you might expect large rocks, loose dirt, sand, mud, or deep water, then you might consider ordering optional off-road items if you're willing to accept the downside of them as well.

## Custom-Ordering a Car

Most people who buy or lease a new car get one from a dealership's stock. When you do this, you can only choose from the configurations that the dealer has ordered or can swap for with another dealership. As a result, you may not be able to find the exact configuration you would prefer.

One option is to special-order a vehicle that's built at the factory to the configuration you want. This has several advantages:

- You can avoid options you don't want. According to Ashly Knapp, an executive with consumer-consultancy Auto Advisor in Seattle, "When you buy a car out of dealer stock you have to take what's there. And dealers frequently over-option cars because they know they can sell them." Being able to choose only the options you desire can save you hundreds or even several thousand dollars.
- The dealer spends less on a special-order deal. Dealers pay a lot for their inventory, and every day that a car goes unsold costs the dealership interest and overhead. Since the dealer invests essentially nothing on a special-order deal, there's more room to negotiate.
- Finally, even a small dealership can custom-order a car, so you can do business with the franchise closest to where you live.

There are also disadvantages to custom-ordering:

- The waiting time can be four to six weeks, sometimes longer.
- While domestic and European automakers make it easy to custom-order, Asian makers such as Toyota, Honda, and Nissan don't take custom orders even on domestically-produced cars. Instead, some offer a "preference order," or similar term, which means that if enough other customers want the same configuration you do, the factory might build them, but it could take months.
- If you custom-order a vehicle, an unscrupulous dealership could check a few extra boxes on the order form, so when the vehicle is delivered, you have to either take it, often at an increased price, or order all over again.
- Finally, there's the "oops" factor. If you don't like the car once it arrives, you may have a difficult time getting out of the deal.

## Options and Resale Value

Generally speaking, vehicles with the most options have the best resale value, but that doesn't necessarily mean you will get the best return on your money by buying a loaded vehicle. There are some options that are absolutely necessary for decent resale value, and there are others that don't enhance resale value—and in some cases actually reduce it.

Those options that make the most sense from a resale perspective are those we strongly recommended earlier in this chapter. The luster and value of some options don't really fade as we look at the "nice to have" category. Options such as sunroofs are truly nice to have, and their value depreciates at about the same rate as the vehicle itself.

Factory-installed options often hold their value in line with the vehicle's general price depreciation, but aftermarket-installed options are another matter. Aftermarket-installed options, such as audio systems, theft alarms, and special paint treatments, are of little value when it comes time to trade in your vehicle, mostly because there is no factory warranty for these features. The same can be said for some towing hitches and almost all off-road modifications. In fact, off-road additions can actually decrease a vehicle's trade-in value because it is an indicator that the vehicle has probably been through some pretty rough experiences. Too many customizations can limit resale value unless you find someone who really wants all those modifications.

# Good and Bad Features: Small Touches Can Make a Big Difference

When you're testing 60 or more vehicles a year, as CONSUMER REPORTS' auto-test staff does, certain features stand out as being especially well-designed and helpful. They are niceties that make a vehicle easier to live with, day in and day out. On the other hand, some features, which need more time at the drawing board, can be minor annoyances on an ongoing basis.

The best items are often simple and inexpensive but well-thought-out. Many of these features are available as standard or optional equipment on a variety of models. Some can only be found on a few models, but we list them partly so other automakers might take notice.

While some of them won't make or break your purchase decision, we recommend that you look for these features when you're comparing cars. They can make a big difference in your ownership experience.

### Features we like (or "Why didn't somebody think of this sooner?")

**Rain-sensing windshield wipers.** If left on the "intermittent" setting, some cars will automatically adjust the intermittent speed for you, depending on how hard it's raining. They will even turn the wipers on and off when the rain starts and stops. If left in this position, some wipers will swipe once at start-up in most cars, even if it isn't raining. Available in Lincolns, Cadillacs, and many luxury European cars, these rain-sensing wipers can greatly reduce distraction in bad weather, provided the sensor is well-calibrated.

**"Rest" feature in the climate-control system.** By pressing the climate-control Rest button in a few Mercedes-Benz, BMW, and Audi models, the system will continue circulating warm air for up to 30 minutes after you turn off the car. It's handy when you leave the car to go shopping and return to a warm car. And it can save gas when you'd otherwise leave the car idling while waiting for someone.

**Stability-control systems that light up the brake lights.** When a stability-control system is activated to keep a car under control, it slows the

## Original cost vs. trade-in value

How much value do options retain over time? Here are some examples that compare the retail price of some stand-alone options for 2003 models and how much those options added to the trade-in value of those models in mid-2005 as used cars, according to Consumer Reports' Auto Price Service:

| Feature | Price when new | Trade-in value |
|---|---|---|
| **2003 Dodge Grand Caravan ES** | | |
| All-wheel drive | $3,800 | $1,200 |
| Leather seats | $1,250 | $450 |
| Sunroof | $895 | $575 |
| | | |
| **2003 Ford Expedition XLT 4WD** | | |
| Rear DVD system | $1,295 | $550 |
| Running boards | $735 | $150 |
| Leather captains chairs | $1,420 | $500 |
| | | |
| **2003 Toyota Camry SE V6** | | |
| Power sunroof | $900 | $575 |
| Navigation system | $3,080 | $525 |

vehicle with the brakes. In Jaguars and Lincolns, the system also illuminates the brake lights when it's activated to warn drivers behind.

**Convex interior mirror for viewing rear passengers in minivans.** With these overhead wide-angle mirrors, you don't have to turn your head around to check on sleepy tots or needy tykes.

**Retractable rear windows in minivans.** The second-row power windows in minivans from Toyota, Honda, and Mazda can be lowered like those in the front doors, which greatly improves ventilation and makes it easier for kids to wave good-bye when leaving their friends.

**Inside trunk pull handles.** Something as simple as closing a trunk lid can be a chore if there's no clear, clean place to grip it. A trunk with a pull handle that's integrated into the inside trim lets you close the lid without getting your hands dirty, or your wax job smudged, and without cutting your fingers on the sharp metal frame inside most unfinished trunks. Usually you can swing the trunk lid closed without touching the lid's top.

**Cruise controls with a cancel function.** This allows you to shut off the cruise control without stepping on the brakes. It also retains your preset speed in the system's memory, so that when traffic clears up enough to reactivate the cruise control, you're ready to resume your pace.

**Arrow on gas gauge that indicates which side the filler is located on.** This is a simple, inexpensive help at the pump that's useful when your car is new or someone else is driving.

**Neck-warming vents.** Often when you drive a convertible at highway speeds with the top down, wind swirls around passengers from behind. These new vents at the base of the head restraints in the Mercedes-Benz SLK blow enough hot air when switched on to counteract the cold wind.

## More kudos and gold stars

**Power-window controls that raise or lower all windows at once.** Many also open or close the sunroof. They're most convenient if you want to cool off the cabin on a hot day before you get in, or when you forget to close a window when you park. Most are controlled by pressing a button on the key fob. Some convertibles also have a separate cabin switch that controls all windows; this comes in handy when you're raising or lowering the top or seeking a little shelter from the wind on the highway.

**RDS radios that display the name of the artist and song.** Short for Radio Data System, RDS radios make it easy to identify that cool tune you heard midway through a 30-song marathon. Some stations also broadcast their station format (news, R&B, classical, etc.), which makes it easy to find stations you like on trips away from home. They are available in General Motors vehicles and an increasing number of imports, even in less expensive models, such as Scion.

**Remote starters.** In cold or hot climates it's handy to get the heater or air conditioner started before you go out and sit behind the wheel, especially if you're loading up the kids. Long a mainstay of the aftermarket, General Motors is beginning to install them as factory options in many models.

**Fold-down rear seats in sedans and coupes.** These provide added cargo-carrying flexibility by letting you carry longer items than you could fit in the trunk alone. The best design is a split-seat version in which one side can be folded down while the other side remains up. Some models also include a front-passenger seat that folds flat, providing additional cargo-carrying space.

**Audio controls on the steering wheel.** They make it easy to change the radio station or adjust the volume without taking your hands off the wheel or your eyes off the road. These are available as standard in a wide range of luxury cars and higher trim versions of more mainstream family sedans, minivans, and small SUVs.

**Heated and cooled seats and heated steering wheels.** They are really nice on hot or cold days, and even better with adjustable levels. Many vehicles are available with heated seats, but cooled or ventilated seats are usually found on more-expensive models. Cooled seats in models from BMW, Lexus, Lincoln, Mercedes-Benz, and Saab use internal fans to blow air onto you, helping to keep you from sweating on hot days. Some of the systems are noisy, however. The best heating designs have separate controls for the seat bottom, backrest, and steering wheel, as well as adjustable levels that provide greater control for better comfort.

**Outside temperature display.** Many give warnings of ice and snow. Even if they don't, it's nice to know what you're facing when you open the door. They're often integrated with auto-dimming rearview mirrors or climate controls on cars that have these options.

**Remote door lock/unlock button that's integrated with the key.** Having the control on the key rather than on a key fob takes up less room in your pocket or purse and makes it easier to find the right button quickly. Acura, Audi, BMW, Lexus, Mercedes-Benz, Toyota, and Volkswagen, for example, use these keys.

**Windshield-wiper heating elements in the windshield.** They keep the wipers from sticking to the windshield and reduce ice and snow accumulation. They're available in Chrysler minivans, Subarus, and other cars.

**Rear wipers that activate automatically in reverse.** This feature turns on the rear wiper automatically if the front wipers are on and the car is put in reverse. It makes it easier to see out the rear while backing up. Available on some European and Japanese wagons, SUVs, and minivans.

**Auto-dimming rearview mirror.** Auto-dimming interior mirrors monitor the amount of light coming in through the rear window, automatically dimming the mirror to reduce glare when a car comes up behind and undimming it when there are no cars. This ensures you don't get unexpected glare from vehicles that suddenly appear behind you.

**Automatic headlights.** These headlights come on automatically when the ambient light level drops to a preset level, even if you forget. Sometimes, however, they're slow to activate in tunnels and parking garages, when the sky is overcast, and at twilight hours.

**Cruise-control systems that remember they're on when you start the car.** If you leave the system's on/off switch in the "on" position when you turn off the car, it will automatically come on when the car's started again. It's convenient not to have to switch the system on every time you drive.

**Rotary or slider sunroof controls.** These controls allow you to quickly set how far the sunroof will open anywhere along its track. You simply rotate or slide the switch to the desired point and the sunroof will open only as far as your set position. It's available on all Volkswagens and some Audis and Nissans.

**Knobs for tuning the radio.** If it's not broken, etc. There's still no beating the simple tuning knob on car radios. In contrast to rocker switches or more cumbersome controls, knobs are easy to find and simple to use, and you can travel up or down the dial as far as you want in one easy step. The ideal setup is to have the tuning knob on the left side of the radio, near the driver; it's often used much more than the volume knob. General Motors, Toyota, Volkswagen, and others use this design.

## Features that need more work (or "Maybe it seemed like a good idea at the time.")

**Active cruise-control systems.** This type of system can vary the vehicle's speed—either slowing down or speeding up—based on the speed of a vehicle that's in front. The systems we've experienced have worked OK on an open highway with little traffic, but are more trouble than they're worth in other situations. They allow the car to gradually fall back in traffic, speed up on empty stretches, and slow down when cars pass by in adjacent lanes.

**Auto-unlocking systems you can't program yourself.** Most such systems unlock only the driver's door or only the front doors. So when you want to retrieve a child or briefcase from the back seat, you must still manually unlock the rear doors. We prefer auto locking/unlocking systems in which you can tailor the locking pattern to the way you like it.

**Instrument lights that come on without the headlights.** They can fool the driver into believing the headlights are on when they're not, especially if the car has daytime running lights. Since high beams don't work without the headlights being turned on, this is often the first indication to the driver that the lights are not on.

**Front seats in two-door coupes that don't slide forward** for better access to the rear seat or don't return to their preset position when the backrest is pushed back. They make it unnecessarily difficult for passengers to access the rear seat or require front passengers to readjust their seat after someone gets in or out of the back. Seat-folding mechanisms that work well have been around for decades. But some manufacturers are backsliding.

**Manual recline levers on power seats.** Sure, this is a cost-cutting measure, but it's difficult to make small adjustments to the seatback in order to relieve pressure or find a better position.

## Annoying switches and controls

**Cruise-control buttons that aren't illuminated.** Vehicle speed is too important to fumble with in the dark. And many cruise-control switches are on steering wheels that also contain unlit audio controls, so you can accidentally change the radio when you want to slow down or speed up. Domestic cars are the main culprit, though we're now seeing more models with illuminated switches. Cruise-control switches that are located on small stalks mounted on the steering column, such as in Toyotas and some new GM models, are intuitive enough that they don't need illumination.

**Cruise controls on the same stalk as turn-signal indicators or on similar stalks behind the steering wheel.** These are easy to confuse and difficult to see and use.

**Rear wiper controls that aren't mounted on a steering-column stalk.** Without variable intermittent settings, rear wipers often need to be turned on and off. Fumbling for a switch on the dashboard takes your hands off the wheel and your eyes off the road. Stalk-mounted controls such as those on Audis, BMWs, and Volkswagens, as well as on most Japanese makes, are much more intuitive. Daimler-Chrysler and General Motors vehicles are the main culprits.

**Remote outside mirror controls that aren't illuminated.** They're often hard to find quickly at night, especially when headlights approaching from behind are blinding the driver.

**Heating and air-conditioning systems without a separate A/C switch.** You can't use the A/C to prevent the car from steaming up in the winter while keeping warm air flowing in the dashboard vents or footwells.

**LCD displays that wash out.** Many are illegible in bright sunlight or at dawn or dusk when the headlights are off. LED displays are more consistently legible.

# More Choices Than Ever, But Watch the Bottom Line

For almost any vehicle you'll find a tempting array of both standard and optional features. Moreover, the auto manufacturers have gotten very good at selling you features and options you never knew you wanted or needed. So it's easy to get carried away when loading up your new vehicle with options, sometimes adding hundreds or thousands of dollars to a vehicle's price. Our best advice is to focus on your needs and let your wants take a back seat when choosing features and options. That way you'll be able to find a vehicle that you'll be satisfied with for years to come and that won't be a financial burden.

# Step 2

## Check Out the Cars

■ CHAPTER 5: Get the Most From Your Test-Drive    **107**
■ CHAPTER 6: How to Evaluate a Used Car    **125**

# 5

# Get the Most From Your Test Drive

**The test drive** is one of the most important parts of the car-buying process. A lot of vehicles look good on paper—especially in glossy brochure photos—but the test drive is the moment of truth. This is your best chance to see how a vehicle measures up to expectations and, just as important, how well it "fits" you. After all, you'll be living with this vehicle every day for the next several years. You don't want any surprises after you've bought it.

The test drive lets you evaluate a vehicle's comfort, ergonomics, and driving characteristics. Often, it's the little, unexpected things you discover on a test drive that can be most influential when deciding between different models. In some vehicles, for example, the seats may not fit you well. Perhaps the seat's contours don't align comfortably with your body, or there's too little or too much lumbar support. A seat you can't get comfortable in should be a deal-breaker.

There are other things you could uncover. Perhaps the driving position is awkward; you may have to choose between having your legs uncomfortably crowded or stretching out your arms too far to reach the wheel. You could find that outward visibility isn't very good, with large blind spots in the rear. Maybe there's isn't enough head room. Controls could be confusing or hard to operate. It could be difficult to get in and out. Or a child seat may be hard to secure in the rear seat. You get the picture.

That's why it's surprising that many people give vehicles only a token test drive or, worse, none at all. This is a mistake, and a sure recipe for buyer remorse after the purchase. The goal of a test drive is to get to know the vehicles you're considering as thoroughly as possible before deciding which to buy. That's why it's critical that you take ample time to conduct a complete test drive and perform a thorough walk-around of any vehicle you're considering. You also get a chance to size up dealerships and salespeople before you get down to the nitty-gritty of talking money.

In this chapter, we'll give you pointers on:

- Planning the test-drive experience so you get the most from it
- Minimizing the sales pressure so you can concentrate on the vehicle
- Knowing what to look for in a vehicle—inside and out
- Evaluating a vehicle's performance
- Taking notes so you can do a meaningful comparison of different cars

# Before Visiting the Dealership

In an ideal world, the best way to pick the vehicle that's right for you would be to take several cars home for a few weeks and alternate among them for your everyday driving. That's the best way to compare vehicles back to back and, in a sense, is what CONSUMER REPORTS' auto experts do (in addition to a full battery of instrumented testing at our 327-acre test track) when testing groups of competitive vehicles for our monthly road-test reports. Unfortunately, that's not a realistic option for the typical car buyer, although some dealers will let you take vehicles home overnight.

The next best option would be to rent the vehicles you're considering, each for at least a few days, but this would be expensive, even if you could find the vehicles in the exact configuration you want.

That leaves the dealership test drive as your best chance to get to know the vehicles inside and out. This is important enough that you should make a separate visit to the dealership just for that purpose. Don't wait until the day you're ready to buy to do your test drive; that won't give you enough time to thoroughly evaluate the cars you're considering.

Whatever you do, don't skip the test drive. It's surprising how many new-car buyers skip the opportunity to take this crucial ride. Some say they're satisfied to have driven a particular make of car all their lives, and they assume that the same brand will be all right the next time around. That's a risky assumption, because when manufacturers redesign their vehicles they often give them different driving characteristics to appeal to different market segments. And just because a friend or relative has suggested that you buy a particular make or model that they've been happy with doesn't mean you will be happy with that car, too.

By test driving several of your potential choices, you'll find out that many vehicles look great in photos and have excellent specifications, but behave differently in the real world. There are good reasons some vehicles get very high ratings and others receive only fair ratings in our tests. Different vehicles can have very different characteristics, in terms of driving feel, performance, comfort, ergonomics, and build quality. You'll never know the whole story until you get behind the wheel for that all-important test drive.

# Plan Your Test-Drive Day

By this stage, you should have narrowed your choices to two or three vehicles that meet your needs, providing the space and features you want, fitting within your price range, and rating high in the areas that you feel are most important. The test-drive visit will take you to the next phase.

Don't waste time test driving cars you have little or no interest in buying. Save those for later, in case your prime candidates don't meet your expectations and you have to look further. If possible, try to test drive all the cars you're interested in on the same day. You'll find it easier to make comparisons.

You'll get the most out of your test-drive experience if you do a little preparation ahead of time:

**Grade your current vehicle.** Make a list of the things you like and dislike about your current car. Then you can compare it with what you expect from your intended purchase so you know exactly what to look for during your test drive. For example, if you don't like the way your present car's transmission shifts, make sure you pay close attention to the new one. Does your existing engine have enough power to keep up with traffic and merge safely? Are there ergonomic problems or irritating shortcomings, like too little storage space in the cabin, cup holders that don't hold drinks securely, or controls that are awkward to use? Put down all your gripes—large and small—so you don't overlook those things in the new car.

**Come prepared.** Take along a notebook so you can jot down impressions as you inspect the vehicle and after the test drive, especially if you're test driving several cars on the same day. It's really easy to mix up impressions of similar vehicles. Also, make several copies of the test-drive checklist at the end of this chapter so you have a separate sheet for each vehicle you plan to drive and a few extras for any spontaneous drives you make. This will help keep you organized at the dealership and make it easier to compare different vehicles later. Be sure to jot down any particular items or features that you want to check out, if they aren't already listed. In addition, if you typically use a child seat, take it along for the test drive. Now is the time to make sure it fits well and is easy to secure.

**Bring a friend.** Try to have someone accompany you to the dealership. He or she can help take notes, act as an impartial observer, and run

## Kids and dealerships

Should you bring your children with you when shopping for a new vehicle? The answer is yes and no. It's a good idea to bring them along when you're doing your test drives because it's important to make sure they'll fit comfortably and securely (and happily) in your new vehicle. They can give you a good "rear-seat" perspective, such as whether the seats are comfortable and whether they can see out of the windows easily. If this can't be arranged, make sure you go back for a second test drive with the entire family for any vehicle you are serious about buying.

If you have a teenager who will be driving the car, you should let him or her take a turn behind the wheel while you're test driving.

When it comes time to visit dealerships to negotiate the best deal you can, however, little ones are best left at home. They can become a distraction during the negotiating process, especially if you end up spending a lot of time in one or more showrooms.

interference with the salesperson so you can concentrate on the vehicle and driving experience rather than being obliged to chitchat.

**Plan your own route.** To get the most accurate impressions from your test drive, you need to drive over the kinds of roads and surfaces on which you typically drive. If a salesperson accompanies you on your test drive, he or she will most likely suggest a quick, well-used route. He may also direct you along roads that are "vehicle friendly" and don't stress the engine or suspension too much. But this will not give you a complete picture of how the vehicle performs.

Ideally, therefore, you should plan your own test-drive route in advance. Choose one that includes as many different types of roads and surfaces as possible. If you normally drive over rough city streets, twisting country roads, or high-speed freeways, make sure you include the appropriate ones as a part of your route.

Ideally, you should plan a route that gives you about 35 to 40 minutes of driving time; the more, the better. The more time you can spend on each test drive, the more accurate your overall impressions will be.

Sometimes you can use a map of the area around the dealership to plot a good route before you leave home. If not, it's worth scouting the vicinity for appropriate roads before you drive into the parking lot.

It can help to drive your current vehicle around a chosen route before visiting the dealership. This will help you become familiar with the route so you can better concentrate on the new vehicle later on. This will also give you a back-to-back comparison between the new car and your current one. But keep in mind that if your current car is several years old, it's likely that any new car is going to feel better by comparison.

If you test drive several cars, be sure to drive all of them over similar roads and in similar conditions. One advantage of visiting different dealerships in the same automall is that you will be able to use the same driving route for each vehicle.

**Drive what you intend to buy.** Be sure that the vehicle you drive is the same trim line and has the same engine and transmission as the one you are thinking of buying. Since most sales "demo" vehicles used for test drives are loaded, top-of-the-line models, a popular sales trick is to offer you a spin in

## You need to know

**Keep an eye on your credit report.** If you're taking a test drive, be sure the dealership's staff isn't taking the opportunity to check your credit history when they make a copy of your driver's license. Tell the salesperson, "You do not have the authority to pull my credit report." Pulling credit reports without consent violates the Fair Credit Reporting Act. If you're not satisfied that the staff acknowledges the lack of authorization, take your business elsewhere. It's easy to verify whether the dealer pulled the report by checking the report under the "inquiries" section.

a model that has all the bells and whistles, when you're really interested in (or can only afford) a lower-trim or less-equipped version. Similarly, if you plan to buy a vehicle with, say, a four-cylinder engine and manual transmission, driving one with a V6 and automatic won't help you evaluate it.

Call ahead of time to make sure that any dealerships you'll be visiting have the exact version you want in their inventory. If you've been dealing with some of the online pricing and buying services, you may already know some dealerships that have the right version.

# The Initial Inspection

## A thorough walk-around

When you arrive at a dealership and greet a salesperson, make it clear up front that you are there only to inspect and test drive the car(s) you're interested in, and that you will not be making any buying decisions that day. This will help keep things simple and allow you to better concentrate on comparing cars.

Throughout the visit, resist any attempts by the salesperson to lure you into making a buying decision or talking about a deal. Despite any sense of urgency that the salesperson tries to instill in you ("We have a great deal that's only good for today" or "I've got another customer coming to look at this exact vehicle later today"), simply remind him that you'll make your decision only after having test-driven all the cars in which you're interested. Being polite but firm with this message can help lessen the sales pressure while you're conducting the test drive. Also, don't get sidetracked by an ambitious salesperson who is trying to move some other model. Stay focused on what you want to see and do.

The first thing you'll want to do is spend some time looking over the vehicle carefully. Now's the time to sit in all the seats, check out the trunk or cargo area, and poke around in all of the vehicle's nooks and crannies. Kids can be especially good at this latter chore, and it will keep them busy while you look at other things. Here are some questions to consider while you do your initial walk-around:

- **Exterior appearance.** Does your test car look as good as you expected? Does the exterior styling suit you? Do the exterior panels line up properly without gaps or irregularities? Do the colors suit you? Is the paint smooth, with mirrorlike reflections?

- **Controls and instruments.** Are the instruments easy to see and interpret? Are all controls easy to identify and operate, and are they within easy reach? Do the audio and climate-control systems have controls that are logical and uncomplicated? The buttons and knobs should be large enough that you can operate them quickly, easily, and without having to take your eyes off the road for more than a second.

- **Steering wheel.** Does the steering wheel feel comfortable in your hands? Is the horn easy to use? Are there audio and cruise-control buttons located on the steering wheel? This can make it easier to perform common functions without taking your eyes off the road. In addition, check to see if the steering wheel is adjustable. Most adjust up and down. Telescopic designs that also adjust in and out make it easier to find a comfortable driving position. Once you have it adjusted to fit you, check that you can see the instrument panel clearly.

- **Audio system.** Is the audio quality satisfactory? Take along a favorite CD or cassette to see if audio quality meets your expectations.

- **Rear seat.** Is it easily accessed and comfortable? Is there a three-point safety belt for all seating positions? Is there a fold-down armrest? Does the seatback fold down for increased cargo space? The most versatile design has a split seatback that allows you to fold either half down separately. If appropriate, does your child's safety seat fit well and can it be fastened securely?

- **Storage space.** Are there sufficient cup holders and special storage spaces for common things like CDs, cassettes, and a cellular phone? Are there enough power points, front and rear, to satisfy the needs of passengers with laptops, cell phones, PDAs, and games?

## Getting in and out

It should be easy to get in and out of both the front and rear seats without having to duck your head or contort your body. Tall SUVs and pickups can be difficult because of their high step-in height. Some cars with low-slung roofs make you duck to keep from banging your head on the edge of the roof, especially in the rear. In others, it can be awkward to step into the rear seat area because there's too little space between the seat and door pillar.

Are the door handles easy to operate? Some designs are easier to use than others. How heavy are the doors, and can you open them with one hand while juggling a bag of groceries? Can kids get in and out by themselves?

How about the back seat? Will it be easy for rear passengers to get in and out of it? If one of your rear passengers is a small child, make sure you can get the child safety seat in and out easily and installed properly. Can you lift a sleeping child out of the seat? You and your family can judge accessibility by climbing in and out of all seating positions.

Look for big doors that open wide, a tall roof, a high seat, grab handles, low doorsills, and plenty of space to get your feet in and out. In a vehicle with three rows of seats, like a minivan or some SUVs, see how much ducking and crawling it takes to reach the back, and how comfortable (or claustrophobic) you feel once you've buckled up.

Be sure to check out access to the trunk. Some require the use of a key to open it from the outside—something that's a real nuisance when your hands are full. Better designs have a covered grab handle that can be pulled to unlatch and open the trunk lid or a power-operated release that lets you open the trunk by pressing a button on the remote control.

Once the lid is open, check to see what kind of hinges it has. This might seem insignificant, but the worst hinges are the ones that swing down into the cargo area, potentially causing damage to luggage and other items if you're not careful. Better designs hold up the lid with struts that don't intrude into the cargo space.

How difficult will it be to load bulky items into the cargo area? It's much easier to load a vehicle when the cargo opening is even with the vehicle's floor. Cargo areas with a high liftover are less useful and more difficult to load. Make sure the cargo area is big enough and configured to carry any odd-sized cargo you may have—like golf clubs. And it's always handy to have a back seat that folds down to extend the cargo area.

## The importance of the interior

A car's exterior styling is designed to grab your attention, evoke emotions, and project an image. But it's inside the vehicle where you'll spend your time. Your long-term satisfaction with a vehicle can be greatly influenced by how well-designed the interior is. This includes how comfortable and quiet the cabin is and how convenient things are to operate. More and more, buyers are concerned about such things as cup holders, luggage capacity, sound systems, and interior quality and appearance.

When comparing vehicles, think about how a vehicle fits you and your

## The night perspective

It's better to visually inspect a vehicle in daylight. If possible, however, you should try to drive any vehicle you're serious about buying at night as well. That's the only way you'll ever be able to tell how well the headlights perform, how the switches, gauges, and controls are lighted for nighttime use, and whether there are any annoying reflections in the windshield at night. If you aren't able to drive the car at night remember that each CONSUMER REPORTS test report includes the results of our headlight testing and any other comments we have from our night-driving experiences. (The latest test reports are available to subscribers of ConsumerReports.org.)

lifestyle. If a seat is uncomfortable or if the controls are awkward to use, you could become frustrated with the car long before the loan or lease is over.

## Seat comfort and your driving position

A comfortable seat is very important and individual preference for seat upholstery is part of that. So be sure to test the upholstery you intend to buy. Some people prefer leather because it makes entry and exit less of a chore— it's easier to slide over leather than cloth. But leather isn't as comfortable when it's cold and can burn bare legs when it's hot, and some leather seats have different padding than cloth seats, affecting overall seating comfort.

A good seat supports your body and lets you sit up and see out without strain. Look to see that your test-car seat is shaped to fit your body's contours and supports you from the thighs to the shoulders. The seat shouldn't pinch or protrude into your back. An adjustable lumbar support is a worthy option, as no two people sit in exactly the same position. Watch out for a seat that feels soft at first—if it gives way beneath your weight, after 20 minutes or so you could wind up tensing your muscles to stay positioned properly.

Look for a firm seat with multiple adjustments, either power or manual. You want to be able to easily move the seat up and down as well as back and forth. Often, having a height adjustment option makes a key difference, particularly for a shorter driver. The most versatile seats have a bottom cushion that adjusts for angle as well as height. And make sure the seat cushion is long enough to support your thighs almost all the way to your knees.

In addition, you want to be able to find a good driving position that lets you reach the pedals without sitting too close to the steering wheel. Your body should be at least 10 inches away from the steering wheel so the air bag has room to deploy when necessary.

If your vehicle is supposed to have adjustable pedals, make sure you try them out. You should be able to see out well in all directions and maintain a relaxed and comfortable posture while driving.

All cars aren't the same inside, and the concept "one size fits all" doesn't apply. Seat and steering-wheel adjustments can help, but so can the car's basic design. A high dashboard and low seats—or high seats and a low roofline—can obstruct the view forward. Wide roof pillars can block your view to the rear, creating dangerous blind spots.

## Driving ergonomics

With good ergonomic design, any driver can see, reach, and use all controls easily. The dashboard layout should be logical and intuitive. Switches you use at night should be illuminated. Knobs you must turn should be large enough to grasp. You shouldn't have to take your eyes off the road for more than an instant to discern one switch from another. Push buttons should give good tactile feedback. Labeling should be clear and unambiguous.

If the vehicle you test drive has a full-feature climate-control or advanced electronics system (such as in-dash navigation, voice-activated controls, hands-free telephone, or multifunction control system), you should consider trying them out. Perhaps the salesperson can help here, since some are very complicated and hard to use without studying the owner's manual first. Since learning a new system can be distracting while driving, begin by going through as much as you can while parked.

Before you start the actual test drive, adjust the seat for the optimal position and view out. Then see if you can reach all the controls without taking your eyes off the road. See if a soda or water bottle, a large cup, or your favorite travel mug fits securely in the cup holders, and whether the cup blocks access to important switches. You might be surprised at how many vehicles have problems in this area. Similarly, some cup holders are positioned directly in front of air-conditioning vents, which can rapidly cool a hot drink while blocking the air coming from the vent.

Finally, if you have kids, are they going to be happy in the area where they could be spending a good bit of time? See if there are plenty of places for drinks, snacks, toys, and books. And if there are high-tech conveniences like rear audio or video systems, make sure your children try them out. No point in buying something they don't like and won't use.

# The Test Drive

You've already done a big part of the test drive without even moving, but now it's time to get the feel of the vehicle in motion. The best way to do that is to eliminate as many distractions as possible. Many dealers will let you do the test drive by yourself, but some still insist on sending someone along. Because the last thing you need right now is someone jabbering in your ear while you're trying to concentrate on the vehicle, this is one of the ways in which having a friend or relative along can help by engaging in conversation with the salesperson.

Unfortunately, the test drive is the perfect opportunity for you to be overwhelmed by a new car—any new car. It's likely newer and better in many ways than the older car you've been driving. That's why it's important to compare the vehicle to other new vehicles in which you're interested, rather than comparing it only to your current car. The more vehicles you test drive, the better perspective you'll get on each one of them.

Listen and feel for the things you like, and look carefully for the things on your list that you might not be happy with. New cars have personalities, and it's important to find one that matches yours. Little things that might seem insignificant now could become major irritants later.

With that in mind, here are a few of the things you should consider during your test drive:

- **Ride comfort.** Is the ride soft, harsh, or somewhere in between? Does the suspension isolate you from the road, or do you feel every bump and ripple? Some softer suspensions feel comfortable over bumps but tend to be floaty, wallowing up and down a bit after a large bump. Look for a vehicle that feels tight and controlled over bumps, but not harsh.

- **Acceleration.** Does the engine give you the kind of feel you expect when starting up from a stop? Can you merge safely into freeway traffic?
- **Braking.** Do the brakes feel responsive, without being too jerky?
- **Steering and handling.** Does the car respond well to quick steering maneuvers? Does the car track well when driving straight ahead on the highway, or does it need small, continual corrections? Does the car feel relaxed or too darty to be comfortable? And does it stay relatively composed on rough roads?
- **Quietness.** Is the sound of the engine annoying during heavy acceleration or highway cruising? Can you hear noise from the tires or wind noise from side-view mirrors? Are there any squeaks or rattles?
- **Visibility.** Do you get a good panoramic view of the road ahead? Do the mirrors give you the kind of side and rear view you need? Or do wide pillars or a small rear window restrict your view? When backing up, is the rear visibility good and can you gauge the length of the vehicle?

**Ride comfort** is determined by a vehicle's suspension, tires, and even its seats, but it's certainly one vehicle attribute that's measured by personal preference. Sporty cars, including some family sedans, typically have a firmer ride, which is a tradeoff to their better handling characteristics. This may not be for everyone. Some buyers who have been enchanted into buying a sporty car have regretted it later because of the stiff ride quality that seems to accentuate every little bump in the road. To confirm your preference, we suggest you drive several comparable vehicles to evaluate the differences in ride. Be sure the ride you experience during your test drive is one you can tolerate for the life of the car.

**Acceleration** depends primarily on the engine power, but it is also closely linked to the transmission. A great engine coupled with a mediocre transmission will deliver less-than-stellar performance. Conversely, a fairly small engine can appear much better in combination with a modern, well-designed manual or automatic transmission.

One of the real benefits of a test drive is to see if you like the powertrain you've selected. If so, that's great, but if not, now's the time to change your selection or keep looking. During your test drives, be sure to try quick acceleration from a stop and a rolling merge into fast freeway traffic.

**Braking** is a vehicle attribute that's hard to evaluate thoroughly without professional help, but you can do a basic assessment. Feel how the vehicle responds when you depress the brake pedal, both softly and with more force. The braking should be nice and smooth, and it should be easy to get just the amount of stopping power you need, without the car stopping too quickly or not quickly enough.

**Steering and handling.** Since vehicle response to quick steering maneuvers is a key factor in avoiding emergency highway situations, it's important that you're comfortable with the way your vehicle responds. It should be easy and controllable to maneuver along the road—not so quick that it feels darty and not so slow that it takes a lot of turning to make a maneuver. You should also get good feedback through the steering wheel about what the car is doing on the road; some steering systems feel numb and disconnected from the road. Many vehicles have variable power steering, which makes them feel one way on the highway and another at slow speeds, such as when trying to maneuver into a tight parking space.

An important note: You won't be able to test a vehicle at its handling and braking limits to see how it would respond in an emergency situation, such as when you're trying to avoid an accident. For this see CONSUMER REPORTS' road-test report. We do a number of different braking and emergency-handling tests on every vehicle we evaluate. We tell you how each car responded and give individual ratings for overall braking and emergency handling.

**Quietness** includes engine, wind, and road noise, as well as other things such as squeaks and rattles. During your test drive, turn off the radio and close all windows so you can hear what else is going on.

Engine noise has a lot to do with the quality of the engine, but it's also related to the engine size and configuration. Four-cylinder engines are the noisiest because they are built to be economical and are usually installed in low-priced entry-level cars. If your four-cylinder test car seems too noisy, try driving a V6 version, if available, to see if it's any better. If any engine sounds coarse and loud under heavy acceleration or at highway speed, it could become more annoying later. Engines don't get quieter with age.

Wind noise is the next biggest annoyance, and side-view mirrors are the major culprits. Better-designed mirrors make almost no noise, while poorly designed ones roar and whistle. You should have little trouble telling which is which during your test drive.

Like mirrors, luggage racks vary in engineering quality, and some are noisier than others. Listen above your head at highway speed for wind noise coming through the roof. Much has been done to eliminate noise from the radio antenna, but some may still make a whistling sound at higher speeds.

High-performance tires on sporty cars and off-road tires on SUVs and pickup trucks tend to create the most tire noise. It can be annoying, but buyers who want those kinds of tires are usually willing to put up with the noise. The test drive is a good way to find out what your tolerance level is.

**Visibility** takes into account a number of design factors, such as seating position, vehicle configuration, mirror effectiveness, and body design. Visibility can vary greatly, even among similar sedans, wagons, SUVs, and minivans. Several back-to-back test drives will tell you quickly which ones have the best visibility. And don't forget to check rear visibility when backing up (see Chapter 3 for more about backup safety).

# After the Test Drive

As soon as you return to the dealership from your test drive, the salesperson will almost certainly try to hustle you into an office to start the buying process. The salesperson is counting on your enthusiasm after driving a new car to seal the deal. This is not a good time, however, to start the negotiating process, especially if you have other cars to test drive. Now's the time to collect your thoughts about your test-drive experience and get them down on paper. This is also the time to check over your notes to see if your test drive answered your questions from your checklist of things to look for.

Even if you don't have other vehicles to test drive right away, you should take time to review your notes and think about your driving experience. And just to make sure you get all of your thoughts organized, there is a complete checklist for the entire test drive at the end of this chapter.

# Evaluating the Dealership

How you're treated during your first visit to a dealership may tell you a lot about any future relationship, so make sure you're comfortable with the atmosphere and test-drive experience.

Your test drives give you a good chance to evaluate a variety of dealerships. Even the lowest possible price usually won't compensate for a bad experience with a particular dealership or salesperson. Salespeople should treat you with respect and honesty. Unfortunately, there are exceptions, so here are some key things to ask yourself when you decide where you're going to buy your next vehicle:

- Has the salesperson been responsive to my inquiries?
- Was I treated with respect?
- Did I get all of the information I needed?
- Did I get honest answers?
- Was it easy to arrange a test drive?
- Were any high-pressure tactics used during my first encounter?
- Was I invited back for additional test drives?

If you answered "yes" to more than a few of the questions above, there's a good chance you might want to do business there. If you answered "no" often, you should think about going elsewhere to buy your new vehicle.

# Test-Drive Checklist

| Walk-Around Checklist | Good | Average | Poor | Comments |
|---|---|---|---|---|
| **Exterior** | | | | |
| Styling | | | | |
| Body panel fit & finish | | | | |
| **Interior** | | | | |
| Driving position | | | | |
| Ergonomics | | | | |
| Quality of plastics, leather, upholstery | | | | |
| Ease of entry/exit, front & rear | | | | |
| Head room, front & rear | | | | |
| Leg room, front & rear | | | | |
| Seat comfort, front & rear | | | | |
| Instruments & controls, layout & usefulness | | | | |
| Storage space inside | | | | |
| Cargo space | | | | |
| Comfort & convenience features | | | | |
| Audio system | | | | |
| **Road-Test Checklist** | | | | |
| Acceleration/passing/hill-climbing | | | | |
| Braking | | | | |
| Handling/cornering | | | | |
| Transmission | | | | |
| Ride comfort/suspension | | | | |
| Driving position | | | | |
| Noise from engine, wind, and tires | | | | |
| Rattles and squeaks | | | | |
| Visibility: front, side, rear, mirrors | | | | |
| **OVERALL EVALUATION** | | | | |

# 6

# How to Evaluate a Used Car

**Buying a used car** is an exercise in finding the right balance of value and risk. A used vehicle can be a real bargain. But there's also an inherent risk. Shoppers often have the nagging thought: "Am I buying someone else's problems?" In the following pages, you'll learn:

- Where to shop for a used car

- Questions you should ask a seller

- Warning signs to look for when inspecting a vehicle

- How to check into a vehicle's past

- Why it's important to have the car inspected by a mechanic

- The problem of rebuilt wrecks

- The pros and cons of certified pre-owned cars

With a little research, you can significantly reduce the chances of buying someone's lemon and increase your chances of getting a long-lasting vehicle that's also a great value.

# Where to Shop for a Used Car

You can buy a used vehicle from a much wider range of outlets than a new vehicle. Prices can vary greatly, but so can the quality of the car. Following are the typical outlets for buying a used car. To find them, check the classified ads in local newspapers and specialty auto-selling publications, as well as those on Web sites specializing in used-car sales (see Appendix A).

**New-car dealers.** Nearly all franchised dealers have a used-car department that sells vehicles they have taken as trade-ins, bought at auction or from another dealer, or that have come back at the end of a lease. Such departments tend to feature late-model vehicles, two or three years old, that often carry the remains of the original factory warranty. Many new-car dealers don't bother with cars more than four or five years old, or ones that are difficult to sell, so their used vehicles tend to be expensive.

**Auto superstores.** Superstores are dealerships with huge lots and scores of cars to sell. CarMax, for instance, is a superstore chain that sells cars at no-haggle prices. There are also independent dealerships that call themselves superstores. Whether they specialize in low-pressure, one-price selling or want you to bargain the old-fashioned way, their key advantage is the quantity and the variety of the stock.

**Independent used-car dealers.** These dealerships are apt to handle any car make, and the vehicles can run the gamut from the almost-new to the junker-in-waiting. Some dealers specialize in late-model cars, and can be affiliated with a franchised new-car dealer. If the dealer has been around for a long time and has a good reputation locally, that's a good sign. As with new cars, many used-car dealerships can arrange financing for you. Still, caution is the watchword. Both price and quality tend to be lower than at a new-car dealership.

**Service stations.** Many service stations have a sideline business selling used cars. They may not have all that many cars to sell, but prices are often better than those you'll find at a dealership. If the station has serviced the car throughout its life, you may have access to the repair history—a real plus. But take it somewhere else for an impartial inspection.

**Private owners.** You can usually get the best price if you buy a car directly from its previous owner. A private party doesn't have to cover the overhead of a business and frequently just wants to get rid of the vehicle. Buying from a private owner, however, also carries the most risk. Even the most honest citizen may be unaware of trouble signs or may suffer a bout of amnesia when asked about problems with a car he is selling. If you're buying a car privately, shop wisely.

## Shopping online

Buying—or at least researching—used cars online opens up a world of possibilities. Its major advantage is your ability to search, sort, and check the marketplace without leaving home. Used cars aren't necessarily any cheaper online, but the Web does provide a way to find out what various models are selling for in your area. You may find, however, that many offerings are located inconveniently far from home.

Used-car Web sites, such as those listed in Appendix A, typically ask you to fill in some search parameters: the make and model you're interested in, your price range, and the region (usually based on your ZIP code) where you'd like to shop. It's a good idea to limit your search to the area within which you're willing to travel to inspect a vehicle. You then get a list of vehicles that fit your buying criteria, along with the sellers' e-mail addresses or phone numbers. Because many sellers are car dealerships, most sites provide direct links to the dealers' Web sites. Many services also let you place a classified ad for selling your old car, either free or for a small fee.

Online auctions (eBay Motors is by far the largest) are another route. The auction system is a little different from standard dickering over price. On eBay, once you enter a bid, it's like signing a contract to buy, whether there's a reserve of not. The buyer is obligated by the bid, and the seller is obligated by accepting it. If there is a reserve, this price must be met before the auction can close. But if no one comes close to the reserve, the seller may remove it. While that means you can snap up a bargain, it also means that you can't get out of the deal unless the seller has made some serious misrepresentation. There is, however, a conditional guarantee by the seller and a short-term service agreement of one month or 1,000 miles. It's still advisable to have the vehicle inspected, and you can arrange this through a paid service on the site.

Problems we've noticed with used-car Web sites include the freshness of the information and the clutter of pop-up and banner ads from other service providers. Sellers must constantly update their Web offerings as inventories change. If they don't, the sites grow stale and inaccurate. That can make locating even common models a challenge. Always call before visiting any seller, whether it's a dealer or a private party, to make sure the vehicle you're looking for is still available.

No matter how much of the transaction you conduct by phone or e-mail, it's important that you inspect the vehicle in person and take it for a test drive.

## Ask the Right Questions

Once you've located one or more vehicles you're interested in, your next step is to contact the seller, whether a private party or a dealership. The easiest way is to call and ask some basic questions about the vehicle, such as those listed below. The answers you get can help you determine whether it's worth a trip to take a closer look. That's especially true when you're buying from a private party. Any strange, far-fetched, or odd-sounding answers to routine questions should put you on guard.

- "What color is the car?" Color may or may not be important to you, but this question can be a good icebreaker.

- "How is it equipped?" Whether they're listed in the ad or not, ask about key features: number of doors; transmission type; air conditioning; antilock brakes; air bags; sound system; power windows, locks, seats, or mirrors; cruise control; sunroof; upholstery material; and so forth. Double-checking on these could produce some telling comments.
- "In what kind of condition are the body and upholstery?" You want to get a general idea of the car's condition.
- "How many miles has it been driven?" If the mileage is higher than, say, 20,000 per year or lower than 5,000, ask why. If a car has high mileage because its owner had a long highway commute to work, that's better than if a car was used for a lot of short trips, stop-and-go driving, or a delivery route. Low mileage is preferable, but a low odometer reading is no guarantee of gentle care.
- "Has it ever been in an accident?" If so, ask about the extent of the damage, cost of repairs, and the sort of shop that did the work. Don't worry too much about minor scrapes, but think twice about buying a car that has been in a serious accident.
- "Do you have service records?" You want a car that has been well-cared-for. That means that it should have had recommended maintenance performed at the manufacturer's specified service intervals. If the owner says he did the maintenance himself but can't produce any receipts for parts, be skeptical. You also want to see the receipts for any new muffler, brakes, tires, or other "wear" parts that have been replaced. Repair-shop receipts normally note the car's odometer reading, helping you verify the car's history.
- "Has the car had any recalls? Has the work been done?" Ask if any safety-recall work was performed or, more important, needs to be done. Dealerships keep records of that. Note the mileage when such work was performed. You can check for safety recalls for a particular model at *www.nhtsa.dot.gov.*

## Where there's smoke...

You can learn a lot about a vehicle's engine by observing the smoke that's emitted from the tailpipe. A little whitish vapor in the first few seconds after start-up is nothing to worry about; it's condensation being blown out of the exhaust system and will quickly disperse. Smoke that persists, however, is cause for concern.

■ Black smoke comes from partially burned fuel. This indicates that the air filter or fuel system needs to be serviced.

■ Blue smoke indicates burning oil—a bad sign. Clouds of blue smoke on start-up may indicate worn valve guide seals, valves, or piston rings, the latter of which can mean a cylinder-head or engine rebuild is needed.

■ Billowy white smoke may indicate that coolant is getting into the engine—another bad sign. This can be a result of a blown head gasket, damaged cylinder head, or even a cracked block—all expensive repairs.

Additional questions for private sellers:

■ "Have you owned it since it was new?" You want to be able to piece together as much of the car's service history as you can. Be wary about a car that has changed hands several times in a few years.

■ "Are you the person who drove it the most?" Ideally, you want to meet the car's principal driver or drivers to see if they strike you as responsible people.

■ "Why are you selling the car?" Look for a plausible explanation rather than an interesting story. If the answer sounds evasive, be wary.

Keep in mind that a salesperson at a dealership may paint an overly rosy picture of any vehicle you ask about. Take with a grain of salt any tale about how the previous owner pampered the car.

You also may not be able to glean all that much information about the car's history from a dealership because the staff simply may not know it.

But you should still ask to see service records and other evidence that the car was maintained properly.

# How to Inspect a Used Car

No matter who you buy from, always look over the vehicle thoroughly and take it to a mechanic for a complete inspection. You don't have to be a mechanical expert to give a car a good, revealing going-over. You can learn a great deal just by using your eyes, ears, and nose. Dress in old clothes and take along a friend to help you out. Do your inspection in broad daylight on a dry day. Floodlit lots tend to make cars look shiny and can hide a lot of body defects. The car must be parked on a level surface and shouldn't have been driven for at least an hour before your inspection.

## Exterior

**Body condition.** Check each body panel and the roof, looking for scratches, dents, and rust. Examine the lines of the fenders and doors. Misaligned panels or large gaps can indicate either sloppy assembly at the factory or shoddy repair. The paint color and finish should be the same on every body panel.

If you think a dent may have been patched up with body filler, put a small magnet on the suspect area; it won't stick to an area with body filler. If parts of the car have been repainted, there may be signs of "overspray," or paint adhering to the rubber seals around the hood and trunk lid.

Minor cosmetic flaws and superficial scratches are no cause for concern, but rust is. Check the outer body for blistered paint or rust. Also, inspect the wheel wells, rocker panels (the sheet metal beneath the doors), and the bottoms of the doors themselves. Use a flashlight when looking inside the wheel wells for rust or corrosion.

Open and close each door, the hood, and the trunk. Gently lift and let go of each door, particularly the driver's door. If the door seems loose on its hinges, the car has seen hard or long use. Also, inspect the rubber seals around all openings for tearing or rot.

**Glass.** Look carefully at the windshield and other windows to make sure there are no cracks or large pocked areas. A small stone chip may not be cause for alarm, though you should bring it up as a bargaining point in negotiations. But cracks in the windshield will worsen and lead to a costly repair.

**Suspension.** Walk around the car and see if it's standing level. Bounce each corner up and down. If the shock absorbers are in good shape, the car should rebound just once; it shouldn't keep moving up and down. Then grab the top of each front tire and tug it back and forth. If you feel play in it or hear a clunking or ticking sound, the wheel bearings or suspension joints may be shot.

**Lights and lenses.** Have a friend stand outside the car and confirm that all lights are working. Make sure all light lenses and reflectors are intact and not cracked, fogged with moisture, or missing.

**Tires.** You can tell a lot from the tires. If the car has less than, say, 20,000 miles on the odometer, it should probably still have its original tires. Be wary of a car with moderately low miles and brand-new tires. The vehicle's odometer may have been rolled back. Also check that all four tires are the same. Any different tires may show that they have been replaced.

Tread wear should be even across the width of the tread. It should also be the same on the left and right sides of the car. Ask if the tires have been regularly rotated. If not, the wear is usually more severe on the drive wheels.

Also, aggressive drivers tend to put heavy wear on the outside shoulder of the front tires, at the edge of the sidewall. Assume that the car has been driven hard if that area is badly worn relative to the rest of the tire.

Tires that have been driven while overinflated tend to wear in the middle. Chronically underinflated tires show wear on the sides. Cupped tires, those that are worn unevenly along the tread's circumference, may herald a problem with the steering, suspension, or brakes.

Check the tread depth, either with a tread-depth tool (available at auto-parts stores) or with a penny. To be legal, tires must have at least ¹⁄₁₆ inch of tread. If you don't have a tread gauge, insert a penny into the tread groove, with Lincoln's head down. If you can see the top of Abe's head, the tire should be replaced.

Examine the sidewalls for scuffing, cracks, or bulges, and look on the edge of each rim for dents or cracks. And be sure to check that the spare is in good shape and that the proper jack and lug wrench are present.

## Interior

It's the inside of a car that may matter most in the long run since that's where you'll be spending the most time with the car.

**Odor.** When you first open the car door, sniff the interior. A musty, moldy, or mildewy smell could indicate water leaks. Remove the floor mats, and feel and sniff for wet spots on the carpet beneath. An acrid smell may indicate the car was used by a smoker. Check the lighter and ashtray for evidence. Some odors can be hard to get rid of. If you don't like what you smell, find another car.

**Seats.** Try out all the seats even though you may not plan to sit in the rear. Upholstery shouldn't be ripped or badly worn, particularly in a car that's supposed to have low miles on it. Try all the driver's seat adjustments to make sure they work properly and that you can find a good driving position.

**Pedals.** The rubber on the brake, clutch, and gas pedals gives an indication of use. A car with low miles shouldn't show much wear. If the pedal rubber is worn through in spots—or brand new—it indicates high miles.

**Instruments and controls.** Turn the ignition switch, but without starting the engine. All the warning lights—including the "Check engine" light—should illuminate for a few moments. They should then go off when you start the engine. Note if the engine is hard to start when cold and whether it idles smoothly. Then methodically try out every switch, button, and lever.

With the engine running, turn on the heater full blast and see how hot it gets—and how quickly. Switch on the air conditioning, and make sure it quickly blows cold.

**Sound system.** Check radio reception on AM and FM. If there is a CD or tape player, try loading and ejecting a compact disc or tape.

**Roof.** Check the headliner for stains or sags; they can mean that water is leaking in through ill-fitting doors or windows. If the car has a sunroof or moonroof, check to see that it opens and closes properly and seals well when shut. Inspect the fabric of a convertible top for tears by shining a flashlight up into it.

**Trunk.** Again, use your nose as well as your eyes. Again, sniff and look for signs of water entry. See if the carpeting feels wet or smells musty. Take up the trunk floor and check the spare-tire well for water or rust.

## Under the hood

If the engine has been off for a few minutes, you can do most under-the-hood checks. Look first at the general condition of the engine bay. Dirt and dust are normal, but watch out if you see lots of oil spattered about, a battery covered with corrosion, or wires and hoses hanging loose.

**Hoses and belts.** Try to squeeze the various rubber hoses running to the radiator, air conditioner, and other parts. The rubber should be firm and supple, not rock-hard, cracked, or mushy. Feel the drive belts to determine whether they are frayed.

**Fluids.** Check all fluid levels. The owner's manual will point out where to look. The engine oil should be dark brown or black, but not too dirty or gritty. If the oil is honey-colored, it was just changed. If the dipstick has water droplets on it or oil that is gray or foamy, it could indicate a cracked engine block or blown head gasket—serious problems you want no part of. Transmission fluid should be pinkish, not brown, and smell like oil, with no "burnt" odor. The dipstick shouldn't leave visible metal particles on the rag—another sign of serious problems. With most cars, you check the automatic-transmission fluid with the engine warmed up and running. On some, the transmission-fluid dipstick has two sets of marks for checking when the engine is either cold or warm. Also be sure to check the power-steering and brake-fluid levels. They should be within the safe zone.

**Radiator.** Check the coolant by looking into the plastic reservoir near the radiator. The coolant should be greenish or orange, not a milky or rusty color. Greenish stains on the outside of the radiator are a sign of pinhole leaks.

**Battery.** Some "maintenance-free" batteries have a built-in charge indicator. A green indicator eye usually means the battery is in good shape; yellow or black usually means the battery is dying or dead. But because these indicators reveal the condition of just one cell, it may not give an accurate reading on how healthy the whole battery is. If the battery has filler caps, wipe off the top of the battery with a rag, then carefully pry off or unscrew the caps to look at the liquid electrolyte level. If the level is low, it may not mean much, or it may mean that the battery has been working too hard. A mechanic can check out the charging system and do a "load test" on the battery.

## Under the vehicle

If you can find the spot where a car was habitually parked, see if that part of the garage floor or driveway is marred with puddles of gasoline, oil, coolant, or transmission fluid. Don't be alarmed if some clear water drips from under the car on a hot day. It's probably just water condensed from the air conditioner.

Feel for any tailpipe residue. If it's black and greasy, it means the car is burning oil. The tailpipe smudge should be dry and dark gray. Look at the pipes—some rust is normal. Heavy rust is sometimes normal but could mean that a new exhaust system might be needed soon.

If the vehicle is high enough to slide under, you may be able to do some basic checks underneath. (If not, make sure you have a mechanic include this as part of a thorough professional inspection.) Spread an old blanket on the ground so you can look under the engine. Use a flashlight. If you see oil drips, other oily leaks, or green or red fluid on the engine or the pavement beneath the car, it's not a good sign.

On a front-wheel-drive car, examine the constant-velocity-joint boots behind the front wheels. They are round, black-rubber bellows at the ends of the axle shafts. If the rubber boots are split and leaking grease, assume that the car has or shortly will have bad CV joints—another item that's costly to repair.

Kinked structural components and large dents in the floor pan or fuel tank are all indications of a past accident. Welding on the frame suggests a damaged section might have been replaced or cut out to perform repair work. Fresh undercoating may hide recent structural repairs.

## Test drive

It's essential that you take the vehicle for a thorough test drive. For advice on what to look for, see Chapter 5.

## Take the car to an independent mechanic

Before you buy a used vehicle, have it scrutinized by a repair shop that routinely does diagnostic work. A dealer should have no problem lending you the car to have it inspected as long as you leave identification. If a salesperson tells you that an independent inspection is not necessary because the dealership has already done it, insist that you want the vehicle looked at by a mechanic of your choice. A private seller may be reluctant to let you drive the car to a shop. You should offer to follow the seller to the shop where the inspection will take place.

Make sure the mechanic puts the vehicle on a lift and inspects the undercarriage. A thorough diagnosis should cost around $100, but confirm the price in advance. Ask for a written report detailing the car's condition, noting any problems found and what it would cost to repair them. You can

## Noises: What they can mean

Part of the diagnostic that's especially tricky is decoding the various mechanical noises a car can make. Some are serious, some not.

**In the engine compartment.** A high-pitched squeal that occurs mainly when revving the engine is probably due to a slipping drive belt. Have the belt replaced. While driving, a light metallic rattling from the engine, especially under acceleration, may be "pinging," which can result from something as simple as using too low an octane gasoline or from something more serious like an overheating engine. If pinging is loud or constant, consult a mechanic. A loud knocking sound within the engine is a sign of serious trouble.

**From the wheels.** A rhythmic thumping that gets faster and slower as you accelerate or brake may mean something is wrong with a tire. A ticking or grinding noise when you turn hard left or right may mean the constant-velocity joints on a front-drive car need replacement—a several-hundred-dollar repair. If the brakes squeal when you're not braking, the brake pads probably need changing. A harsh grinding noise accompanied by vibration when you hit the brakes may mean the brake drums or disc rotors are in bad shape.

then use the report in the negotiation with the seller, should you decide to buy the vehicle.

If you don't know of a repair shop with which you feel comfortable, try to get a referral from someone you trust. You could also ask for the name of a good shop at a local auto-parts store. Other sources include the Yellow Pages or an organization called the Car Care Council, which lists facilities on its Web site. To check for complaints about any shops you aren't familiar with, go to the Better Business Bureau's Web site and type in the name of the business. If you're an American Automobile Association (AAA) member, use one of its recommended facilities. You can get recommendations through its Web site; type in your member number, the city, and the radius in miles in which you're willing to travel.

If you're visiting a shop for the first time, see if it looks clean and well maintained. There should be up-to-date electronic diagnostic equipment next to the service bays. Look for framed certificates or window decals from AAA or the National Institute of Automotive Service Excellence (ASE). AAA-certified garages must meet certain quality standards. ASE grants certificates to mechanics who pass exams in any of eight areas of expertise. The ASE does not certify a shop as a whole, but if 75 percent of the employees are ASE-certified, the shop can carry the seal.

## You need to know

Every passenger vehicle sold in this country has a 17-digit serial number known as the Vehicle Identification Number, or VIN. It's found stamped on a metal plate in a number of places, including where the windshield meets the dash in front of the driver. It's also printed on the car's title document and registration. If you understand the VIN code, you can confirm the vehicle's place of manufacture, model year, and other information.

**The first character** of the VIN code indicates the country of manufacture: 1 or 4 means USA, 2 is Canada, 3 is Mexico, J is Japan, K is Korea, S is England, W is Germany, and Z is Italy.

**The 10th digit** is a letter or number indicating the model year. The letters T, V, W, X, and Y stand for 1996, 1997, 1998, 1999, and 2000, respectively. The digits 1, 2, 3, 4, 5, and 6 stand for 2001, 2002, 2003, 2004, 2005, and 2006.

There are several free VIN-decoder services available on the Internet. A couple of the better ones are from CarFax *(www.carfax.com)* and the Car Care Council *(www.carcarecouncil.org,* under "Helpful Stats & Info"). A quick check can confirm that the car you are looking at is the same as what the documentation says it is.

# Looking Into a Vehicle's Past

You should always try to check out the history of a used car before you buy. You can piece some of the history together by interviewing the former owner and looking at any service records that come with the car.

If you have a car's vehicle identification number (VIN), you can also buy a vehicle history report from at least two companies that track vehicle histories. CarFax (*www.carfax.com*) and Experian Automotive (*www.autocheck.com*) offer fee-based background reports using information from motor vehicle records, police and fire departments, and elsewhere. These reports can alert you to a vehicle that has had its odometer rolled back or sustained flood damage, or may be a salvaged vehicle that has been rebuilt or repaired after being totaled in an accident.

Don't assume a clean report is a guarantee that there is nothing wrong, however. The company's data might be incomplete or insufficient to form a judgment. If, say, a car was in a crash that wasn't reported to police, or if the police officer incorrectly copied the VIN number, then that collision won't show up in your vehicle history report. Regardless of what the report or service records indicate, always have a mechanic check out the car completely.

If you're buying from an individual, examine the title document carefully. It might disclose that the vehicle had been classified junk or salvage, or that it was repurchased by the manufacturer under a state Lemon Law program (see "Beware of Rebuilt Wrecks," below).

# Beware of Rebuilt Wrecks

Repairing and reselling "salvage" vehicles, those that have been written off by insurance companies as a total loss, is a larger business than you might expect. According to the National Association of Consumer Advocates, about one million salvage vehicles are returned to the road each year.

While it is possible to restore such a vehicle to good condition, rebuilders often must cut costs to make a profit. Even if they try to do an acceptable job, no one can predict the crashworthiness and mechanical reliability of those vehicles.

Similar issues affect the estimated 60,000 or so vehicles that are repurchased by manufacturers under state Lemon Law programs. Many are resold at retail. Lemons usually don't have the severe problems you'd expect with salvage cars. But it can be very difficult verifying that the chronic defect has been corrected.

State laws differ, sometimes dramatically, on what they define as salvage and lemon vehicles and on how—or even if—these vehicles need to be inspected and buyers informed before resale.

Many states require a "brand" to be printed on the vehicle's title document. Washington State, for example, mandates the words "WA REBUILT" in large type if the vehicle is less than 6 years old or worth more than $6,500. In Colorado, salvage vehicles are distinguished only by a small "S" in front of the vehicle's make. Call your local Department of Motor Vehicles office to find out how to spot a salvage title in your own state.

All this has led to the interstate trafficking of salvage and lemon vehicles, a practice in which titles are "washed" through the more lenient states to remove signs of a dubious history. Even if titles of former lemon and salvage vehicles are conspicuously branded, those who buy a used car from a dealership often never see the previous title.

If you discover that you've unknowingly purchased a salvage vehicle or recycled lemon, contact your state consumer and motor vehicle officials. You also can check with the National Association of Consumer Advocates (*www.naca.net*), which keeps a list of lawyers who specialize in such cases.

Before you buy, check to see what protection your state offers and what's required of the seller. New York and New Jersey, for instance, have lemon laws for used cars. In addition, the Federal Trade Commission requires that used-car dealers must post a Buyers Guide on every used car, which details in writing all warranty information. Buyers should keep this after the sale.

# The "Certified" Option

Because the risks of buying a used car can make some buyers uneasy, most automakers and some dealerships have now developed certification systems that are intended to give buyers greater peace of mind. Certified used cars are billed as the cream-of-the-crop, inspected, and reconditioned according to stringent guidelines. But they can cost hundreds or thousands of dollars more than noncertified vehicles.

All manufacturer programs require that candidates for certification have less than a specified age and mileage, typically no more than 5 years old and with less than 60,000 or 70,000 miles. Manufacturer programs also routinely exclude cars that have a suspicious title history or other serious flaws.

With a typical manufacturer-certification program, the dealership screens, inspects, and reconditions the chosen vehicles. The automaker then certifies that the car is sound and gives it a manufacturer-backed warranty. The terms of the warranties, however, can differ significantly from one brand to another, with coverage lasting from three months to several years. Some warranties extend the manufacturer's original new-car warranty, with the coverage listed from the date the car was first sold. Other warranties begin when you buy the certified vehicle.

Certification programs also typically throw in enhancements such as roadside assistance and trip-interruption insurance. Since these items are generally available through an auto-club membership or other source, the extras probably shouldn't be a deciding factor.

The term "certified" doesn't actually mean much. Any used-car dealer can call any car "certified." The term has no legal definition, and no watchdog agency polices its use. As a result, you'll sometimes see a car labeled "certified" that has not undergone any reconditioning process. It may carry only a service contract, the cost of which is rolled into the vehicle's price.

You might also see aftermarket warranty programs that look like a manufacturer certification. These "dealer certification" programs are underwritten by one of a number of warranty companies, which are essentially insurers that sell a program to dealers who then resell it to consumers. Because the quality and terms of such contracts vary widely, it's especially important to read the fine print carefully. Some unscrupulous dealers mislead car shoppers about the certification status of a given car, so it's important to be wary.

Don't assume that a certified car is worth the premium price. If you're buying a late-model, low-mileage car, you should expect it to be in good condition anyway. Negotiate the price as you would any other used car.

When considering any certified car, ask the dealer specific questions:

- Is the vehicle covered by a manufacturer-certified program or by a third-party plan sold by the dealer? Nonmanufacturer plans are wild cards because they can vary greatly in quality.
- What does the warranty cover, and for how long? Ask to see a copy of the warranty contract, not just a glossy brochure. Read the fine print.
- Is there a deductible? If there is a charge for service, find out how much it is, and whether you must pay it for each item serviced or for each service call. Ask about other fees, such as a "diagnostic" fee that's added to the deductible.
- Who provides the service? Ask whether you have to bring the car back to the original dealership for warranty work, or whether any same-brand dealership is fine. Ask what you're required to do in an emergency.

If you are buying a well-maintained car with a good record of reliability, you aren't taking much of a risk if you skip the certification route. But, once again, the real key for your peace of mind when buying a used vehicle is to have it thoroughly inspected by an independent mechanic.

# Step 3

## Crunch the Numbers

■ CHAPTER 7: Set a Target Price                         **145**
■ CHAPTER 8: Get Top Dollar for Your Trade-in           **157**
■ CHAPTER 9: Understand Your Insurance Options          **175**

# 7

# Set a Target Price

**When buying most products,** from a refrigerator to a high-definition television, you typically assume that the price marked on the product is the figure the store expects you to pay. If you went to a cashier and said you wanted, say, $500 off the marked price, he or she would probably smile politely and quietly notify security.

That's usually not the case when buying a car. Sure, there are some so-called "no-haggle" dealerships, but in the vast majority of the cases, auto salespeople expect you to negotiate the price of a car. The figure on a car's window sticker is only a suggested retail price set by the auto manufacturer. As separate businesses, dealerships are free to sell their vehicles at whatever price they want.

Of course the salesperson would like you to pay something close to the sticker price; that means more commission for him or her and added profit for the dealership. But an informed buyer, prepared with the right information, can often buy a vehicle for hundreds or thousands of dollars below the sticker price.

This is why it's important to calculate a reasonable target price before you go to the dealership to buy. By researching what the dealership paid for the car, you know how much profit margin the dealer has to work with. Then you're not negotiating in the dark.

Many people are intimidated by the prospect of haggling. Approaching the negotiation with accurate price information, though, puts you in control and puts the burden on the salesperson to come up with the best price possible. In Chapter 15, we'll cover how to negotiate effectively. In this chapter, we'll show you how to prepare, by covering the ins and outs of auto pricing, where to find key pricing information, and how to arrive at a reasonable target price. All of this information will help you be a better negotiator in the showroom.

In the following pages, you'll learn:

- Auto-pricing terms
- How to decipher the window sticker
- How the dealer-invoice price differs from the actual dealer cost
- Why you should know about dealer incentives
- What the dealer holdback is
- How vehicle demand affects the price you pay
- Pros and cons of no-haggle sales

## Auto-Pricing Terms

The most effective way to negotiate a new car's price is to start with the dealer's cost and bargain up from there, rather than starting with the sticker price and trying to hammer that downward. To figure out the true dealer cost, you have to piece together the various elements of the auto-pricing puzzle.

## Manufacturer's suggested retail price (MSRP), or sticker price

This is the price that the automaker publishes for any given model and trim line. Because it's "suggested," dealers are free to sell a vehicle for a figure that's higher or lower than the MSRP. The "base price," excluding any options, destination charge, or other fees, is the initial figure you'll find in pricing guides, most car reviews, and on pricing Web sites. The "total MSRP," commonly called the "sticker price" because it's the bottom-line figure on a car's window sticker, is the base price plus any options, option-package discounts, and destination charge. Unless a model is in very high demand, you can generally buy a vehicle for less than the sticker price.

## Dealer-invoice price

The "invoice price" is the figure printed on the dealer's invoice from the manufacturer. Once difficult to find, invoice prices are now commonly available online and in printed pricing guides, such as Consumer Reports' Auto Pricing & Ratings Guide. The reports also include the date when the incentive expires, which is important to know. Information about incentives can also be found on various auto-pricing Web sites (see Appendix A). In fact, dealer-invoice prices have become so ubiquitous that they are even listed on some automaker Web sites. In addition, at many dealerships salespeople will show you the invoice for the car you're interested in, often as a way to let you know how "little markup" there is on what they're asking.

The dealer-invoice price, however, is not necessarily what the dealer really paid for the car, because there are often behind-the-scenes payments, such as dealer sales incentives and holdbacks, that give the dealer extra profit margin. What you see on the invoice is only part of the pricing puzzle. You'll need a few more pieces to make the puzzle fit together for a complete picture.

## Dealer sales incentives

These are unadvertised payments that the manufacturer offers the dealer for selling certain models. The dealer can pass along the incentive to the buyer in the form of a price reduction or keep it as added profit. They are usually used to push sales of slow-selling or overstocked models. Incentive programs can come and go quickly, depending on supply and demand, and some can be regional in nature, depending on local market conditions.

## Holdbacks

You can think of a holdback as a refund for the dealer that he gets after the vehicle has been sold. Depending on the automaker, a typical holdback is about 2 or 3 percent of either the MSRP or invoice price. For example, if a vehicle has an MSRP of about $25,000, a dealer's holdback might be as much as $800. Holdbacks are a way of reimbursing dealers for the financing costs of keeping vehicles in inventory. Because the dealer will receive the entire holdback amount, the sooner he can sell a vehicle—thereby reducing his finance costs—the more of the holdback he can keep as profit.

Dealers usually won't bargain away their holdback, but knowing about it gives you more perspective on how much profit margin they're working with. So, when the salesperson pleads that they're not making any money on a car, you'll know whether it's just a line or not. CR's New Car Price Reports also include the vehicle's holdback price, information that's hard to

## You need to know

When negotiating the price of a vehicle, it's important to remember that the rebate comes from the automaker, not the dealer. Therefore it doesn't affect the dealer's profit margin or room to negotiate. Don't let a salesperson make you feel like you're getting a good deal simply because you'll get a rebate. You'll get that rebate no matter how little you pay for the vehicle. So negotiate the vehicle's price as if the car didn't have a rebate. There's no reason you shouldn't get the lowest price you can—and the rebate, too.

find elsewhere. To make the negotiation simpler, every price report includes the CR Wholesale Price, which subtracts any incentives, rebates, and the holdback from the dealer-invoice price to give you a good starting point for your negotiations.

## Rebate

This is a direct-to-the-buyer payment from the manufacturer to encourage you to buy a particular vehicle. Many buyers use it as part of the down payment to reduce the amount that needs to be financed. Rebates are widely promoted in vehicle advertising, but they can be national or regional, and they don't last forever. It pays to check out the details.

## Market adjustment

Sometimes if there is exceptional demand for a model, dealers tack on an additional charge that can be hundreds or thousands of dollars over the manufacturer's sticker price. You'll typically find these on a highly anticipated model that's been recently introduced or one that has a long waiting list. You can try to negotiate this figure, but if the vehicle is selling well, the dealer won't have much incentive to work with you. If you have to be the first on your block to have a hot new model, this could be the premium you have to pay. If you wait a while to buy, however, these dealer adjustments will usually disappear.

## The window sticker

Here's what you can expect to see on a typical window sticker:

- **Standard equipment.** These are the core features included for the vehicle's base price, or MSRP.
- **Vehicle identification number (VIN).** Make sure that this is the same number that's on the vehicle and that it's the same in all documentation. On the vehicle, you can see the VIN when outside of the car by looking

## Automakers discourage market adjustments

Even though dealers have the right to charge whatever the market will bear for a vehicle, especially for those in high demand, automakers generally discourage such a practice. That's because once the sought-after vehicle is readily available, those who paid a premium price will start to experience "buyer's remorse" when they see friends and neighbors buying the same vehicle for hundreds or thousands less. That breeds discontent with the brand—the last thing automakers want. Some dealers, however, just want to make as much money as they can while a model's hot and don't take a longer-range view.

through the windshield at the point in front of the driver's position where the dash meets the windshield.

- **Manufacturer's suggested retail price.** The MSRP is the base price, before options and delivery charges are factored in.
- **Optional equipment.** These are extra-cost features that get added onto the base MSRP. Option packages often can be more cost-effective than choosing individual items but can also force you to buy items you don't need to get one or two you want.
- **Destination charge.** This covers the delivery of the vehicle from the factory to the dealership. Normally, this is the same for all models within the same brand. It doesn't depend on actual shipping distance.
- **Market adjustments.** Sometimes you'll see a line on the window sticker or a separate sticker that adds an additional charge to the vehicle's price. This is a fee the dealer tacks on, usually to cars that are in high demand, in an effort to make additional profit.
- **Fuel economy.** City and highway figures are based on the EPA standard driving cycle. Real-world figures tend to be slightly lower, particularly for the city rating.
- **Total.** The "sticker price" is the total retail price, including the MSRP,

options, option-package discounts, and destination charge. This may or may not include market adjustments made by the dealer.

# Calculating a Starting Price

When you walk into a showroom, the window sticker on every new car displays the manufacturer's suggested retail price, including the cost of all the options. As we've said, don't assume that the sticker price is what you should pay. Typically, you should be able to negotiate a lower price with little resistance. In fact, don't even use the sticker price as your gauge when negotiating a deal. For example, dealer advertising might tout a price that's, say, "$500 below the MSRP," and many consumers will accept such an offer, concluding—often mistakenly—that they got a good deal. Unless the vehicle is in big demand and short supply, you can often get an even lower price by doing your homework before you visit the dealership.

As we discussed, to get the lowest price, you have to start with a figure that's based on how much the dealer actually paid for the vehicle. By knowing the dealer's cost, you'll know how much profit margin the dealer has to work with. Your goal then is to get the lowest price you can while allowing the dealer to make a fair profit.

## Putting it all together

To figure out the dealer's actual cost for a vehicle, you need to find the dealer-invoice price, any current dealer sales incentives, and the holdback amount. As we said, dealer-invoice prices are now so common that you can find them on many Web sites and pricing guides, but you'll have to do a little more digging to find behind-the-scenes dealer incentives.

To point you in the right direction, Consumer Reports' New Car Price Reports do this work for you (see Appendix C for details on the reports). Each report shows you all three factors: the dealer-invoice price, the amount of any national or regional dealer sales incentives, and the holdback amount. Alternatively, you can look up current sales incentives yourself at some auto-pricing Web sites (see Appendix A).

A reasonable price for a vehicle is about 4 percent to 8 percent over the dealer's cost, depending on how popular the model is. If a model has been on the market for awhile and isn't selling well—indicated by the automaker often offering rebates or special financing—you might be able to buy the vehicle for a little over the dealer's cost. If there's more demand, you should expect a higher percentage over cost. Occasionally, if the model is very popular, you may not get much less than the sticker price.

If you have the time, it can also be helpful to check your target price against those offered by dealerships affiliated with Web sites. To do this, see the auto-buying Web sites listed in Appendix A. On these sites, you can ask for a price quote on a vehicle that's configured the way you want it and one or more dealerships will reply by e-mail. CarsDirect.com will also give you a no-haggle price that their contracted dealerships have agreed to honor.

You can compare these quotes against the target price you calculated based on the dealer's cost. Usually, the quotes will be higher. But if, by chance, a quote is lower than your figure, this gives you more leverage with which to bargain. Of course, once you do this, you'll be on the contact list for those dealerships and will likely be receiving a number of e-mails and, perhaps, phone calls.

Another point of comparison could be so-called transaction prices posted on some auto-buying Web sites. These are intended to reflect the average of what other buyers are actually paying for new vehicles. These prices are available on sites such as Autobytel and Edmunds.com, which posts its True Market Value (TMV) price.

Since these transaction prices are an average of nationwide sales prices, they might not necessarily apply to your area. Prices will vary by region, depending on the local cost of doing business, and of course, what the market will bear. In addition, keep in mind that posted transaction prices are average prices, meaning some actual prices were higher and some were lower.

By having a target price based on the dealer's cost and following the advice in Chapter 15, you may be able to do better than those transaction prices. At the very least, during your negotiating process, it's really comforting to know approximately what you should be paying.

How should you use your target price to get the best deal? We'll discuss this in more detail in Chapter 15.

Ideally, your best chance to get a rock-bottom price is to get different dealerships bidding against each other. You simply tell them you want the lowest markup over your target price, that you will be asking other dealerships for the same, and that you will buy from the one who gives you the lowest price. This helps keep the negotiating process straightforward, and keeps you in command without having to be an ace at haggling.

# "No-Haggle" Prices

One-price, no-haggle, no-hassle, upfront pricing, or value pricing are different names for the practice of selling a vehicle at a non-negotiable price. GM's Saturn division has been using a no-haggle approach since its inception in 1990. Scion, Toyota's "youth-oriented" brand, also uses no-haggle pricing. While no other brands have adopted this strategy, some individual dealerships and other outlets also use this approach.

At the auto-selling Web site CarsDirect.com you can choose to take either a single, no-haggle price for the vehicle you want or get price quotes from contracted dealerships, just as you can at other Web sites.

As an alternative, you can go to places like Sam's Club, Costco, or BJ's Wholesale Club and get a set price that's been pre-negotiated with local dealerships. Once you make the purchase, you then go to the appropriate dealership to get the car.

No-haggle pricing is intended to take the stress of negotiating the vehicle's price out of the buying process. No-haggle outlets often discount their prices below the manufacturer's suggested retail price (MSRP), but you can often get an even lower price by negotiating.

Not having to negotiate the vehicle's price may seem to make things simpler, but you still shouldn't go in unprepared. There are other variables beyond the vehicle's price that can cost you extra money. If you don't get the full value of your trade-in, for example, this could substantially alter the effectiveness of your deal. In addition, many times you'll still be pressured to buy options and/or unnecessary extras that will inflate the overall price (see Chapters 4 and 12).

Even if you intend to negotiate the price, you can use no-haggle outlets just as you do other research tools. If you know that one dealership is willing to sell a vehicle at a set price, then you know that no matter which dealership you negotiate with, you don't need to pay more than that price.

## Regional auto price incentives

Most price incentives offered to consumers on new cars, such as cash rebates or low-interest financing, are nationally based; they usually apply to all buyers throughout the country and are often advertised on national TV or in nationally distributed publications. Incentives are very expensive for the automaker and aren't always needed on a national level. More and more auto manufacturers now also are offering regional incentives that only apply to a specific geographic area.

By offering buyers regional incentives, manufacturers can target individual areas where sales are lower. Some manufacturers offer both national and regional incentives simultaneously, with the regional incentive often being more generous.

If you're eligible for both, you'll have to make a choice, since dealers won't let you combine the offers.

To help, Consumer Reports' New Car Price Reports list both regional and national incentives currently in effect.

Many automakers are additionally offering their dealers regional incentives. These are behind-the-scenes, unadvertised rebates that the dealer receives for selling certain models.

Knowing about regional dealer incentives can help you gauge the dealer's profit margin on an individual model, which in turn can help you get a better deal.

# Knowledge is Power

The best approach going into the shopping process is to be armed with accurate pricing information and a target price range. That helps level the playing field with the salesperson, and gives you the perspective to know if a price he or she is quoting is competitive. Knowledge is power, and with it, you'll be negotiating from strength.

## Worksheet: Setting a Target Price Range

### Manufacturer's suggested retail price (only for comparison)

Base MSRP                                          $ _____

Add: Total of options (at retail price)            $ _____

    Destination charge                        $ _____

Total MSRP                                         $ _____


### Customer rebate (if any)                       $ _____


### Estimate the dealer's actual cost

Dealer-invoice price (for base vehicle)            $ _____

Add: Total of options (at dealer-invoice price)    $ _____

    Destination charge                        $ _____

Subtract:  Dealer sales incentive (if any)         _____

       Holdback                            $ _____

Estimated dealer cost*                             $ _____

**Target price range**                             $ _____

(4% to 8% over dealer cost)


### Internet price quotes (for comparison)         $ _____


\* This is the same as the CR Wholesale Price, which is included with each Consumer Reports New Car Price Report (see Appendix C).

# 8

# Get Top Dollar for Your Trade-In

**In addition to the homework** and price negotiations you need to do to get the best deal on a new car, most people have to address another important issue: what to do with the current vehicle. This might seem like a secondary concern in the emotional swirl of getting new wheels, but be careful. You could get a great deal on your new car and lose all of the savings—and more—on your trade-in.

Of course, you don't have to trade in your current car. You can typically get more money by selling it yourself. But trading in is a relatively low-hassle option that about 55 percent of new-car buyers choose, according to the National Automobile Dealers Association.

In this chapter we'll cover the pros and cons of the various options open to you, including trading the vehicle in or selling it yourself. We'll also give you important advice about how to assess your current vehicle's true value and how to get the most money for it. We'll cover:

- The difference between a used car's wholesale and retail prices
- The factors that affect your car's value
- Used-car pricing sources and how they can be used against you
- Trading in vs. selling it yourself
- How to maximize your car's "curb appeal"
- When to discuss your trade-in with the salesperson
- Sales tax and other financial implications

# What Is Your Car Really Worth?

Whatever you decide to do with your current car, it's important to know its current cash value. Assessing the value of a used car, however, is far more complicated than with a new car. It depends on a number of factors, including the vehicle's age, mileage, condition, trim level, optional equipment, and even the region in which it's being sold.

For any used car there are two prices to consider: retail and wholesale.

**Retail price.** This is the higher of the two. The retail value is what you would expect to pay for the car if you were buying it at a dealership and is likely the most you should expect to get if you sold it yourself. This takes into account the cost of acquiring the vehicle, reconditioning it, and holding it in inventory until sold—plus profit. This is considerably higher than the price you'll likely receive for your trade-in.

**Wholesale price (trade-in value).** This is the car's value to someone, such as a dealer, who wants to turn around and resell it to someone else for a profit. The wholesale price is essentially the same as the trade-in value. Understandably it is notably lower than the retail price in order to allow room for profit. This price, for all practical purposes, assumes that the dealership can clean it up and sell it quickly.

To show you the difference between a car's retail and wholesale values, here are the base prices of several popular three-year-old models (with 33,000 miles) as they were listed in Consumer Reports' Used Car Price Reports in mid-2005:

| Model | Trim Level | Retail Price | Wholesale Price |
|---|---|---|---|
| Chevrolet Impala | LS | $13,042 | $11,022 |
| Ford Explorer | 4WD XLT | $17,480 | $15,037 |
| Dodge Ram 1500 | Quad Cab SLT | $16,907 | $14,512 |
| Honda Civic | EX | $12,145 | $10,225 |
| Toyota Camry | LE V6 | $14,937 | $12,767 |

If you decide to trade in your current car, you should expect to get something close to its wholesale value, after taking all variables (options, mileage, condition, etc.) into consideration. Some dealerships will try to give you less money for it so they can make more profit when it's resold.

If you sell the vehicle yourself, you will usually be able to get a price that's notably higher than the wholesale price, but because private buyers are usually looking for a good deal, you may not be able to get the full retail value.

## Find the book value

There are many sources from which you can get a basic idea of a vehicle's value, including printed pricing guides and Web sites that provide used-car prices. The first figure you'll see when you look up a vehicle in these pricing guides is the car's base value. To get a more accurate figure, you must factor in any options as well as the vehicle's mileage and condition. Some Web sites let you do this online and then give you adjusted figures.

To help in this area, CONSUMER REPORTS offers Used Car Price Reports that are tailored to specific models. Each report gives you the retail and wholesale/trade-in value of the model and walks you through the process of adjusting the value according to options, mileage, and condition. For information, see Appendix C.

Alternately, you can check Web sites or pricing guides published by companies such as Edmunds (*www.edmunds.com*), Kelley Blue Book (*www.kbb.com*), National Automobile Dealers Association (*www.nadaguides.com*), and VMR (*www.vmrintl.com*). The printed guides can often be found at libraries.

An important consideration: Since prices tend to fluctuate constantly and different pricing sources provide different values, you'll likely find that one model can have different retail and/or wholesale prices, depending on the source. Usually the difference isn't great, but it points out that there's no such thing as a precise price for a used car. It's best to check out several sources to get an average value.

## What are other sellers asking?

While pricing guides and Web sites can give you a general idea of a vehicle's value, you can often get a better fix on its worth in your region by checking the classified ads and dealer ads in local newspapers and classified-ad publications. Sometimes it's difficult to sort out the private sellers from the hidden dealer ads, but it's a good place to start. Look for vehicles that are similar to yours in terms of model year, mileage, trim level, options, and condition.

You can also check online used-car selling sites such as Autobytel (*www.autobytel.com*), Auto Trader (*www.autotrader.com*), UsedCars.com (*www.usedcars.com*), or eBay Motors (*www.ebaymotors.com*). You can limit your search to your general geographic area and instantly get a listing of the cars for sale and the prices. Keep in mind that prices in other regions may vary from those in your area.

Also remember that the listed prices are only the asking prices, not necessarily what people are paying. You should assume that all such prices are negotiable. One advantage to eBay Motors is that you can check completed auctions for the actual sale prices.

## Get quotes from dealerships

If you're trading in and want to find an easily obtainable rock-bottom price, make your car presentable (see "Maximizing Your Car's Curb Appeal" on the next page) and take it to the used-car department of several local dealerships. Ask what they would give you in a straight-out sale. That will tell you the minimum to expect if you trade your car in, and it gives you a price

### Condition means a lot

Just because your car has been reliable and still looks OK doesn't mean it's in good condition. A spot or two of rust, a dent or ding, stained upholstery, or worn-out tires can change the condition of your car from good to fair, or worse yet, from fair to poor. Make sure you understand the definitions of mint, good, fair, and poor condition when researching the value of your car. And try to look at your car objectively—just as potential buyers will be doing.

to compare with the salesperson's offer when you're buying your new car. Another advantage of having this information: If you're being lowballed on your trade-in, you can always simply refuse the trade-in offer and take your vehicle to one of the places that gave you a quote.

If you're selling your car, your final price will likely be somewhere above what the used-car departments offered but below the highest asking prices you uncovered.

Once you're armed with the vehicle's true value, you can negotiate with confidence and avoid being scammed.

## Maximizing Your Car's Curb Appeal

Whether you trade in your current vehicle or sell it yourself, making it look as good as possible can pay big dividends by improving both its value and sales appeal.

Depending on the vehicle's condition, you can do a lot or all of the work yourself. Alternately, you can take your vehicle to a professional detailer, where prices can start around $100 but can go rapidly up, depending on the region, type of vehicle, and the amount of work to be done. As with other do-it-yourself projects, the more elbow grease you invest, the less you'll need to pay someone else to do it. Here are some tips about how to get the

## Trading In vs. Selling

| Trading in | Selling it yourself |
|---|---|
| It's an easy way to dispose of your current car. Just turn it over to the dealership. | This requires more effort, including placing ads, taking phone calls, dealing with strangers, and giving test drives. |
| You will get less money than selling it yourself. At best, you should expect to get the vehicle's whole-sale value. | You'll usually get the most money for your car; likely somewhere between the vehicle's retail and wholesale values. |
| You can use the trade-in amount as the down payment on the new car. | You likely won't be able to sell your current car until after you buy your new car. So you won't be able to use the money as a down payment. If the old car isn't paid off, you could have an overlap of car payments until you sell it. |
| To get the best price, you will likely need to haggle with the salesperson over the trade-in value. | You still will need to negotiate with a buyer, but private buyers usually aren't as experienced in haggling or manipulating the process as a professional car salesperson. |
| Sales-tax advantage. Most states only charge sales tax on the difference between the trade-in value and new-car price. | You may need to pay more sales tax on the new car, but if you get more money for the old car by selling it yourself, you could still be ahead. |

best results. Most of the specialty products mentioned can be found at an auto-parts store or in a dealership that handles your car's make.

### Outside appearance

Give your vehicle a thorough cleaning with car-wash detergent and water. Alloy wheels should be scrubbed thoroughly to remove road film and grime. Use a stiff-bristled brush and a good all-purpose detergent or wheel cleaner. If you use the latter, look for one that says it's safe for all wheels. Once everything is dry, you can apply a tire dressing to give your rubber a new-car look.

Then inspect the paint surface and assess any damage you see. Note any scratches, stone chips, and dents in the sheet metal. If the paint is in good condition, a coat of wax may be all it needs. If your vehicle's paint is the original factory finish, it likely has a clearcoat outer paint layer. If so, make sure the wax you use is marked "safe for clearcoats." Avoid abrasive products, which are meant for removal of paint defects or to put a shine on a dull finish. On the other hand, if your paint finish is a little dull, look for a product that both polishes and protects.

You can fix small scratches and chips yourself with touch-up paint, available for a few dollars from your dealership. Make sure you get an exact color match, or your repair job will look worse than the original defect. Use the application brush or a small, pointed artist's brush and fill in the scratch by going over it in tiny dabs. Let the paint dry for at least a day or two before polishing the car.

Fine surface scratches in the paint can be professionally buffed out at a body shop or professional car wash center. This will greatly improve the car's overall appearance, but it costs between $100 and $200. Alternatively, you can hand polish the car yourself using an appropriate polish and old terry-cloth towels or T-shirts. If you know how to use an electric rotary buffer, you can borrow, rent, or buy one. If you don't know what you're doing, though, don't attempt it because you can easily burn through the paint or leave permanent swirl marks.

## First impressions are all-important

Nothing can turn off a potential buyer faster than the sight of a dirty car. It conveys the impression that the car hasn't been maintained very well—and the buyer will have to pay to get it cleaned up. Whether fair or not, shoppers also might assume that if the outside wasn't maintained well, neither were the engine, transmission, and other critical mechanical systems.

## Dent removal

Having a body shop fix unsightly dents and dings can be costly. If there is no paint damage, you may be able to use a service called paintless dent repair, sometimes franchised under names such as Dent Doctor *(www.dent doctorusa.com)* or DentPro *(www.dentpro.com)*. They use special tools to massage out small dents from the inside. Your local mechanic, body shop, or car dealer can help you find a dent fixer, or try using the Yellow Pages. Typical costs range from about $50 to $150 per dent.

Some do-it-yourself dent-removal kits have come on the market as well. They're advertised using TV infomercials and cost from about $20 to $30 (plus shipping and handling). Essentially, they work by hot-gluing a suction cup onto the dent and then pulling the dent out with a special tool. Two kits that CONSUMER REPORTS tested were Ding King *(www.dingking.tv)* and DentOut *(www.dentout.net)*. Our testers found that they worked about equally well, but the results were not perfect. Generally, the more experience you have, the better the results. The user has to be careful with the hot glue and should avoid pulling the metal out too far. Small dents less than 1 inch in diameter were the toughest. The kits worked best on dents about 4 inches across.

## Fixing window glass

It's very common for a windshield to pick up "star" or "bull's-eye" damage from a flying stone. These dings can be filled by an auto-glass repair service, so that they are less noticeable and don't develop into larger cracks. Figure on spending about $50 to $60 to treat a small glass ding. For larger cracks, you'll have to replace the glass.

Consult your auto-insurance policy first. If you have glass coverage, the replacement is free, except for a possible deductible.

## The inside dirt

Clean the inside of the vehicle as though you were looking at it for the first time with the intention to buy it. Remove all of your personal clutter from the

## Investing in your current car

Does it make sense to invest time and money in making a used car look really good? To find out, in 2000 Consumer Reports started with a 1995 Subaru Legacy sedan that had been used as a family car for five years and 92,000 miles. Although well-maintained, it looked a little shabby. The body had numerous superficial scratches, there was a small dent in the driver's door, and a dime-sized "star" marred the windshield. Inside, the carpets and upholstery were sound but dirty. A child safety seat had left a long rust-colored stain on a rear seat.

By looking in price guides and local classifieds, we determined that the retail value was more than $10,500. But the wholesale value was closer to $5,000. Without making any improvements to the car, we took it to some dealers and asked what they'd buy it for. A Toyota dealer declined to make an offer. A multibrand dealer offered $5,500 without looking at the car. One Subaru dealer offered $6,000 after a lengthy inspection. A second Subaru dealer offered $6,700.

Then we went to work. A windshield-repair specialist charged $50 to treat the blemish in the windshield, so that it now looked no bigger than a pinhead. A "paintless dent repair" specialist performed a nearly flawless repair on our door dent for $50. We used a carpet-cleaning spray ($6), which did a good job on the seats. We took the front floor mats to a carpet-cleaning service ($15). We cleaned the battery and terminals with diluted baking soda and sprayed the battery with a clear sealer we bought at an auto-parts store.

Then we had a body shop buff and touch up the exterior. For $200 the finish came out gleaming. After investing $321, we took the Legacy to a couple more Subaru dealers. The first offer, $5,065, was the lowest yet. But the second was better: $8,000.

One clear lesson: It pays to shop around. That and our $321 investment increased what we could make by anywhere from $1,300 to $3,000.

glove box, ashtrays, and other storage spaces. Check under the seats for lost toys, trash, or wayward french fries. Then go to work on the windows, dash, upholstery, and carpets.

You can buy special cleaners for upholstery, carpet, vinyl, and leather. For hard plastic surfaces, use any general purpose cleaner. Use a good glass cleaner to remove smudges and film from the insides of all windows, paying special attention to the windshield and rear window.

If a cleaner doesn't do the job on carpeted floor mats, they can be taken to a carpet-cleaning service and cleaned for about $15 to $20 a pair. Or just replace worn ones.

Ridding cars of odors can be a real challenge. First get all of the interior fabrics clean with pet-spot cleaner or another odor-fighting product. Don't forget to wipe down the overhead fabric, called the headliner. Also, don't forget to clean inside the trunk and spare-tire well.

To remove stale odors from the ventilation ducts, try spraying odor eliminator into the system's air intake, which is usually located at the base of the windshield. Then run the air conditioner full blast for at least 10 minutes.

## Under the hood

Cleaning the outside of the engine and other under-hood components can be a chore, but a clean engine bay is impressive.

If battery terminals are corroded or caked with white powder, use an old toothbrush dipped in a mixture of water and baking soda to clean off the residue. Then coat the terminals with battery terminal grease. Always wear eye protection and gloves when working around car batteries.

You can certainly clean engine parts with old rags and plain soap and water, though you may have better luck with an aerosol engine degreaser. Be careful not to get electrical connections wet. Loosen dirt and rust from iron and steel parts with a soft-bristle brass wire brush and soft abrasive cleaner.

### Minor and major repairs

It just makes good sense to fix or replace broken or missing items. A missing wheel cover or a broken mirror are signals to the buyer that your car has not been well-maintained and that other repairs will probably be needed. Major repairs are another matter, however. Most buyers probably won't want to make a major repair right after buying a vehicle.

Suppose, for instance, your air conditioner doesn't work, and you have an estimate that it will cost $600 to repair. Obviously the air conditioner isn't necessary for the proper operation of the vehicle and, if you're selling the car yourself, some buyers might not care as long as the selling price is adjusted accordingly. But most potential buyers will likely lose interest when they find out about it. The big question is whether you can recoup the cost of the repair in your selling price. Most of the time you can't—so be prepared to take a beating if you have major repair problems. You'll have the same dilemma if you decide to go the trade-in route.

## Trading In: Minimum Hassle, Less Money

Many new-car buyers prefer to trade in their current vehicle because it's easy. All you have to do is drive to the dealership with your current

### You need to know

Different pricing sources list different values for the same vehicle. Salespeople can use this to their advantage by using the source that's best for a particular situation. For instance, if you're trading in a vehicle, a salesperson might quote a source that lists a lower value, but when selling a used car, he might use a source with a higher value. Whatever figure he uses, don't assume it's gospel information. Do your own research, and have the various prices written down so you can refer to them if you feel the salesperson isn't giving you a fair figure.

## Too good to be true?

Be wary if a dealership offers to pay off the remainder of your current vehicle's loan if you buy a new car from them. A former car salesperson told our reporter that he sometimes made this offer for customers, but would quietly add that cost into the new loan, purposely filling out the contract in a confusing way.

vehicle, sign a few papers, and drive away in a new one. You can apply the trade-in amount to your down payment, reducing the amount you need to finance.

There can also be tax advantages. Most states require that sales tax be paid only on the difference between the selling prices of your new car and your trade-in—not the full selling price of your new car alone. This tax benefit does not apply if you sell your old vehicle yourself. Check with the Department of Motor Vehicles in your state for details.

The downside of trading in, however, is that you might leave behind hundreds, if not thousands, of dollars in the dealer's pocket. As mentioned before, the best you can hope for when trading in is to get the car's wholesale value, which is significantly less than what you would expect to get if you sold it yourself. In addition, even if you've checked all the pricing sources and you think you know what your vehicle is worth, you'll likely have to haggle with the salesperson to get the best deal.

Another problem you could encounter: If a dealer already has six used silver Camrys on the lot, he isn't likely to pay top dollar for your silver one. And if your trade-in is one the dealer doesn't want on his lot, it will be sent to auction—and your trade-in will be discounted accordingly.

Just remember, no matter how tired you may be of your old car, a dealership isn't doing you a favor by taking it off your hands. If the dealership buys your car, it's because there's a profit at the end of the transaction.

## How to get the most money for your trade-in

There are several things you can do to maximize the value of your trade-in:

- The appearance of your vehicle is an important consideration when the used-car manager estimates its value. See the previous section on improving "curb appeal."
- If your car needs repairs, it could help to get a repair estimate to take with you for a little bargaining power when the dealer's estimator starts deducting the repair's cost from the figure to be offered to you.
- Shop your trade-in around. If the new car you want is readily available at several dealerships, get a second or third quote from other dealers. That way, you can make your trade-in value the focus of the deal. Keep in mind, though, that all other factors need to be the same to compare deals. The dealer who offers an exceptionally high trade-in value could be planning to make it up with a higher price on your new car. Do the math carefully.
- Try to sell your car to a used-car dealer. They're always looking for clean, low-mileage vehicles for their lot. If yours falls in that category and is a popular model, you just might be able to get more than wholesale price for it. If you've done your homework, you can discourage lowball offers because you will know the car's real value.

## What to look for when negotiating your trade-in

The key to getting the most for your trade-in is to keep the new-car and trade-in negotiations separate. If you allow the salesperson to mix the negotiations together, it gives him too much opportunity to manipulate the deals so that one deal could cancel out a good price for the other.

We suggest that you nail down the price of the new car first, then discuss your trade-in allowance. If the dealership isn't willing to give you the full value of your trade-in, you can always take it elsewhere or sell it yourself. Since dealers usually make more money by reselling your trade-in than on selling you a new car, there is some incentive for the dealer to be competitive with a trade-in offer.

**Shhhhh!**

Dealership insiders have told us that they often preyed on customers' willingness to divulge too much information, such as the amount other dealers have offered them for their old car. They say customers should refuse to discuss a trade-in until negotiations are complete on the car they're buying.

Keep your eye on the bottom line. What's important is the net amount you have to pay. In addition, be sure to read and understand any sales contract before you sign it. If you have a problem with any of the terms or conditions, ask questions. After you sign, you'll have little recourse.

# Selling It Yourself: More Money, More Effort

As we mentioned, selling your current vehicle on your own will get you a higher price than trading it in. Sellers can always expect to get more than wholesale price, and unless the vehicle is in big demand, buyers should expect to pay less than the retail price. Selling your car yourself, however, takes a lot more work than the easy alternative of just driving to the dealer for a trade-in. You'll have to go through the hassle of advertising, taking phone calls, and showing the car.

## Set a competitive price

By following the advice under "What is your car really worth?" earlier in this chapter, you should have a good idea of what the retail and local asking prices are for your vehicle. If you checked to see what a local dealer will offer on a straight-up sale, you should have plenty of information to price your car reasonably.

Remember, it's always smart to price your vehicle just a little bit higher than the least you are willing to take for it. That way, the buyer can negotiate for a slightly lower price and feel good about it. Don't get greedy, though. You could scare off potential buyers who don't think they have a chance to negotiate down to a reasonable price.

## Advertise effectively

There are many ways to advertise your car. Some are more effective than others, and their cost can vary from free to quite expensive. Don't feel limited by the suggestions you see here for advertising. Use your imagination and go with what you think will work.

- Word of mouth is a very effective way to advertise. Tell your friends, relatives, colleagues, and anyone else you know that you have a car for sale. If your network is big enough, you might be surprised at how much interest you generate. And it's free.
- Online classified ads are quickly becoming the most effective way to advertise your car. Autobytel.com offers a deal for around $30 that links your ad to four other Web sites: Autoweb.com, CarSmart.com, AutoSite.com, and Car.com. Cars.com, which operates in partnership with Kelley Blue Book *(www.kbb.com),* charges $30 for a single ad with one photo. Edmunds.com works in cooperation with AutoTrader to list your car for $29. Often, the ad will run for two weeks, but many sites will let you renew the ad at no additional charge.

## Words of caution

Selling a car privately can involve an element of risk, so be careful. If you don't want stranger to come to your home, offer to meet the prospective buyer at a neutral location, such as a supermarket parking lot. You should also ask to have the agreed-upon price paid by certified check or some other guaranteed payment method.

- Daily newspaper ads still work, but aren't as effective as they used to be. Some newspapers will give you both a print and online ad for one price. Depending on the newspaper, rates can run about $30 to $40 for a week or two, although some major metropolitan papers are higher.
- Ads in weekly shoppers and free newspapers can also work, but some are better than others.
- There's always the old-fashioned way: Just put a "For Sale" sign in the window with your phone number on it, and wait for the phone to ring.

## Showing your car

Once you've placed your ads, make sure you have your car's specifications, mileage, and other particulars on hand by the phone. Interested callers will want to see the vehicle. Have your schedule ready so you can designate a day and time. That said, don't be surprised if the caller never shows up. No-shows are one of the frustrating aspects of selling your own car.

When you show the car, answer all questions honestly but briefly. Be prepared to provide service receipts and to accompany the prospective buyer on a lengthy test drive.

## The pre-purchase inspection

Just about any savvy buyer will want to have your car inspected by a mechanic before the sale takes place. If the buyer is a friend or relative, there should be little risk in allowing them to take the car for an inspection. If the potential buyer is a total stranger, however, you'll probably want to drive it to the shop yourself. It shouldn't take more than an hour.

## Know what paperwork you need

The paperwork requirements for selling a car vary from state to state. In some, transferring the title of a vehicle to another person is as simple as entering the odometer reading, sale price, and your signature on the back of the certificate of title. In others, you must fill out official title-transfer forms. Contact your state's DMV to see what you should do.

## More work, more satisfaction

"A trade-in is like prepackaged food. It's not as good as homemade, but it's convenient," says Mark Perleberg, an auto expert with the National Automobile Dealer Association. "Selling it yourself is like a home-cooked meal. It takes more effort, but it usually tastes better."

If there's still an outstanding loan on your car, you and the buyer will have to go to your lending institution to make sure the lender gets its money before you get what's left.

Frequently a bill of sale is required by the buyer for sales-tax purposes. Preprinted forms are available at any office supply store, but a handwritten version can also acceptable. See the following sample for what's required.

## Wrapping up the details

Buying a new vehicle is an exciting experience, but not getting the full value out of your current car can leave a bad taste in your mouth. By knowing your vehicle's true value, spending a little time making it look its best, and by sticking to your price during the negotiations, you can get your car's full value—whether you trade it in or sell it yourself. And this will only add to your overall satisfaction with your new vehicle.

# Bill of Sale

**Received from:**

Seller's name _____

Street address _____

City _____ State _____ ZIP _____

Phone _____

Co-owner's name (if any) _____

in consideration of $ _____, receipt of which is hereby

acknowledged,

**Do hereby transfer to:**

Purchaser's name _____

Street address _____

City _____ State _____ ZIP _____

Phone _____

Co-purchaser's name (if any) _____

**The following described motor vehicle:**

Year _____ Make _____

Model _____

Body style (e.g., 4-dr. sedan) _____ No. of cylinders _____

Color _____ Odometer reading _____

Vehicle ID No. (VIN) _____

Certificate of Title No. _____

Signature of seller _____

Signature of buyer _____

**On this date:** _____

*Permission is granted to photocopy this page.*

# 9

# Understand Your Insurance Options

**Aside from your payments** for an auto loan or lease, the largest ongoing payment you'll face once you've bought the vehicle is typically the insurance premium. According to the National Association of Insurance Commissioners (NAIC), the average insured driver pays about $880 per year for auto-insurance premiums. This can vary greatly, though, depending on the vehicle, the driver, where you live, how much you drive each year, and other factors. So it pays to get a good idea of what your insurance cost will be before you sign on the dotted line for that new car.

First, assess your insurance needs by reading this chapter. Then contact an insurance agent or broker, or go online to see what the coverage you need will cost for each model you're considering. This could influence your decisions on which vehicle to buy.

In the following pages, you'll learn:

- Basic insurance terms you should know
- The different types of coverage
- What affects the price of insurance
- How to hold down your insurance cost
- Where to shop for auto insurance

# The Language of Insurance

Understanding basic insurance terms can help you when determining your needs and communicating with insurers or their agents. Here are ones with which you should be familiar:

**Agents.** If they are employees of an insurance company, they represent that one company exclusively. Independent agents, on the other hand, are self-employed and represent many insurance companies. In theory, they are free to shop for the best policy and offer it at the best price to customers such as you. They may sometimes be called brokers, but true brokers work primarily with commercial clients.

**Carrier** is another name for an insurance company.

**Deductible** is the amount of money you must pay before your insurance company pays the remainder of your covered loss. There is typically a deductible on collision and comprehensive coverage but not on liability.

**Exclusion** refers to a type of loss your policy won't cover.

**Insured** refers to a person covered by a policy.

**Limit** is the maximum amount your insurance company will pay for a loss, regardless of the claim amount.

**No-fault insurance** requires each insured person's insurance company to pay for certain financial losses, regardless of who caused the accident. This type is required in some states.

**Personal injury protection** (PIP) covers medical expenses for the driver and passengers when in the policyholder's car. It's required in states with no-fault laws.

**Premium** is the amount of money you pay to the insurance company for a policy.

**Term** is the length of time that a policy is in effect.

**Underwriters** work for insurance companies to analyze insurance applications and determine whether the risk is acceptable and will not result in a loss for the company.

**Usage** refers to the primary purpose of your vehicle—for example, commuting, business, travel, running errands.

# Types of Auto Insurance

Every state requires you to have at least some kind of auto insurance, but many drivers will want more coverage than the state's minimum. Selecting an insurance policy can get complicated, however, so it's a good idea to understand the different parts of an auto-insurance policy and know what's required in your state.

There is no such thing as a standard auto-insurance policy. This is because each policy is a package, or bundle, of several different types of coverage. Each part can be tailored to meet your specific needs and satisfy your state's legal requirements. The individual parts of a typical auto-insurance policy are described next.

### Liability insurance

The heart of your auto-insurance coverage is liability insurance. If you are found to be at fault in an accident, your liability insurance will pay for the bodily injury and property-damage expenses caused to others in the accident, including your legal bills. Liability coverage also protects you if the other party decides to sue you to collect "pain and suffering" damages.

If you have a nice home and substantial savings, you should consider having more liability insurance, because in most states drivers are allowed to sue other drivers who injure them in car accidents. If you're sued and your liability insurance doesn't pay for all of the damages, your personal finances are on the line, and a judgment against you is a frightening possibility.

Two types of liability insurance are required in most states:

- Bodily injury coverage protects you if you have been judged responsible for an accident in which someone is hurt or killed. This coverage pays for the claim against you, as well as for your legal defense.
- Property-damage insurance covers damage that you or anyone covered as a driver under your policy causes to another vehicle or property.

Insurance policies frequently describe the levels of liability coverage as a series of three numbers, commonly called split limits. For example, suppose your policy says you have 50,000/100,000/50,000 liability coverage. Typically what this means is that the insurance company will pay a maximum of $50,000 for bodily injuries that result from an accident to any one person. The second number refers to the maximum amount the insurance company will pay for all bodily injuries, no matter how many people incur those injuries in the accident. The third number in our example, $50,000, is the maximum the insurance company will pay for damage to someone else's property.

Some insurance companies, however, may confuse you by combining the first and last numbers in the above sequence. So, make sure you get a clear explanation from each company as to what the numbers represent.

Almost every state requires a minimum level of liability-insurance coverage, but if you look carefully, the requirements are barely adequate. There's almost always a big gap between what's required and what you really should have. Moreover, even if the state laws focus only on liability coverage, you should consider a broader range of coverage.

The bodily injury portion of your liability insurance is perhaps the most important coverage in your insurance policy. In the event of a serious accident, the liability claims against you for medical bills, lost income, and pain and suffering can be hundreds of thousands of dollars. Property-damage claims can also be significant, should you damage

## What is loan gap insurance?

What happens if you total your car and the insurance company payout is less than the balance on your auto loan? That can happen if you're upside-down with your loan, which means your vehicle's current cash value is less than the amount you owe on your loan. Some insurance companies offer loan gap insurance to cover such a situation, but this only adds to the total cost of your vehicle. The best option is to choose the right loan in the first place to avoid getting upside down (see Chapter 10).

some expensive commercial property or several expensive vehicles. Liability coverage is definitely one area where you don't want to be underinsured.

You can find out what the minimum insurance requirements are in your state by asking an insurance agent or broker, or by going online. One Web site that provides this information is that of the Insurance Information Institute *(www.iii.org/individuals/auto/)*. Later, we'll discuss how to protect yourself with uninsured/underinsured motorist coverage.

Deductibles don't apply to liability insurance, so the upper limits are the most important consideration.

## Collision and comprehensive insurance

Collision coverage is one of the most expensive components of auto insurance. If you cause an accident, collision coverage will pay to repair or replace your vehicle, but you usually can't collect any more than the actual cash value of your car.

Comprehensive coverage covers repair or replacement of your vehicle from damage that isn't caused by a collision. This includes theft, fire, vandalism, natural disasters, falling trees, or hitting a deer.

Collision and comprehensive coverages don't usually pay for the total amount of the claim. In most cases, you have a deductible, which is an amount you must pay before your insurance company begins to pay. Further, your insurance will reimburse you for the actual cash value of your loss, not the original cost of your car. So, if your two- or three-year-old car is a total loss, you will get only what the car is worth at the time of the claim—that is, its depreciated value.

Many factors—such as vehicle age, usage, and location—influence the cost of collision and comprehensive insurance. One of the biggest influences on your rate is the amount of your deductible. The lower the deductible, the higher the cost of coverage, so it's usually best to choose the highest deductible you can afford. Keep in mind when you decide on your deductible that the whole purpose of insurance is to protect you from huge losses, not to reimburse you for every dime's worth of damage.

The cost of collision and comprehensive coverage can run as much as half of your insurance premium. If you have a new car with a sizeable loan, collision/comprehensive insurance is almost a necessity. In fact, many lenders require proof of such insurance before approving an auto loan. If you've had your vehicle for a long time and it isn't worth much, however, you might think about dropping it altogether. This approach is not with-

## You need to know

Replacement cost is the actual amount it would take to repair or replace your vehicle, without considering depreciation. Depreciation is the decrease in value of your vehicle because of age or wear. Actual cash value is the value of your vehicle at the time it is damaged or destroyed. This figure is usually determined by subtracting depreciation from replacement cost.

Typically an insurance settlement for even a late-model vehicle that has been totaled will not cover the total cost for a new car of the same type and price range. You will need to pay off any remaining loan balance and then put the remainder of the settlement toward a new car. This is just one of the reasons there are no winners in an auto accident.

out risk, since you will have to pay for any damage or replacement if your vehicle is wrecked or stolen. Some people can afford that risk—many can't.

## Medical payments and personal-injury-protection insurance

Regardless of the type of mishap, collisions and crashes often result in some type of injury to you or your passengers. The cost of medical care, even for seemingly minor injuries, can be substantial, so don't overlook coverage for medical payments.

Sometimes there's more to an injury than just medical care, so there's personal-injury protection—a benefit that offers expanded coverage beyond just medical payments.

**Medical payments** is the portion of your auto-insurance policy that covers you and your passengers for medical expenses resulting from an accident, regardless of who is at fault. Nonfamily passengers should qualify for this coverage if they get injured in your car.

Normally the other driver's insurance should cover your medical payments—if he or she is at fault. Your medical-payments coverage goes into effect when the accident is your fault. If you have good health-insurance coverage for you and your family, you might think you don't really need much in the way of medical-payments coverage. Think again—your health insurance won't cover passengers who aren't members of your immediate family.

**Personal-injury protection (PIP)** is a form of no-fault insurance that's required in states that have no-fault insurance laws. This coverage is a more extensive type of medical-payments insurance, since it pays for medical care, lost wages, and replacement services for the injured party.

## Uninsured (or underinsured) motorist

This coverage pays your legal bills, rehabilitation, and funeral costs, as well as losses for pain and suffering incurred by you or passengers in your car, if you are involved in an accident that is caused by a hit-and-run driver or by someone who has little or no insurance.

# A quick guide to insurance coverage

Below is a summary of what insurance companies typically offer, what you have to buy, and how much coverage you should consider.

| Type | What it pays for | Necessary? | Suggested coverage | Comments |
|---|---|---|---|---|
| Liability | Medical, rehabilitation, and funeral bills for your passengers, the other driver, and his passengers; pain and suffering; and legal costs. Also, repair or replacement of the other driver's car. | Required by most states. | For bodily injury, $100,000 per person and $300,000 per accident. For property damage, $100,000. | If you have an expensive home or other large assets, increase your bodily-injury limits to at least $250,000 per person and $500,000 per accident. The extra coverage will increase your premium by 10 percent. |
| Uninsured /under-insured motorist | Medical, rehabilitation, and funeral bills for you and your passengers from an accident caused by a driver with insufficient or no coverage. | Required by most states. | Same as above. | Same as above. |
| Collision and comprehensive | Repair or replacement of your car if it is damaged in an accident or as a result of theft, vandalism, fire, or natural disaster. | Yes, if you lease or finance your car. | Keep the deductible as high as you can afford, but no less than $500. | Drop coverage when the premium equals or exceeds 10 percent of the car's book value. |

| Type | What it pays for | Necessary? | Suggested coverage | Comments |
|------|------------------|------------|--------------------|----------|
| Personal-injury protection (PIP)/medical payments | Reimbursement for lost wages; medical bills for you and your passengers. | Optional. | $5,000. | Even if you have good health insurance, you might want this for uninsured passengers. |
| Roadside assistance | Towing. | Optional. | The minimum. | Unnecessary if you have auto-club membership or if it's included as part of your car's warranty. |
| Rental reimbursement | Rental-car payment while your car is in the shop. | Optional. | The minimum. | Unnecessary if you own a second car. Otherwise, it costs about $30 a year. |

Some states require uninsured motorist coverage; it is optional in others. If you live in a state that requires no-fault coverage, uninsured coverage might not be necessary because your auto insurance will have to cover your losses even if the other driver was at fault. Considering the high number of uninsured, underinsured, and hit-and-run motorists on the road, this is one segment of coverage you don't want to skimp on.

## No-fault insurance

In most states, insurance companies pay for damages based on each person's degree of fault for a particular auto accident. Fixing the blame for an accident is often determined by the outcome of a lengthy, expensive court battle. To minimize the time and expense of going to court, some states have instituted an alternative called no-fault insurance.

In a no-fault state, each insured person's insurance company pays for damages resulting from an accident, regardless of who caused the accident. No-fault insurance speeds up the payment of claims and reduces litigation, but in exchange you'll give up your right to sue in some cases.

Another function of no-fault insurance is to reduce auto-insurance premiums by reducing the number of cases clogging up the courts, by limiting payments for pain and suffering, and by limiting payment for other losses.

### Pure no-fault vs. modified no-fault

With pure no-fault coverage, your insurance company pays for all economic damages such as medical bills and lost wages, and you're prohibited from suing a negligent driver for noneconomic losses such as pain and suffering. No state that requires no-fault insurance operates this way.

Instead, the no-fault states have chosen a modified no-fault system. Modified is the key word here. It means that your insurer still pays for your economic losses up to the policy limit, but you have more freedom to sue for noneconomic damages. Be sure to check with your insurance agent or broker on the thresholds and limits for these noneconomic claims.

# What Affects the Price of Insurance?

Since each insurance company has the right to set its own prices in most states, premiums can vary from insurer to insurer. But there are other important factors that can influence your rates even more. They include:

**Your coverage.** As mentioned earlier, your insurance policy is really a bundle or collection of individual coverages, and each one has its own price tag. That gives you the freedom to mix and match to suit your individual needs. Many people are underinsured rather than being overinsured. Still, it's important to be realistic about how much coverage you need.

**What you drive.** One of the biggest factors affecting the price of your policy is what kind of vehicle you drive. For a number of reasons, a sports car, for instance, costs more to insure than a family sedan. Likewise, four-wheel drive may add dollars to your premium. Certain models may be considered high risk because they cost a lot to repair, cause more damage when involved in an accident, or are frequently stolen. Owning one of these cars could significantly increase your collision, comprehensive, or liability premiums. For everyone else, the price of coverage will be determined primarily by the value of the vehicle.

**Where you drive.** If you live in an area with a high rate of theft, vandalism, or accidents, your insurance will cost more than if you live where those problems are less frequent. City dwellers tend to pay higher rates than those who live in small towns or rural areas. Other variables include regional weather patterns and local auto-repair prices. Keep in mind, if you have a high-value vehicle, your insurance company will want to know where it will be parked—in a garage or on the street. This will affect your premium cost.

**How much you drive.** How far and how often you drive will affect your insurance rate. The insurance companies have plenty of statistical evidence to prove that the more you drive, the higher the odds are that you'll be in an accident. Obviously those who have long-distance commutes will pay more than those who live close to work. And those who drive to work, regardless of distance, will pay more than those who use their cars purely for pleasure or for running errands. Again, it's a matter of statistics that determines the cost of coverage.

**Your age.** Statistically, drivers under the age of 20 have the highest rate of fatal crashes relative to other age groups, including the elderly. So their premiums are higher. Drivers between 50 and 65 have low accident rates, and are sometimes offered discounts. After age 65, the accident rates begin to climb, and so do the premiums.

**Your gender.** A man can expect to pay more than a woman of the same age. That's because insurance-company records show that mens are involved in more accidents than women.

**Your marital status.** Statistically, young married drivers have fewer accidents than young singles, so they usually pay less.

**Your driving record.** It almost goes without saying that drivers who have a record of traffic violations or accidents will have to pay more for insurance than safe drivers. That's because insurance-company statistics indicate such drivers generally have repeat accidents or violations within just a few years. Drivers with poor records may not be able to find regular coverage and might have to participate in state-regulated plans called "assigned risk pools," where the state assigns an insurance company to provide coverage. That higher risk commands a very high premium.

**Your credit record.** More insurance companies are evaluating credit records to determine whether there's financial risk involved in offering auto-insurance policies to certain individuals. Consumers Union, publisher of CONSUMER REPORTS, feels that this is unfair and advises you to demand that insurers tell you how your credit score will affect your premium. This is another reason to check your credit reports ahead of time and have any errors corrected as quickly as possible. (See Chapter 10 for more information on credit reports.)

# Shopping for Auto Insurance

You can make your insurance shopping project quick and easy by being prepared to answer the questions you'll be asked. If you fill in the form later in this chapter, you'll have all of the necessary information at your fingertips.

## Where to shop

Friends, relatives, and colleagues always seem willing to talk about their auto-insurance experiences, whether they're good or bad. They might be able to give you some valuable information about how some insurers treat their customers. Remember, the insurer with the lowest price might not be the best choice if it turns out that their customer service and reputation for paying claims is subpar.

There's also the phone book. Try to get quotes from different types of companies. Some sell through their own proprietary agents, while others sell through independent agents who offer policies from several insurers. Some companies sell directly to customers over the phone.

The Internet provides another way to shop for auto insurance. By visiting Web sites, you can get competing quotes, find the best deals, and purchase a policy. One major concern about shopping online, however, is giving out personal information to a site that might not treat it confidentially. Check for e-ratings of auto-insurance sites at Consumer Reports' WebWatch (*www.consumerwebwatch.org*).

## How vehicle type affects your premium

To see which types of vehicles cost the most and least to insure, CONSUMER REPORTS did a study in 2002. The reporter created a standard driver profile— a 30-something couple with good driving records—and gave them home-address ZIP codes in Oakland, Calif., Frontenac, Mo., and Yonkers, N.Y. Then he got auto-insurance price quotes from five national auto insurers for the same full-coverage package on 45 different models. The results showed that there's typically a wide range of premiums for any given model as well as a wide range among different vehicle types, as show below:

| Vehicle size & type | Average premium |
| --- | --- |
| Small sedan | $1,489 |
| Minivan | $1,501 |
| Midsized family sedan | $1,554 |
| Large pickup | $1,679 |
| Midsized SUV | $1,679 |
| Large SUV | $1,817 |
| Midsized sports car | $1,906 |
| Midsized high-end sedan | $1,929 |

---

## Auto-Insurance Information

---

### Car Information:

Year _____     Make _____

Model _____     Body style _____

Vehicle ID
No. (VIN): _____     City _____

County _____     State _____

ZIP code _____     Miles driven per year _____


Vehicle's primary use:

❑ To and from work  ❑ To and from school  ❑ Pleasure
❑ Farm  ❑ Business  ❑ Other_____


Car-safety features_____

_____

_____

Anti-theft devices _____

_____

_____


### Driver Information:

|  | Principal driver | Driver No. 2 | Driver No. 3 |
|---|---|---|---|
| Name | _____ | _____ | _____ |
| Relationship | _____ | _____ | _____ |
| Date of birth | _____ | _____ | _____ |
| Sex | _____ | _____ | _____ |
| Marital status | _____ | _____ | _____ |
| Occupation | _____ | _____ | _____ |
| List moving violations | _____ | _____ | _____ |
| Convictions for past 3 years | _____ | _____ | _____ |

You can find more general information about auto insurance at the Insurance Information Institute's Web site, *www.iii.org*.

# Holding Down Your Insurance Cost

There are various ways to minimize your payments, starting with choosing a vehicle that costs less to insure, shopping around among insurance carriers, looking into any premium discounts for which you may be eligible, and tailoring your coverage to fit your needs and budget.

## Sizing up the insurance costs of your vehicle

The overall price of your auto insurance is largely driven by vehicle-related factors, such as the type of vehicle and how much it costs to repair. Some models, such as sports cars, luxury cars, and four-wheel-drive trucks and SUVs, typically carry a higher premium than, say, family sedans, because the insurer feels there is more risk of damage and/or these models can cost more to repair.

Many accidents involve property damage only. As the CONSUMER REPORTS bumper-basher tests and the Insurance Institute for Highway Safety crash tests have consistently shown, some cars suffer much more physical and financial damage from the same impact than others.

After gathering and sorting some policy price data, CONSUMER REPORTS discovered differences among broad classes of cars. For example, shoppers who need lots of cargo room and want to save on insurance may want to pass on a large SUV and opt for a minivan, which costs between $200 and $300 a year less to insure, on average, than the midsized and large SUVs we studied. Similarly, CONSUMER REPORTS found that midsized high-end sedans cost $375 more a year to insure than midsized family sedans.

Bottom line: Before you buy a new car, take a careful look at what it's going to cost to insure it. The Insurance Institute for Highway Safety (*www.iihs.org*) can provide valuable information about vehicle choices with regard to insurance costs. Don't commit to purchasing a new vehicle until you have a solid understanding of what your auto-insurance costs will be.

## Other tips for saving money

You must be vigilant in order to control your auto-insurance cost. Keep the following suggestions in mind when shopping for a new policy, and even after you've purchased one. Just because you don't qualify for a particular discount at first doesn't mean you won't down the line as your circumstances change. Check on your eligibility on a regular basis.

- Keep shopping. Even after you've had a policy in effect for a while, it's in your best interest to keep your eyes open for a better deal.
- Don't forget about higher deductibles. You may be surprised, but changing from a $200 to $500 deductible could reduce your comprehensive and collision premium by as much as 30 percent. Moving up to a $1,000 deductible will probably save you 40 percent or more. A word of caution is in order here—before going to a higher deductible, make sure you have the cash to pay for the deductible you've selected in case you have a claim.
- Most full-line insurers will give you a discount if you buy several types of insurance, such as auto, home, and personal liability. See about a discount if you have more than one vehicle insured with the same company. A few insurers will give you a break if you're a longtime customer. But it still pays to shop around. An agent can get complacent, thinking your business is guaranteed.
- Maintain a good credit record. Whether fair or not, a growing number of insurers are using credit information to price auto-insurance policies.
- Take advantage of low-mileage discounts. As discussed earlier, the more you drive, the higher the odds you'll have an accident. So it stands to reason that the fewer miles you drive, the lower your risk will be for your

insurer. Be sure to ask about a discount, especially if you drive less than 7,500 miles per year. If appropriate, tell your insurer if you carpool or take public transportation to work.

- Good-driver discounts are frequently offered to those who haven't had any moving violations or accidents in a number of years.

Here is a list of possible discounts you might explore, as provided by the Insurance Information Institute:

- Deductible of $500 or more (a deductible of $1,000 is better)
- Two or more vehicles
- No accidents (3 years minimum)
- No moving violations (3 years minimum)
- Drivers between 50 and 55 years of age
- Driver training or defensive driving course
- Anti-theft device
- Low annual mileage
- Antilock brakes
- Daytime running lights
- Good grades for student drivers
- College kids away from home
- Longtime customer
- Multipolicy customer (homeowner's, life, business)

Just remember to keep your eye focused on the bottom line. Discounts are important, but it's still the overall price that should be the primary influence in your decision on which auto-insurance policy to select.

# Ensuring Your Peace of Mind

For many of us, shopping for insurance is about as exciting as buying a new battery. You may be tempted to skip the details and buy what an insurance salesperson tells you is a standard policy. Still, all insurance coverage isn't the same, so you need to choose carefully just as you would when buying the right vehicle or getting the right financing deal.

Further, after you've filed a claim you don't want to discover that your coverage is inadequate. So take the time to inventory your insurance needs to be sure that you get the best insurance for you.

# Step 4

## Arrange Financing

■ CHAPTER 10: Find the Best Financing      **195**
■ CHAPTER 11: Is Leasing for You?      **213**

# 10

# Find the Best Financing

**Next to buying a home** or paying for your children's education, buying a new vehicle is probably the biggest purchase you'll ever make. Of course, the cheapest way to buy a vehicle is with cash, but few people are able to just write a check for the full amount of the purchase. The vast majority either finance or lease a new vehicle and make payments over time. Because the interest on a car loan can amount to a fairly tidy sum in itself, there's a huge benefit to paying close attention to the details of your financing arrangements so you don't end up spending more than you need to.

Borrowing money and paying it back with interest seems like a fairly straightforward concept, but it's amazing how complicated it can get when it isn't done right. You might be a real whiz at finding the right car at the right price, but if you don't choose your financing as carefully as you do your car, you could lose everything you saved on the vehicle's purchase price. As the old saying goes, you can make it on the peanuts but lose it on the popcorn.

Interestingly, consumers will spend days shopping for vehicle prices, yet many don't bother to shop for auto loans. A car shopper who doesn't have financing in place is fair game for whatever loan programs the dealer has available, and those could cost you much more than a low-interest loan you get elsewhere on your own.

The dealer's goal is to sell you a car, which usually means offering whatever financing it takes to make the sale. Such loans might have monthly payments that fit your budget, but they can wind up costing you hundreds or even thousands of dollars more over the term of the loan. Dealers also often mark up the interest rate of a loan over what you actually qualify for, which can cost you hundreds of dollars extra.

That's why it's critical to comparison shop and prequalify for an auto loan *before* you go to the dealership to buy the vehicle. You may be surprised at how interested various lenders are in loaning you money. In fact, auto loans are relatively easy to get because the lender has built-in collateral: If you don't make the payments, it will take back your car. Still, like cars, all loans are not the same.

So to help guide you through this phase of the buying experience, this chapter gives you advice on:

- How financing works: the basics of an auto loan
- Financing terms: the language of auto loans
- The effects of interest and the length of the loan
- Checking your credit rating
- Shopping for a loan
- How to compare lenders and loans
- Loan alternatives
- Refinancing auto loans

# How Financing Works: Auto Loan Basics

There's nothing mysterious about borrowing money to pay for a new vehicle, but it's still important to understand the main parts of an auto loan. There are five basic pieces to the auto-loan puzzle: the annual percentage rate (APR), down payment, interest rate, loan term, and principal. Understanding them and how they fit together is crucial when shopping for loans.

**Annual percentage rate (APR).** The APR is essentially the only piece of information you'll need to compare one loan (of the same length) with another, because it includes not only interest from the lender, but also all of the fees and other costs associated with making the loan available to you—document-preparation fees, filing fees, and so on.

These extra fees have the effect of increasing the lending rate slightly above the basic interest rate. Thus, APR is the true cost of financing. It's easy for anyone to compare most loans because federal law requires lenders to disclose the APR in writing.

## APR does matter: 5% vs. 6%

|  | 5 percent | 6 percent |
|---|---|---|
| Amount financed | $16,000 | $16,000 |
| Loan term in months | 48 | 48 |
| APR | 5.000% | 6.000% |
| Monthly payment | $368 | $376 |
| Total of all payments | $17,664 | $18,048 |
| Total interest paid | $1,664 | $2,048 |

(The advantage of the 1 percent lower rate is a saving of $384, a little more than one payment, over the life of the loan. For a higher-priced vehicle, the difference would be greater.)

**Down payment.** The down payment is a portion of the vehicle's price that must be paid in cash at the time you sign the contract. The larger the down payment you can make, the better, because that decreases the amount of money you need to borrow.

**Interest rate.** The interest rate is the part of the APR that the lender receives on the loan. The interest rate is important only to the lender, while the APR is of more importance to the borrower. Unfortunately, the interest rate is the cause of more confusion about auto loans than any other single factor. People tend to compare the interest rate when they should be comparing the APR. Be sure to keep this distinction in mind when comparing loans.

## Simple vs. precomputed interest

Most auto loans are structured to charge so-called simple interest. That means your interest rate is applied to the loan's declining balance over time. Some subprime lenders, however, offer loans that are "precomputed." It's very important to understand the difference.

When you pay off a simple-interest loan early, all you owe is the remaining loan balance, plus any interest that might have accrued since your last payment.

Precomputed loans generally use the "Rule of 78s" formula to calculate the finance charges when you pay off the loan early. The formula is complicated, but it's based on the fact that a lender usually collects three-quarters of a loan's interest in the first half of the loan's term.

And you are obligated to pay back not only the principal but also the full amount of interest. Over the full term, this method doesn't affect the total finance charge, but the earlier you pay off one of these loans, the larger your prepayment penalties.

## Long term vs. short term: Which is better?

A longer term means a lower monthly payment but more interest over-all. The short-term loan in this example will save you $720. You'll save more on a longer loan.

|  | Long term | Short term |
|---|---|---|
| Amount financed | $14,000 | $14,000 |
| Loan term in months | 48 | 24 |
| APR | 5.000% | 5.000% |
| Monthly payment | $322 | $614 |
| Total of all payments | $15,456 | $14,736 |
| Total interest paid | $1,456 | $736 |

**Loan term.** This is the length of the loan, usually expressed as the number of months (or payments) it will take until the loan is paid off. The longer the loan term, the lower the monthly payment, but the more total interest you'll pay and the longer you'll have to make car payments.

Even more important, you run the risk of getting "upside down" with your loan, where you owe more on your loan than your car is worth. This happens when your payments don't keep up with your vehicle's depreciation. When shopping for a loan, look for the best combination of APR and term that fits with your monthly budget while keeping your overall interest payments as low as possible.

**Principal.** Principal is the amount you're borrowing without the interest added in. It's the amount on which you'll be paying interest. Here's how to figure your loan principal:

- Determine the vehicle's final sales price.
- Add all relevant fees (taxes, titling obligations, etc.).
- Subtract the amount of your down payment.
- Subtract the value of your trade-in (if applicable).

## What if you're upside-down with your loan?

It is estimated that about one-quarter of consumers are upside-down with their auto loans, meaning they owe more on their loan than the vehicle is worth. This makes it difficult to sell or trade a car before the loan is paid off.

The worst-case scenario for someone who's upside-down is if the car is totaled in an accident. Because the insurer will typically reimburse you only for the current value of the vehicle, you may be left with some remaining loan payments while simultaneously trying to buy a new car.

There is no graceful, painless, or easy way to get out of an upside-down loan, but here is some advice about how to make the best of it:

■ Regardless of how much you want a newer car, keep the one you have until it's paid for. Then you can start fresh with a new round of financing.

■ Remember that you can always refinance with a loan that has a shorter term and higher payments, but you'll probably have to come up with some cash to pay off the difference between your car's value and the loan amount. No lender will loan you more than your collateral (car) is worth.

■ If you really need to get rid of your vehicle, try to get the most for it by selling it yourself. You probably won't come out ahead, but at least you'll cut your losses. (See Chapter 8 for advice about selling your car.)

■ Subtract any rebates or incentives. The number you come up with after this process is the principal.

This process may vary slightly from state to state, depending on how the state sales tax is calculated. Most states allow the final price for the new car to be reduced by the trade-in amount, while some states tax the sales price prior to any reductions.

# Your Credit Report

If you're about to start shopping for a car loan, one of the first things you should do is get a copy of your credit report. This document contains all of the data that goes into calculating your credit score, a single three-digit number that's used by most lenders to determine what interest rate they will charge you (or whether you'll be able to get an auto loan at all).

Your credit report is a surprisingly detailed account of your credit payment history. If you've ever had a bank loan or credit card, information regarding your account activity will be shown on your report. You can expect to find four categories of information:

**Personal information.** This includes your name, spouse's name, Social

## Bumping the interest rate

Dealerships sometimes use so-called interest-rate bumping to make extra money on auto financing. Here's how it works: The finance company or bank used by the car dealership runs your credit history and determines that you are eligible for a loan at a rate of, say, 6 percent a year. But the dealership might bump the rate by as much as 3 percentage points or more to, for instance, 9 percent. Moreover, it doesn't have to tell you that you could get a lower rate elsewhere.

The practice, which is allowed by finance companies, pays incentives back to the dealer for this additional profit. On an $18,000, five-year loan, that 3 percent increase in the annual interest charge would add $1,560 to the cost of the loan.

A former salesman told us that if the customer questions the rate, he'd say, "I'm really sorry. It's not up to us; it's up to the bank." The best way to prevent this is to shop for a loan at banks and credit unions instead of the dealership. For more information, see page 240.

Security number, current and previous addresses, birth date, and current and previous employers. This data comes from past credit applications, so its validity depends entirely on how accurately you filled out past credit applications.

**Credit information.** Included in this category is information about each of your accounts with banks, retailers, credit card issuers, and other lenders. Credit limits as well as loan amounts and balances are detailed, along with past payment patterns.

**Public information.** This includes bankruptcies, tax liens and monetary judgments, and, in some states, overdue child support.

**Inquiries.** Included are the names of those who requested and obtained copies of your credit report.

## Your credit score

For years, creditors have been using these credit-scoring systems to determine whether you'd be a good risk for credit cards and auto loans.

Information about you and your credit experiences, such as your bill-paying history, the number and types of accounts you have, late payments, collection actions, outstanding debt, and the age of your accounts, is collected from your credit application and your credit report. This information is used to calculate a credit score, which is used to help predict who is most likely to repay a debt. The total number of points—or credit score—helps predict how creditworthy you are—that is, how likely you are to repay a loan and make the payments on time.

Although there are several scoring methods, the one most commonly used by lenders is known as a FICO because it was invented by Fair Isaac Corporation, an independent firm that came up with the scoring method used by banks and lenders, insurers, and other businesses. Each of the three major credit bureaus (Experian, Equifax, and TransUnion) worked with Fair Isaac in the late 1980s to come up with the scoring method.

FICO scores range from 300 to 850, with the higher scores indicating

## Best, worst, and in between

According to Fair Isaac, the following is a breakdown of actual credit scores among the U.S. population in 2003. The higher the number, the better:

Up to 499: 2 percent

500 to 549: 5 percent

550 to 599: 8 percent

600 to 649: 12 percent

650 to 699: 15 percent

700 to 749: 10 percent

750 to 799: 27 percent

Over 800: 13 percent

better credit ratings. The formula for exactly how the score is calculated is proprietary information and owned by Fair Isaac.

The earlier you check your credit score, the better. Ideally, you should check it a few months before you intend to buy a car, so you have plenty of time to correct any errors or work with any bad-credit marks before you arrange your auto financing. If an error needs to be corrected, it's done at all three credit-recording companies: Equifax, Experian, and Trans Union (see below).

To help, Consumers Union, the publisher of CONSUMER REPORTS, maintains a Web site (*www.consumersunion.org/issues/creditmatters.html*) that's designed to help you understand and your credit. It offers a wide range of information, including how to get free copies of your reports, how to read reports, what to do if you find errors, and more.

A new federal rule specifies that you can get a free credit report from the three major credit-reporting agencies once per year. Details are available at *www.annualcreditreport.com*. You'll have to pay a fee, however, to get your credit score. You can also get an annual copy of your free report and your score from the following sources:

- Equifax: 800-685-1111; *www.equifax.com*
- Experian (formerly TRW): 888-397-3742; *www.experian.com*
- Trans Union: 800-916-8800; *www.transunion.com*

- MyFico: *www.myfico.com*
- True Credit: *www.truecredit.com*

Some dealers advertise that they will work with buyers who are credit risks, but in that case you should count on paying a high APR.

# Where to Shop for a Loan

Walking into a dealership with a guaranteed new car loan in your hand gives you bargaining power and flexibility. This also helps you easily avoid the common dealership trap of mixing up the vehicle price with financing costs (see Chapter 15 for more information on getting the best price). On the other hand, going into the dealership without the foggiest notion of how you are going to finance your purchase is setting yourself up to be manipulated and possibly overpay.

In this time when automakers are offering aggressive low-interest financing incentives on many models, a dealership may be able to offer you the best financing terms. But you should do your homework beforehand by carefully shopping around for the best loan offers so you have a comparison point. Here are several general categories of places to look for a loan:

- **Banks** have been in the auto loan business for almost as long as there have been autos. They generally have very specific, conservative loan policies and may only cater to those with better credit references. As such, banks are in a position to offer some very competitive loan rates. Since you probably already have a relationship with at least one bank, that might be a great place to start your financing search. Most banks have Web sites where you can check their current loan rates, but if you decide to apply for a loan, you should stop by a branch office and deal with a real person, not a phone or keyboard. It's a good way to control where your personal information goes, and by avoiding mistakes or misunderstandings, you might just walk out the door with a pretty good interest-rate offer.

- **Credit unions** operate a lot like banks, but they lend money only to their members, who are also owners of the credit union itself. Because they are nonprofit, their operating costs are fairly low and their lending rates can be quite competitive. Many people belong to credit unions just to take advantage of their easy, reliable, and honest loan policies.

- **Finance companies.** Almost every automaker has a company-owned finance company such as GMAC or Ford Credit, but there are also literally hundreds of independent finance companies. Large or small, they all operate like a retailer, but what they sell is money. They borrow money at wholesale rates, mark it up, and lend it out at retail rates. Finance companies are typically less conservative than banks and other lending institutions, but you'll pay for their "generosity" with higher interest rates. Dealerships that refer you to a finance company usually get a piece of the action—a financial reward for their efforts. If your credit rating is such that you can't get a loan from a bank or credit union, a finance company might be your last resort. Because of their willingness to lend to those who might be higher credit risks, finance companies are generally the most expensive sources of auto financing. The rationale is that higher lending rates are needed to cover potential credit losses.

- **Dealerships** are always willing to arrange financing because doing so is profitable, and most have several sources readily available. The big appeal of dealer financing is its simplicity for the consumer. There's no need to shop around—all you have to do is show up, sign a few papers, and drive away. But that convenience is likely to cost you money. Many people don't realize that dealer financing is just another product that the dealer sells, and the profit motive is alive and well there. Frequently, what you think is an auto loan is really what's known in the car business as a retail installment sales contract, or

RISC. The dealer signs the RISC with you, then sells it to a bank or other lending institution. Dealers usually get a cut of the interest rate, so the higher the APR they can charge you, the more money they make. As we've mentioned, many dealers also bump up your rate artificially to earn more profit. Fortunately, you don't have to buy their products just because they're convenient. Unless there is a subsidized low APR from the manufacturer, you'll almost always find lower loan rates elsewhere.

- **Online financing** has changed finance shopping in the same way that online car shopping has changed the way you can look for a new vehicle. Just to illustrate how your choice of online lenders has exploded, go to a search engine, such as Google or Yahoo, and search for "online auto loans." You'll be amazed to see the vast number of listings that pop up. Online financing is not without a downside, however. It may be difficult to control where the information you provide about yourself goes, and you may be bombarded with e-mails and phone calls from lenders you never heard of or contacted in the first place. Be sure to check each Web site's privacy policy before providing personal information.

Whether you arrange your financing online or not, it can be helpful to check out Web sites such as Bankrate.com (*www.bankrate.com*), Capital One Auto Finance (*www.capitaloneautofinance.com*), and E-Loan (*www.eloan.com*) to get a quick read on what APR rates are currently available. This will give you a clearer idea of which loans are most competitive as you talk to other lenders.

## The Incentive Game

These days, you can't turn on a TV or radio without hearing about special factory rebates or low-interest financing. Such automaker incentives have long been used to push slow-selling or outgoing models, but in recent years they've become prevalent even for newly released cars.

Some of the more alluring incentives are 0 percent APR financing or other ultra-low rates, but there are catches:

- Some low rates are available only for 36-month loans, meaning the payments will be quite high.
- Without a stellar credit record, you may not qualify. Always phone the dealership before you pay a visit to learn what credit score qualifies a borrower for the lowest financing rate and, if you don't qualify, what the next best rate would be.
- As a rule, you won't find incentives on vehicles in short supply, some high-end models, and new or redesigned models in high demand.
- You often have to make a choice between a low interest rate and a cash rebate. You will have to run the numbers both ways to see which offer saves you the most money. You'll find an auto-financing calculator that lets you make these types of comparisons at *www.ConsumerReports.org/smartcar.*
- The dealer is less likely to negotiate with you on the car's price.

## Don't let special offers stop you from haggling

Factory cash rebates and low-interest financing incentives typically come from the auto manufacturer, not the dealer. Therefore, they don't affect the dealer's profit. Nevertheless, in a survey of new-car buyers that CONSUMER REPORTS conducted, many respondents said that they didn't negotiate the price of the vehicle because they felt—or were told—that the dealer wouldn't haggle because they were already getting special incentives on the car.

Don't hesitate to negotiate the vehicle price even if there are special deals. You will get the rebate or financing no matter what you pay for the vehicle. So there's no reason you shouldn't get the lowest price you can on the car and the incentive, too.

As tempting as special incentives can be, you're buying the vehicle, not the deal. Keep the big picture in mind—as well as all your other vehicle research—and don't let yourself be romanced into buying a car that you'll regret long before the payments are over.

# Auto-Financing Alternatives

In addition to conventional auto loans from the types of lenders mentioned above, there are other ways to finance an auto purchase, each with its own pros and cons. These include a home-equity loan, home-equity line of credit (HELOC), and credit card.

### Home-equity loans

You can borrow against the equity in your home with a home-equity loan, which is really a second mortgage. Banks will usually loan you up to 80 percent of your equity in the house, and the APR can be lower than a conventional auto loan.

Another major benefit of a home equity loan is the ability to deduct the interest as an itemized expense on your income tax. That could be enough to make up for fees typically charged to initiate the loan.

Just a word of caution, though. Remember that a conventional auto loan uses the vehicle as collateral, and home equity loans use your home. If something happens so that you can't make the loan payments, your home ownership could be in jeopardy. That's a big price to pay for an auto loan, so consider it carefully.

### Home-equity line of credit (HELOC)

This is an open-ended revolving line of credit, which is based on the equity of your home. To purchase a vehicle using a HELOC, you write a check drafted from this line of credit. Advantages of HELOCs are tax-deductible interest, payment flexibility, and a comparatively low initial interest rate.

The rates are variable, however, so the interest rate could go up before you have it paid off, costing you more money overall.

And some HELOCs charge interest only; you have to make a balloon payment on the principal several years out. Or you can convert to a fully amortized loan over a specified repayment period.

Like a home-equity loan, this line of credit is tied to the equity of your home, so you could risk a lien on your home if payments are not met.

### Credit card

You can also purchase a car with a credit card using a credit-card draft, which is a cash advance that works like a personal check. You may have received a draft in the mail from your credit-card company with a letter encouraging you to pay off other credit balances or make large purchases with them. With low introductory rates, cash-advance fee waivers, and high credit limits (sometimes reaching way past $20,000) it may be tempting to use one to purchase a car. We don't advise this, however.

Like a HELOC, this is a revolving line of credit, and you have flexibility in how much you pay every month. Still, interest rates climb promptly once the attractive introductory rate has expired since your credit-card debt is secured by neither your vehicle nor your home equity.

## Auto Refinancing

Just like home loans, your auto loan can be refinanced. Here are some cases in which you may wish to consider refinancing your auto loan:

- If you're always looking for ways to improve your financial situation, you probably follow the rise and fall of interest rates. Knowledge of current rates is key to saving money through successful refinancing, and in a climate of falling rates, you may be able to save some money by refinancing your auto loan.

- Buyer's remorse may set in if you made a bad financing deal, especially if you later find out that someone else you know got a significantly better deal. Perhaps you financed through a dealer who tacked on a few points, thinking that you'd never notice. The only way to fix this embarrassing and expensive mistake is to refinance your loan.

- You may have signed up for a short-term loan with higher payments to minimize the total cost of your loan. That's perfectly acceptable as long as you can continue to make the substantial payments. But what happens if your financial circumstances change and you need to reduce your monthly expenses? Refinancing can extend the term of your loan and lower the payments to a more affordable level.

- If you're considering buying your leased car when the lease is up but you don't have the cash, a form of refinancing called a "buy out" may be arranged. Essentially, you purchase the car and establish a loan at the same time.

Perhaps you're thinking about refinancing to fix a mistake you made on your original auto loan by not reading all of the fine print. If so, read on. Refinancing may have its pitfalls too. Before you start looking for a better loan, check to see if your original loan is a simple-interest loan or a precomputed loan. Most are simple interest, but don't count on it.

If it's a simple-interest loan, you're in good shape. With a simple-interest loan, you're charged interest each day, based on the balance you owe. The faster you pay down your loan, the less interest you'll pay. The best simple-interest loans are those that have no prepayment penalty. Even so, you should find out how much your lender charges for prepayment. Fees can vary from $25 to $200.

If your existing loan is precomputed, you may have already paid a hefty portion of the interest and still owe most of the principal on the loan. With a precomputed loan, you typically pay three quarters of the interest in the first half of the life of the loan. This may make refinancing your vehicle less appealing.

# Get a Good Financial Fit

In many ways, shopping for an auto loan is like shopping for the car itself. When you decide which vehicle to buy, you check to make sure it's a good fit for your circumstances. And so it is with financing. If the terms and conditions of your auto loan don't fit your financial circumstances, you could be unhappy with it for a long time. That unhappiness can come from payments so high that you have to give up things you enjoy or a term so long that you can't trade cars because you're upside-down with your loan.

Before you sign on the dotted line, be sure to check out all the details and options available to you. It's a competitive world when it comes to financing, and the profit motive is alive and well with all lenders. Shop around for a good deal—and make sure it offers the right fit for you.

## Refinancing can make sense

You may be able to save by refinancing, but only if your old rate was significantly higher than one you can get now. Remember that when you refinance, your car may be considered used and will therefore qualify for a higher used-car rate. The table below shows how a refinancing might play out if the new loan is started a year after the initial purchase. Fees and a prepayment penalty on your old loan will diminish your savings.

|  | Original loan | Refinanced loan (After one year of payments) |
| --- | --- | --- |
| Principal | $20,000 | $16,575 |
| Interest rate (APR) | 7.5% | 6.0% |
| Monthly payment | $400.76 | $389.26 |
| Total cost of interest | $4,045.45 | $3,494.51 |
| **Total savings** |  | **$550.94** |

# Worksheet: Low-Interest-Rate Financing vs. Rebate

| | ___% dealer financing | Cash rebate |
|---|---|---|
| Negotiated vehicle price | _____ | _____ |
| Trade-in value | _____ | _____ |
| Rebate | _____ | _____ |
| Principal (amount financed) | _____ | _____ |
| Loan term (months) | _____ | _____ |
| Interest rate (APR) | _____ | _____ |
| Monthly payment | _____ | _____ |
| Total cost of loan | _____ | _____ |

## How to use this worksheet

Subtract the trade-in value and rebate from the negotiated vehicle price to get the principal.

Plug in the number of months you anticipate the loan term to be.

Go to *www.ConsumerReports.org/smartcar* or use another auto-financing calculator to figure the monthly payments for the two cases.

Multiply each monthly payment by the number of payments to get the total cost of the loan under the two scenarios. The lower of the two total cost figures is the best deal.

# 11

# Is Leasing for You?

**A few years ago, about one out of every three** new-car shoppers chose to lease rather than buy their vehicle. The appeal of leasing has fluctuated in recent years, but it remains a popular option for many people. Leasing is attractive in a number of ways. It offers lower monthly payments than buying does. You can drive a higher-priced, better-equipped vehicle than you might otherwise be able to afford. You're always driving a late-model vehicle that's usually covered by the manufacturer's warranty. And there's no hassle having to sell or trade in the car when you're ready for a new one; you simply give it back to the dealership. Most lending institutions, manufacturers, and other lenders offer leases in a variety of shapes and forms.

Still, there are a number of compromises and disadvantages to leasing, which means that it's not right for everyone. The best way to decide whether leasing suits your needs is to learn how leasing works and then compare it with buying. You'll have to crunch the numbers so you can make an intelligent financial decision.

In this chapter, we'll cover all aspects of leasing, including:

- How leasing works
- The advantages and disadvantages of leasing
- How leasing compares with buying
- Who benefits the most from leasing
- Key leasing terms
- The different types of leases
- Negotiating your lease
- Minimizing penalties and other pitfalls
- The leasing alternative of balloon-payment loans

## How Leasing Works

Even though leasing an auto is sometimes likened to a long-term rental, the two are quite different. Renting is the short-term use of a vehicle, where you have nothing to say about its cost or the terms and conditions of its financing. You just pay a set (i.e., daily or weekly) rate, drive the vehicle, and return it when you're finished.

When you lease, you are paying for the depreciation of the vehicle for the time that you use it, as well as paying loan interest and profit for the vehicle owner (usually the dealer). You can negotiate the vehicle price and the terms of the lease, including its length and the amount of the monthly payments you're obligated to make. When you lease, you also are responsible for the ongoing maintenance and repair of the vehicle.

It's easy to see why consumers find leasing so seductive. After all, with little or no money down and for a relatively low monthly payment, you can drive an automobile you never imagined you could afford to own. Then, after enjoying the most trouble-free two or three years of the vehicle's life, you simply bring it back to the dealer, turn it in, and lease another new one. Gone are your worries about paying for the upkeep of an older car or haggling over trade-in values. With a lease, the scent of fresh leather upholstery need never leave your nostrils.

But the hassle-free image of leasing that auto manufacturers and dealers are eager to project can be a mirage. There are several notable drawbacks to leasing:

- Once you're in the leasing habit, monthly payments go on forever.
- You have a limited number of miles in your leasing contract and will have to pay extra if you go over that limit.
- You must maintain the vehicle in good condition; if you don't, you'll have to pay penalties for excess wear and tear.
- If you need to get out of a lease before its term expires, you may be stuck with thousands of dollars in early-termination fees and penalties—all due at once.
- Leasing is rarely a better financial arrangement than buying. The financial advantage of buying increases the longer you keep the vehicle after the loan is paid off.
- At the end of the lease, you have no equity in the vehicle to put toward a new car.
- You can't customize your vehicle in any permanent way.

In addition, arranging a lease can be a confusing, complicated process that can easily leave you paying more than you should for a vehicle.

CONSUMER REPORTS evaluated scores of lease ads appearing in 10 metropolitan newspapers across the U.S. and turned up dozens of offers that could mislead or even deceive an inattentive shopper. The editors' analysis of terms quoted by the behind-the-scenes finance companies that actually write the contracts for 30 of the most commonly leased cars, SUVs, and light trucks revealed that the cost of leasing identical vehicles can vary by thousands of dollars over the life of the lease. And a special survey of a nationally representative sample of 305 recent lease customers showed that a majority had done a poor job of shopping for the vehicle, negotiating the most favorable terms, or steering clear of costly end-of-lease charges.

This is not to say that leasing can't be a satisfying and cost-effective way to acquire a new vehicle, but it's a mistake to think that leasing is easier or less expensive than purchasing. Indeed, for all its superficial simplicity, a lease transaction is a tangle of arcane language and buried details that can ensnare even an experienced customer.

# Who Should Lease?

A lease comes with lots of limitations on how you can use your new vehicle. Do you drive a lot? Do you load your trunk or roof rack with paint-gouging flea-market treasures? Is your car a magnet for parking-lot dents and dings? Are your kids apt to turn its interior into a finger-painting studio? If so, you face a potentially costly problem trying to live within the tight strictures of a lease. First, you'll have to pay for what the leasing company determines to be excessive wear and tear to the vehicle when you return it at lease-end. Second, you'll have to ante up anywhere from 10 to as much as 25 cents for every mile you drive beyond what your lease allows. Driving 5,000 miles over your limit can cost you between $500 and $1,250.

## Should you lease?

Leasing generally makes sense only if:

- You don't exceed the annual mileage allowance—typically 12,000 to 15,000 miles, but sometimes as little as 10,000 miles a year.
- You keep the vehicle in very good shape. "Excess-wear-and-tear" charges can be steep.
- You plan to get a new vehicle every two or three years. If you drive your vehicle much longer than that, you're better off buying it from the start.

# Leasing vs. Buying

This chart shows 10 areas where the differences between leasing and buying really stand out. To calculate the financial difference between a specific loan and lease deal, use the calculators at *www.ConsumerReports.org/smartcar.*

|  | Leasing | Buying |
|---|---|---|
| Ownership | You don't own the vehicle. You get to use it but must return it at the end of the lease unless you decide to buy it. | You own the vehicle and get to keep it as long as you want it. |
| Up-front costs | Up-front costs typically include the first month's payment, a refundable security deposit, a down payment, taxes, registration and other fees. | Up-front costs include the cash price or a down payment, taxes, registration and other fees. |
| Monthly payments | Monthly lease payments are almost always lower than monthly loan payments because you're paying only for the vehicle's depreciation during the lease term, plus interest charges (called rent charges in leasing), taxes, and fees. | Monthly loan payments are usually higher than monthly lease payments because you're paying off the entire purchase price of the vehicle, plus interest and other finance charges, taxes, and fees. |
| Early termination | If you end the lease early, the early-termination charges can be almost as costly as keeping the lease. | You can sell or trade in your vehicle at any time. If necessary, money from the sale can be used to pay off any loan balance. |
| Vehicle return | You can return the vehicle at lease-end, pay any end-of-lease costs, and walk away. | You'll have to sell or trade when you decide you want a different vehicle. |

*continued on next page*

| | Leasing | Buying |
|---|---|---|
| Future value | With a typical closed-end lease, you have no risk, but you don't own the car either. | The vehicle will depreciate, but it will still be worth something. |
| Mileage | Most leases limit the number of miles you may drive (often 12,000 to 15,000 per year). You can negotiate a higher mileage limit. You'll have to pay charges for exceeding your limits. | You're free to drive as many miles as you want. (Higher mileage lowers the vehicle's trade-in or resale value.) |
| Excessive wear and tear | Most leases hold you responsible for wear and tear to the leased vehicle. You'll have to pay extra charges for exceeding what is considered normal wear and tear. | You don't have to worry about wear and tear, except in how it could lower the vehicle's trade-in or resale value. |
| End of term | At the end of the lease (typically 2 to 4 years), you'll have a new payment either to finance the purchase of the existing vehicle or to lease or buy another vehicle. | At the end of the loan term (typically 4 to 5 years), you have no further loan payments and you have built equity to help pay for your next vehicle purchase. |
| Customizing | Because the lessor wants the vehicle returned in salable condition, any custom parts you add will need to be removed before you return the car. If there is any residual damage, you'll have to pay to have it fixed. | The vehicle is yours to customize as you like. |

Leasing novices are particularly at risk of running up these costs. Nearly one-third of the first-time lessees in a CONSUMER REPORTS survey were hit either with excess mileage or wear-and-tear charges.

Of course, the value of any car—whether leased or purchased—will be reduced if it is abused or driven hard, but if your driving patterns expose you to these risks, it's better to be aware of them before you even entertain the possibility of leasing. To determine whether the leasing lifestyle is for you, look ahead to the full term of your lease. How likely are you to change jobs or move to a new home that requires you to rely on your leased vehicle for a long daily commute? Will one of your children begin driving in the coming few years? If so, leasing may not be the right choice.

Drivers who are hard on their vehicles aren't the only poor lease candidates. Driving too little can also saddle you with unnecessary costs. In the same CONSUMER REPORTS survey mentioned above, 20 percent of the drivers older than 55 returned their leased vehicles to the dealer having driven at least 10,000 fewer miles than their lease allowed. Since they got no credit for that unused value, they gave the leasing company what amounted to a windfall when it resold the vehicle. Valuing those unused miles at 10 cents apiece, that subsidy to the dealer can add up to $1,000 or more.

# The Language of Leasing

Like most other things in the financial world, leasing has its own language and, to successfully navigate the process, it helps to be familiar with the following common terms.

- **Acquisition fee:** A charge that covers a variety of administrative expenses, such as obtaining a credit report and verifying insurance coverage. It's usually paid up front but can be rolled into the overall lease package, in which case you'll be paying interest on it.
- **Adjusted capitalized cost:** The agreed-upon value of the vehicle at the

beginning of a lease, not including items such as taxes, fees, service contracts, insurance, and any other prior credit or lease balance.

- **Base monthly payment:** The portion of the monthly payment that covers depreciation, any amortized amounts, and rent charges. Monthly sales/use taxes and other monthly fees are added to this base monthly payment to determine the total monthly payment.

- **Closed-end lease:** Otherwise known as a walk-away lease, this is a lease in which you are not responsible for the difference if the actual value of the vehicle at the end of the lease is less than the residual value that was set at the beginning. This is typical of consumer leases.

- **Depreciation and any amortized amounts:** The amount charged to cover the vehicle's projected decline in value during the lease term, plus other items that are paid for over the lease term. It's calculated as the difference between the adjusted capitalized cost and the vehicle's residual value. This amount is chiefly what your monthly payment is based on.

- **Disposition fee (disposal fee):** A fee charged by the lessor to defray the cost of preparing and selling the vehicle at the end of the lease.

- **Down payment:** An initial cash payment in a lease that reduces the capitalized cost or is applied to other amounts due at lease signing.

- **Early termination:** Ending the lease before the scheduled termination date for any reason, voluntary or involuntary. This happens if you return the vehicle early or default on the lease, or if the vehicle is stolen or totaled. In most of these cases, you must pay an early-termination charge.

- **Excess mileage charge:** A charge by the lessor for miles driven in excess of the maximum specified in the lease agreement. The excess mileage charge is usually between 10 and 25 cents per mile.

- **Excessive-wear-and-tear charge:** The amount charged by the lessor to cover wear and tear on a leased vehicle beyond what is considered normal. The charge may cover both interior and exterior damage, such as upholstery stains, body dents and scrapes, and tire wear beyond the limits stated in the lease agreement.

- **Gap coverage (guaranteed auto protection, or GAP):** A plan that provides financial protection in case your leased vehicle is stolen or totaled in an accident. There are two types of gap coverage. One is a waiver by the lessor of the gap amount if the vehicle is stolen or totaled. The other is a contract by a third party to cover the gap amount. See page 225 for more information.

- **Gross capitalized cost (gross cap cost):** The agreed-upon value of the vehicle at the time you lease it, which generally may be negotiated, plus any items you agree to pay for over the lease term (amortized amounts), such as taxes, fees, service contracts, insurance, and any prior credit or lease balance.

- **Lessee:** The party to whom the vehicle is leased. In a consumer lease, the lessee is you. The lessee is required to make payments and to meet any other obligations specified in the lease agreement.

- **Lessor:** A person or organization that regularly leases, offers to lease, or arranges for the lease of a vehicle.

- **Mileage allowance (or mileage limitation):** The fixed mileage limit for the lease term. This can be negotiated, but if you exceed this limit, you may have to pay an excess mileage charge. You can pay for extra miles upfront, but you won't get your money back if you don't use them.

- **Money factor (or lease factor):** A number, often given as a decimal, used by some lessors to determine the rent (interest) charge portion of your monthly payment.

- **Purchase option:** Your right to buy the vehicle that you have leased, during or at the end of the lease term, according to terms specified in the lease agreement. Your lease agreement may or may not include a purchase option.

- **Residual value:** This is the projected end-of-term value of the vehicle, as established at the beginning of the lease and used in calculating your base monthly payment. The residual value is deducted from the adjusted capitalized cost to determine the depreciation and any amortized amounts. It is determined, in part, by using residual value guidebooks. Because the residual value is only an estimate that's set at the beginning of the lease, the vehicle's actual value at the end of the leasing term may be either higher or lower.

- **Sales/use taxes:** Taxes assessed on leased and purchased vehicles. States differ in which amounts are taxed and when the taxes are assessed. In a lease, sales/use taxes may be assessed on (1) the base monthly payment, (2) any capitalized cost reduction, or (3) in a few states, the adjusted capitalized cost. In most states, the sales/use tax on the base monthly payment is paid monthly; in some states, however, the tax is due at lease inception. Sales/use taxes on the capitalized cost reduction and the adjusted capitalized cost are usually due at lease inception. If you exercise any purchase option, separate taxes may apply.

- **Security deposit:** An amount you may be required to pay, usually at the beginning of the lease, that may be used by the lessor in the event of default or at the end of the lease to offset any amounts you owe under the lease agreement. Any remaining amount may be refunded to you.

- **Subvention:** This is a program or plan in which certain vehicles or items are subsidized by the manufacturer. For example, a manufacturer might offer a special deal on a slow-selling vehicle, or one with an unpopular engine, a manual transmission, or other option that isn't in demand.

# Types of Leases

Just as there are many different kinds of auto loans, there are several distinct kinds of vehicle leases.

## Closed-end vs. open-end leases

As we said, in a **closed-end lease** agreement, you are not responsible for the difference in value when the vehicle's actual value at the end of the lease is less than the residual value on which the lease contract was based. You may still be responsible for excess wear charges, excess mileage charges, and other lease requirements. This type of lease is popular because it takes much of the risk away from leasing. You don't have to gamble with the value of your vehicle when the lease ends. This is typical of most consumer leases.

An **open-end lease** is a lease agreement in which the amount you owe at the end of the lease term is based on the difference between the residual value on which the lease contract was based and the vehicle's actual cash value at the end of the lease. You will need to pay the difference if the actual value is less than the residual value. Or you may get a refund if the actual value is greater than the residual value at scheduled termination. This type of lease is used primarily for commercial leases.

### Single-payment vs. multiple-payment leases

A **single-payment lease** requires a single large payment made in advance rather than periodic payments made over the term of the lease. Because you are making this payment in advance, this lump-sum payment should be less than the total amount you would pay in periodic payments. This type of lease requires that you understand and can calculate the time value of money. Businesses often lease vehicles on a single-payment basis.

A **multiple-payment lease** is a lease agreement in which you make incremental payments, usually monthly. Most leases are multiple-payment leases. It's difficult to calculate how much more it costs to go to a multiple-payment rather than a single-payment lease. Most of us who lease tend to prefer multiple payments because almost everyone understands monthly payments and it's easier to budget a monthly lease payment over time. For many people, it could be difficult to come up with a single payment.

## Negotiating Your Lease

Many people assume when they see a monthly payment printed in a leasing ad that the figure is etched in stone. What they don't realize is that the monthly figure is based on the manufacturer's suggested retail price (MSRP), which can be negotiated just as if you were buying the vehicle. Negotiating a lower price for the vehicle can dramatically lower your monthly lease payment. Many consumers, however, don't attempt to negotiate any part of their lease.

Similarly, you can save thousands of dollars over the life of your lease by shopping around and comparing the leases that are available. You'll be surprised at how much difference there is among the leases offered by dealers, banks, and other leasing sources. Why is there a general reluctance to negotiate or shop for a lease? Perhaps it's because the very language of leasing is so opaque that it obscures the simplest elements of the transaction. Ordinary words like "purchase price," "down payment," "finance charge," and "trade-in value" have morphed in leasing parlance into "gross capitalized cost," "capitalized cost reduction," "money factor," and "residual value," respectively.

Take heart—there are some very specific things you can do to negotiate a good lease and save a lot of money in the process. To see an example of a typical leasing form, go to *www.federalreserve.gov/pubs/leasing/form.htm*.

## Negotiate the purchase price

If you tell a salesperson up front that you're interested in leasing a car, he or she will want to focus on just one number—the monthly payment. Indeed, the entire process of leasing appears designed to throw up intimidating barriers, making it hard for you to consider anything else.

So it makes sense to approach the negotiation as if you intend to purchase the vehicle. Don't even mention your desire to lease until after you and the salesperson have arrived at a final purchase price for the vehicle.

You can potentially shave thousands of dollars from the capitalized cost portion of your lease by ignoring the MSRP and determining a target price beforehand, as described in Chapter 7, and then by following the negotiating advice described in Chapter 15.

## Why do you need gap insurance?

Gap insurance complements your regular auto insurance. If your leased vehicle is stolen or destroyed, and you owe more money on the lease than you insurance company will reimburse, gap insurance makes up the difference. Gap is actually an acronym for Guaranteed Auto Protection, a bit of insurance lingo, so you'll sometimes see it spelled GAP in lease documents.

Because most cars depreciate rapidly, it's possible for you to owe more than the car is worth for most of your leasing term. And since regular collision and comprehensive insurance covers only the book value of the car at the time it's totaled or stolen, you could be on the hook for hundreds or thousands of dollars unless you have gap insurance as well.

In some leases, gap insurance is included in the lease—this is called a "gap waiver"—so there's nothing to decide. If gap insurance is extra, we recommend that you shop around before accepting a car dealer's program. Prices can vary dramatically, so get a number of quotes. If your own insurance company provides it, that could be your best bet. Some companies won't sell it unless you buy their regular auto-insurance policy.

One note of caution: Gap insurance covers the leasing company's potential loss, not yours. Your down payment and any other upfront fees and taxes you paid at lease inception are gone forever. That's another reason to pay nothing down if you can.

Is gap insurance a good idea? Yes, if it's available at a modest cost. Be sure to read the terms of the gap agreement carefully, though. Make sure it covers you for events besides theft and collision, such as flood, fire, and other natural disasters.

Whether buying or leasing, it's important to base your negotiations on what the dealer paid for the vehicle. For example, leasing a Ford Expedition based on a price that's just a few percentage points above the dealer's true cost could drop the monthly cost by as much as $140 below what you'd pay

# Worksheet: Documenting the Deal Purchase vs. Lease

| Purchase Agreement | Amount to be Paid | | Lease Agreement |
|---|---|---|---|
| Purchase price | $ | $ | Capitalized-cost |
| Less: Trade-in allowance | | | Less: Trade-in allowance |
| Rebate or other cash incentive | | | Rebate or other cash incentive |
| Down payment (due on delivery) | | | Down payment (due on delivery) |
| Deposit | | | Deposit |
| | | $ | Equals: Capitalized-cost reduction |
| | | | Less: Residual value |
| Equals: Amount to be financed by loan | $ | $ | Equals: Amount to be financed by lease |
| Interest rate (Enter annual percentage rate) | % | 0. | Money factor (Enter four-digit decimal figure) |
| | | _____ mm/dd/year | Lease start date |
| | | _____ mm/dd/year | Lease termination date |
| Loan term (in months) | | | Lease term (in months) |
| Compute: Monthly purchase payment | $ | $ | Compute: Monthly lease payment |
| Total value of payments (over duration of the loan) | $ | $ | Total value of payments (over duration of the loan) |
| Odometer reading (at time of purchase) | | | Odometer reading (at time of purchase) |
| | | | Mileage allowance (over duration of the lease) |
| | | $ | Disposition fee (amount due when lease ends) |
| Delivery date | mm/dd/year | mm/dd/year | Delivery date |

Vehicle: _____
        Make, Model, and Trim Line

Signature: _____
        Dealership sales manager

Vehicle Identification Number: _____

Signature: _____
      Your name

Date: _____

for a lease based on MSRP for the same vehicle—a savings of about $5,000 over the life of a 36-month lease. You may not realize such big savings on vehicles that are in short supply, where you may end up paying closer to full retail price, but it's always in your best interest to negotiate.

## The money factor

The cost of funds, commonly called the money factor, is the term used in leasing that means roughly the same thing as the interest paid in an auto loan. The money factor is always stated as a decimal amount (for example .00333333) that reflects the return on the lessor's investment in monthly terms. So, if you want to convert the money factor to an APR equivalent, all you have to do is multiply it by 2,400. Thus, a money factor of .00333333, multiplied by 2,400 is 8.0 percent APR.

The money factor should be as good as the best rate you can get for an auto loan, but as you might expect, different leasing companies offer different money factors, just as different banks offer different interest rates on their auto loans. Shopping for the best money factor is a critical part of negotiating a lease, and when comparing leases, be sure to compare money factors.

## Read between the lines of leasing ads

It takes a sharp-eyed skeptic to deconstruct a lease advertisement. Many ads that we've seen reveal less for what they say than for what they omitted or obscured. Typically, the most prominent piece of information is how much you can expect to pay per month; but you have to scrutinize the fine print to discover, as mentioned above, that the monthly payment is most commonly computed on the basis of the MSRP, in effect making you pay top dollar for the vehicle.

Here are other common ad twists and tricks you should watch out for:

- **Act fast.** A careful shopper needs time to visit dealers and weigh com-

## You need to know

To make sure you're comparing apples to apples, you need to evaluate each of the following elements when comparing leases:

- The agreed-upon value of the vehicle
- Up-front payments and adjustments—down payment, trade-in, and various fees
- The length of the lease
- The money factor
- The monthly lease payment
- End-of-lease fees and charges
- Mileage allowance and per-mile charge for excess miles
- The option to purchase at lease-end or earlier
- Cost of gap insurance

peting offers—time that a lease ad might not let you have. For example, an ad might promote an attractive-sounding monthly figure. But to qualify for those terms the customer has just one day to sign the lease and then take delivery of the vehicle within three days after that.

- **Minimal mileage allowances.** Some lease ads base their offers on an allowance of 12,000 miles—pretty skimpy for anyone who depends on a car to make a long daily commute. We've also seen mileage limits as low as 10,000 miles a year. Exceed that low limit and you would have to pay an extra charge—perhaps as high as 18 cents or more for each additional mile.
- **Leases that outlast the vehicle's warranty.** One ad we've seen offered what at first seemed to be an unbeatable $169-per-month lease on a new midsized sedan. A closer look revealed that the low monthly payment applied only to cars leased for a minimum of 60 months—longer than the car's 3-year or 36,000-mile bumper-to-bumper warranty. That puts the lease customer at risk of having to pay hefty out-of-warranty repair

bills on a vehicle he or she doesn't own. We've also seen ads for lease terms as long as 5½ years.

## Compare lease-finance companies

Most auto dealerships work with at least four leasing companies, and terms can vary significantly among them. The savings from choosing the right leasing company can be big. Generally, the finance subsidiary of the manufacturer whose vehicles the dealer represents—General Motors Acceptance Corporation (GMAC), for example, or Ford Motor Credit— will provide the most attractive terms. This option is worth asking about first, but don't stop there. Your bank, or one of the many leasing companies, might be able to come up with a better offer.

Just as you should explore your financing options before you go to the dealership to buy a car, it's also important to compare leasing terms before you visit the dealership. This helps keep your negotiations simpler so you can focus on the vehicle's price.

As you gather vehicle prices and lease-cost information, keep an eye on the automotive section of your local paper for so-called subvented lease offers. These special deals are typically offered by auto manufacturers through their subsidiary finance arm (and labeled as such in the fine print). Unlike the standard terms independent leasing companies offer, subvented deals usually provide attractive incentives, such as lower financing charges and manufacturer rebates. They can be useful in identifying the most-competitive lease terms for the vehicles that interest you.

## Plan your exit strategy

The end of your lease might be two or three years down the road, but you should still plan how you want to handle it. If you don't do it now, you could get burned later. The lease contract will spell out conditions you'll be expected to meet when it comes time to return your vehicle, so the time to decide whether you can live with those terms is before you sign. Here's what to do for lease-end advantages:

## 10 tips for a smart lease

1. Negotiate the vehicle's purchase price as if you were going to buy the car. Only after you have a firm price should you bring up leasing.

2. The mileage limit, down payment, and purchase-option price can also be negotiated.

3. Negotiate the money factor. To turn the decimal money factor into an approximate annual interest rate, multiply the money factor by 2,400.

4. Buy gap insurance to protect yourself in case the vehicle is stolen or is totaled in an accident.

5. To keep your monthly payments as low as possible, look for cars that don't depreciate faster than average. CONSUMER REPORTS publishes a "predicted depreciation" rating that's accessible in CR's automotive publications or on ConsumerReports.org (see Appendix C).

6. Avoid leases that extend beyond the car's factory warranty.

7. Note any end-of-lease procedures and fees.

8. Buy extra miles up front if you expect to run over the standard allotment.

9. Ensure your trade-in is deducted from the leased car's "capitalized cost." (See Chapter 8 for advice on how to get the most value for your trade-in.)

10. After the lease has ended, if you choose to buy, try to bargain down the purchase price.

■ **Choose the right mileage allowance.** If you exceed the mileage limitation stipulated in the lease, you could end up paying as much as 25 cents for each additional mile you drive. You may be better off purchasing additional miles at a discount before you take possession of the vehicle. The savings can be significant, since most lease-financing companies will let you boost your mileage limits at the lease inception for about 10 to 16 cents a mile. Keep in mind that the more miles you drive, the more likely you may be to incur charges for excessive wear and tear. So make sure you understand what the dealer deems excessive before you sign the lease.

- **Consider your end-of-lease purchase option.** You may end up liking the performance and reliability of the vehicle you lease and ultimately decide you want to buy it when your lease is up. That's why it makes sense to pay close attention to what the lease sets as the residual value, or what the auto would be expected to sell for used. The lower the residual value, the less you would have to pay to buy. Still, a lower residual value will result in a higher monthly lease payment, so you should weigh your potential interest in purchasing at lease-end before you sign the deal.

Regardless of how the residual value is determined, you're better off insisting that your lease name a specific purchase-option price so you'll have a clear idea of what you can expect to pay if you ultimately choose to buy the vehicle. Some leases are deliberately vague about that price and instead designate a formula to determine the vehicle's ultimate cost when the lease expires. Keep in mind, however, that if you have any interest in eventually buying the vehicle, it makes more sense to buy it in the first place instead of leasing first and then buying it.

# Preparing for the End of Your Lease

A satisfactory leasing experience can unravel expensively at lease-end if you let your guard down. Because you'll be giving up your leased wheels, the dealer knows that you probably have little choice other than to buy or lease another vehicle. Indeed, some dealers will try to strengthen their bargaining hand by telling you that you will be charged for excess wear and tear on the vehicle, then offer to forgive those charges if you agree to lease a new vehicle.

If, on the other hand, you drove many fewer miles than your lease allowed, you may want to investigate whether it makes sense to buy the vehicle at the purchase-option price the lease stipulates and then resell it on your own if its market value is higher. See Chapter 8 to determine the value of a used car.

Here are several other ways to minimize end-of-lease expenses:

- **Have an independent garage repair your vehicle, if necessary.** You're under no obligation to have the dealer who originally leased you the car do the end-of-lease repairs. At least one month before your lease is due to expire, have the vehicle pre-inspected. (Many leasing companies provide this service free.) If repairs are needed, collect bids from mechanics or body shops you trust to determine the least expensive way to make them. When you return the vehicle, insist on getting a signed vehicle-inspection worksheet documenting its condition before you turn over the keys. That way, you can't be held responsible for damage that may occur later.

- **Buy your own tires.** If you've driven your full allotment of miles or more, you may also need to replace the tires—something you can do less expensively with a bit of shopping than simply by allowing the auto dealership to charge you top dollar for its treads. If you do replace tires, expect to pay for all four. Most leases specify that tires must match.

- **Be careful of "loyalty" leases.** Dealers like nothing better than to persuade existing lease customers simply to roll over into a new lease when their contract expires. Indeed, 60 percent of respondents in a CONSUMER REPORTS survey told us they went back to their old dealer for another lease. Fewer than half bothered to shop around first. You owe it to yourself to shop as carefully for your new lease as you did for your original one. If after testing the market you decide to lease anew from your original dealer, make sure that any forgiven end-of-lease charges aren't simply rolled over into the next lease you sign.

- **Get your security deposit back.** Many leasing companies require customers to ante up the equivalent of a month's payment as a security deposit when the initial lease is signed. If you have a good credit history, you may be able to persuade the dealer to waive that fee. If you do have to pay it, though, don't forget to ask for your refund.

# Lease Alternative: Balloon-Payment Loans

Because New York has strict liability laws that hold leasing companies responsible on their leased vehicles, large finance companies such as GMAC, Ford Motor Credit, and Chase Manhattan Bank no longer lease cars there. Instead, you can get a special balloon-payment loan that is essentially a cross between a lease and a loan, and have the same type of low monthly payments and restrictions of a lease. Offered under such names as GM's "SmartBuy" and Ford's "Red Carpet Option," these loans have taken leasing's place in New York and may be offered alongside leases in others states.

Under these programs, you own the car, yet pay only for its depreciation over the length of the loan. Unlike leasing, you have to pay sales tax on the full price of the car, not just the depreciation. With the last payment, the balance of the car's value is due. Like a lease, you can turn the car in at the end of the term, no matter its value, though you may incur fees for excess mileage or excess wear and tear. Another option is to sell the car to pay off the loan or to refinance the balloon payment at the end of the term.

If you have a choice between a lease and a balloon-payment loan, run the numbers both ways to see which is the better deal. As with leasing, if you're considering keeping the vehicle beyond the balloon payment, it's usually better to get a conventional loan in the first place.

## Look before you lease

As with every aspect of buying, financing, or leasing, you have to look out for yourself. It's highly unlikely that anyone at a dealership or leasing company will help you save money or make sure the lease you're about to sign fits you. That's why it's so important to become familiar with the terms and conditions of your proposed lease. Armed with that knowledge, you can avoid common pitfalls that could spoil your new car experience.

If the terms of your lease are fair and leasing suits you, it can be a very enjoyable way to acquire your next new vehicle. Just remember that the conditions of a typical lease are a lot more restrictive than outright ownership. If you're attracted to the lower monthly payments of a lease but concerned about the restrictions, you might want to consider other alternatives, such as buying a car with a longer loan term or buying a used car.

# Step 5

## Get the Best Deal

■ CHAPTER 12: Avoid Dealer Tricks       **237**
■ CHAPTER 13: Size Up the Dealerships       **253**
■ CHAPTER 14: Pros & Cons of Buying Online       **271**
■ CHAPTER 15: Negotiate the Best Price       **289**
■ CHAPTER 16: Close the Deal       **305**

# 12

# Avoid Dealer Tricks

**Ideally, a dealership should help you** find the right vehicle for your needs at a fair price, but some dealers place more emphasis on their own profit margins than on satisfying their customers. This can dramatically affect how the sales staff treats you.

Many salespeople, for instance, have well-rehearsed routines that are intended to put you off-guard and manipulate the car-buying process so they can squeeze more money out of you. At CONSUMER REPORTS, our anonymous auto shoppers have seen these tricks while buying hundreds of vehicles over the years for testing. We've also talked to many current and former auto salespeople, consumer advocates, lawyers, state consumer-protection officials, and other car-buying experts about some of the most common sales tactics.

Going in unprepared is the surest way to overpay for a new car. That's why it's important to be aware of these sales tactics and how to counter them.

In this chapter, we'll cover many of the more common—or more devious—tactics. You'll find more detailed information about many of these subjects in the appropriate chapters of this book. Here you'll learn:

- How salespeople can work the numbers so you think you're getting a good deal when you're not

- How you can overpay in financing interest without knowing it

- What clues to watch for as a tip-off that you could be manipulated

- How used-car salespeople can mislead you about a car's history and condition

- How dealerships can bury hidden fees or extras in the contract

In addition, a series of sidebars in this chapter called "Between the Lines" helps you decode the carefully crafted—and often misleading—language that dealer newspaper ads use to lure you into the showrooms. We'll show you how to ferret out what's really going on behind those too-good-to-be-true offers by studying the ads' footnotes and fine print.

## The Negotiation Shell Game

There are several areas in the car-buying process where a dealership can make a lot of profit off of you: on the vehicle price, trade-in, and financing terms. Most salespeople, for instance, will try to get you to pay top dollar to buy or lease the new car. If you are trading in your current vehicle, the salesperson may try to lowball you on its value so the dealership can make more money when reselling it. Finally, if you're financing through the dealership, it can try to arrange loan or leasing terms that yield the highest return to the dealership.

Naturally, the dealer wants to make as much money as he can on each part of the transaction, but it is the deal's overall profit that matters most.

The easiest way to beef up the overall profit while still making the customer think he or she is getting a good deal is for the salesperson to focus on only one figure: the monthly payment.

Indeed, "how much were you thinking of paying each month?" may be one of the first questions to greet you when you meet a salesperson. Don't take this bait. Like most people, you may find it much simpler to think about the cost of a new car in terms of how paying for it will affect your monthly budget, but that's not how you should approach the negotiations. If you give the salesperson a monthly figure to work with, he will try his best to meet it, but not necessarily in a way that's in your best interests.

On the other hand, if you give a figure that's higher than it needs to be, the salesperson may pad the deal with unnecessary extras, such as an extended warranties, undercoating, maintenance packages, and other items. In extreme cases, customers aren't told their sales contracts have been "padded" with these extras, or the dealer will say the items will be provided at no charge in exchange for an immediate sale.

By mixing the elements together, the salesperson has more room to juggle the figures, so he can give you a good deal in one area while making up for it in another. For example, if he determines that you are fixated on getting a generous trade-in allowance for your used car, he may give you what you want while distracting you from the fact that you are paying more than you should for the new vehicle. Likewise, he might accept a low bid on the new car but compensate for it by masking a handsome profit in the terms of the loan or lease. When you're only looking at the monthly payment, the parts that make it up can become blurred.

If a low monthly payment is a priority, the salesperson can put together a loan that spreads your payments over a long payback period. Yes, your monthly payment will be lower, but you will end up paying far more in interest payments than with a shorter-duration loan. In addition, when it comes time to trade in the car, you risk ending up owing the lender more to pay off the loan than the car is worth.

Or a salesperson might try to encourage you to lease instead of buy, pointing out that the monthly payment on a lease will be lower than if you bought the vehicle, without informing you of a lease's limitations or of the possibility of paying excess fees.

**How to respond:** Focus on one thing at a time. Tell the salesperson that rather than talking about a monthly payment, you're interested in getting the lowest price on the new vehicle, and that only if you can get a good deal on the car will you consider a trade-in or financing.

Once you've completed your negotiations on the vehicle price, you can tackle the trade-in, financing, or any other elements one at a time. By obligating the dealership to offer competitive terms for each part of the transaction independent of the others, you improve your prospects of driving away with the best overall package.

## Bumping the Rate

Dealerships routinely use so-called interest-rate bumping. Though not illegal, the practice drives up your financing costs.

Here's how it works: When a buyer asks about a dealer-originated loan, the finance manager runs a credit check to determine the best interest rate available for that customer.

The dealer often bumps up the rate by a few percentage points for people with good credit and by several points for those with poor credit. The practice is encouraged by the finance companies, which pay incentives back to the dealer for the additional profit. On a $22,000, five-year loan, a 2.5-percent hike in the initial annual interest rate of 6.3 percent would add $1,569 to your cost over the life of the loan.

Another type of interest-rate shuffling involves the "yo-yo" delivery, says Laura MacCleery, of Public Citizen, a Washington, D.C., advocacy group. You drive the car off the lot with dealer financing at a relatively low interest rate. The fine print might make the sale contingent on the approval of the financing agreement. If any finance terms aren't approved, the bank may request or seek to change the terms of the loan.

At this point, the dealership calls and says you need to sign some more papers. When you do, the loan terms have changed and the interest rate may be higher or the loan term longer. If you don't sign, the dealer might threaten to say you stole the car.

**How to respond:** If you're financing through the dealership, you can avoid this by not driving the car off the lot until you're sure the bank has signed the paperwork. The best strategy is to shop for your own car loan ahead of time. Get approved for a loan before you go to the dealership. The dealership may even match or beat the loan for which you've qualified.

## BETWEEN THE LINES I:

### THE MONTHLY PAYMENT YOU SEE MAY NOT BE THE ONE YOU GET

**The pitch:** A 2005 advertisement from an Infiniti dealer highlighted a low monthly payment of $299 on a G35X AWD.

**The catch:** There are two key points in this ad that you might miss. The first, buried in the fine print, is that actually getting this monthly payment is contingent on "Tier 1 credit approval with credit score of 700 or higher." If your credit score doesn't make the grade, you won't qualify for these terms. (For more information about credit scores, see Chapter 10).

Second, as with virtually all leasing ads, the monthly payment is based on the full manufacturer's suggested retail price (MSRP) for the vehicle. But customers rarely pay full MSRP when buying, so why should you when leasing? Before you even mention leasing, you should negotiate the vehicle's price as if you were buying it. Only after you settle on that figure, should you talk about leasing terms. Lowering the vehicle's price will also lower your monthly lease payments. (For more information on leasing, see Chapter 11).

# The Waiting Game

Sometimes a dealership's strategy is to wear you down gradually with long waits and increase the time you've spent in the showroom so you will eventually be ready to agree to or sign just about anything just to complete the deal. The salesperson, for instance, may keep you waiting for long stretches of time while he is supposedly conferring with his sales manager about your deal.

**How to respond:** Fatigue and frustration put you at a great disadvantage in any negotiation. If you get caught up in this kind of time-consuming process in which you spend a lot of time waiting while seeing little real progress, tell the salesperson firmly that you have a limited amount of time to close this deal. If he or she is not the person who can approve the price you're looking for, then you want to deal directly with someone who can. If the pace of the discussion and your energy start to lag, get up and leave.

# The Walls Have Ears

In any negotiation, the greatest edge either side can have is to know just how far the other side is willing to go to close a deal. Some unscrupulous car salespeople try to exploit that advantage by surreptitiously listening in on your private conversations while you're left alone in the showroom.

Here's how it's done: The salesperson excuses himself for one of his mysterious absences. On his way out, he hits the "intercom" button on the phone console on his desk or leaves a connection open to the business office and presses "hands free." We've also been told of salespeople who hide a baby monitor or other eavesdropping device in their desk to listen to their customers' conversations.

Using these techniques, the salesperson and any other dealership staff can listen in as you and your spouse or partner plot your next move or talk over how much more you are willing to pay. Knowing this, the staff can direct the negotiations to get as much money as they can from you.

## BETWEEN THE LINES II:

### BE WARY OF PRICE LEADERS THAT MAY NOT BE THERE WHEN YOU SHOW UP

**The Pitch:** A 2005 advertisement by a Hyundai dealer touted low prices on Accent, Sonata, Tiburon, and Santa Fe models.

**The Catch:** There were only a few (between three and five) of each model from which to choose. What the ad is really offering are a few specific vehicles that are being used as price leaders to generate showroom traffic. If they're gone by the time you arrive, other vehicles on the lot may not be such good deals. Even if the price leaders are still there, the sales staff will often try their best to upsell you into another vehicle from which the dealer stands to make more profit.

There are other restrictions spelled out in the ad's fine print. Only a customer with a top-rated credit score—750 or higher—will qualify for the advertised prices. Others will likely face higher financing charges that will boost the monthly payment. Still, you might think you've got an ace in the hole. The ad proclaims that the dealership will beat any advertised price or payment. Don't waste your time sifting through the competitors' ads, though. The tiny type says you'll have to find one from a dealership that lists the exact make and model—in the same color—as being in stock.

A similar ad we found from a Subaru dealership had several other catches. To get the advertised deals, the customer had to bring the newspaper ad (it was considered a "coupon"), take same-day delivery, and finance through the dealership.

**How to respond:** Take nothing for granted, and keep your private conversations confidential. Assume that any discussion you have within listening distance of a salesperson's desk can and will be used against you. If you want to talk over your strategy during a break in your negotiation, step outside. There may be a bonus to this evasive strategy: If the salesperson notices that you are disappearing whenever he does, he may be more likely to give you more of his undivided attention rather than take the risk that you may not come back.

## Beware the Cream Puff

When buying a used car, the condition of the vehicle is everything. Yet some used-car salespeople that we've talked to say they rarely knew the history or condition of used cars on their lots. When customers asked, most salespeople admitted they just made something up. A common tale that customers like to hear, for instance, is that the vehicle was a trade-in from a frequent customer and the dealership regularly serviced it.

Salespeople told us that if they knew something was wrong, they would often attempt to conceal it. For example, one salesperson told us that he might ask the dealership's mechanics to put refrigerant into a leaky air conditioning system before test drives, a practice he called "juicing the A/C." These charges typically only last a few days. Others we spoke with said that dealerships discourage the practice of letting buyers have vehicles inspected. One told us that he'd say the dealership service department already took care of it. A salesperson in California said that in preparing a used car for sale, some dealerships did little more than check the brakes and change the oil, and that despite advertising claims to the contrary, they didn't do a "120-point inspection" on any car.

**How to respond:** Inspect any used car as thoroughly as possible, using the tips in Chapter 6. And protect yourself from hidden damage by insisting that you have it inspected by an independent mechanic. If any damage is discovered, you should get an estimate for how much it will cost to be repaired and subtract that from your final negotiated price for the car.

## 'Show Me the Money!'

After a couple of rounds of dickering back-and-forth over the price of the vehicle, you make what you hope will be a final offer that the sales manag-

# BETWEEN THE LINES III:

## THIS GREAT PRICE IS REALLY A NOT-SO-GREAT LEASE

**The Pitch:** A Lincoln Mercury dealer advertised in 2005 that you could "own" a 2005 Mercury Mariner for $199 per month or a 2005 Lincoln Aviator for $379 a month.

**The Catch:** If you think these prices are too good to be true, you're right. Read past the monthly payment and you'll watch bargain-basement "ownership" morph into a lease. You get to keep the vehicle for a few years, then must either turn it back in or make a sizeable balloon payment. With the Mariner, it's yours for 23 months, then you owe a final payment of $16,500. The Aviator term runs for 38 months before a payment of $19,860 comes due. After that, if you want to keep the car, you can either plunk down the money or take out a car loan.

As with a conventional lease, the customer can also opt to return the vehicle to the dealership. But not without some pitfalls common to leases. Although not stated in the ad, you would be responsible for excess wear and tear. Then there's the mileage allowance, a stingy 10,500 per year for either vehicle—only 875 miles per month. Although no price for excess miles was listed in the ad, the average cost runs between 15 and 20 cents per mile. So if you drive a not-unreasonable 12,000 each year (1,000 miles each month), at the end of your Mariner contract you could wind up owing between $431 and $575 for 2,875 miles. At the end of the longer Aviator term, the extra-mileage cost could be from $712 and $950 for those extra 1,750 miles. (For more information on balloon-payment loans, see Chapter 11.)

er will accept. The salesperson is encouraging and thinks there's a good chance your bid will be approved, but he tells you that your odds will be improved if you hand over a check as a down payment to demonstrate that you are serious.

**How to respond:** No money should change hands until after both you and the salesperson have agreed on a price and a contract reflecting your terms has been prepared. If the staff won't take your offer seriously unless you write a check to back it up, then you would be better off finding another dealership.

By giving the dealership a check prematurely, you are only setting yourself up to be a hostage to a deal. You risk having the dealership hold on to your check even if the terms you offer are rejected or a less advantageous counteroffer is put on the table. In a worst-case scenario, you may have to stop payment on the check.

## 'We'll Pay Off Your Upside-Down Loan'

As new cars become more expensive and lenders' financing terms more flexible, consumers have been increasing the amount of money they borrow and stretching out the term of their loans—to as long as 72 months—in an effort to keep their monthly payments affordable. But those long car loans can come back to bite you when it comes time to buy a new vehicle.

When they inquire about the trade-in value of their current car, many buyers are surprised to discover that their vehicles are worth less in trade than they owe to pay off their loans. As they say in financing lingo, their loans are "upside down." For example, if the wholesale value of your used car is $6,000, but you still owe the lender $9,000, you're $3,000 in the hole.

The new car dealer may be only too happy to suggest a solution that sounds too good to be true ... and it is. The dealership's finance department may offer to advance you enough to pay off the full loan amount for you and take your old car off your hands. But that $9,000 "advance" simply substitutes the dealer as your creditor in place of your former lender, and it does nothing to change the fact that your old car was still worth just $6,000. That difference of $3,000 does not disappear; instead, it will be rolled into the new car loan the dealer arranges for you.

The dealership may be able to minimize the monthly impact of that extra $3,000 by putting you in a loan with a long payout period, which keeps the monthly payment affordable. Still, you will be paying interest on that $3,000 throughout the life of the new loan, and you will be virtually guaranteed of facing the same problem the next time you buy a new car.

**How to respond:** Rolling over an old car loan into a new one is an expensive and unnecessary waste of money, and if a dealer offers to do this, just say, "No, thanks." As disagreeable as it is to be anchored to an upside-down loan, the only way to get out from under it is to pay it off yourself. If you must replace your old car, you may consider buying a less expensive one to conserve the cash you'll need to repay your creditor.

Another option: Instead of trading in your current vehicle, you can usually get more money by selling it yourself, which would allow you to pay off more of the loan balance. To keep from getting upside down on a loan in the first place, we suggest that your down payment on a new vehicle be at least 20 percent of the selling price, and, if you must borrow, limit the term of your loan to four years or less.

## Invoice Padding

Just when you think your new car deal is tied up neatly with only the papers to be signed, some dealerships will try to slip in extra fees that pad your contract and get them a little more profit.

Among fees that you should question is a dealer preparation charge. It is customary for the vehicle's manufacturer to compensate the dealership to clean and ready the vehicle for final delivery. This is not a service that you should be asked to pay for as well.

Documentation fees cover nothing more than the effort required of the dealership to prepare the paperwork to complete the sale. Ideally, you shouldn't have to pay for this service any more than you would pay a fee to a supermarket for ringing up your purchases at the checkout counter. Those fees are not always negotiable, but it's worth a try.

Equally problematic are charges that might appear for a range of over-priced insurance products you do not need or should consider purchasing elsewhere. The dealer may tell you that the terms of your loan or lease require you to purchase credit life insurance to guarantee that your car payments will continue to be made in the event of your death. Lenders and leading companies require no such thing. Or he may try to sell you disability insurance to cover you in the event that an illness or injury renders you unable to work. Typically, you will have disability coverage through your job, and in any event, you can purchase a less costly policy that's better suited to your needs through your insurance agent.

Finally, if you will be leasing the new vehicle, you may see a charge for gap insurance on the invoice that would cover the vehicle's full value if it were damaged beyond repair during the period of your lease. This is important coverage to have, but you can probably find lower premiums through your car insurance underwriter. For more details on all of the closing pitfalls to avoid, see Chapter 16.

**How to respond:** You can avoid nasty closing surprises by having the dealer fax, e-mail, or mail a copy of all of the final paperwork to you at least 24 hours before you intend to pick up the vehicle. Read it over carefully and call the dealership for an explanation of anything you don't understand. Once you sign and hand over your check, you will have to live with the consequences, so question everything that strikes you as suspect.

# Overpriced Extras

Dollar for dollar, some of the dealership's biggest profit margins are on extras—pinstriping, fabric guard, rust protection, paint sealant, and the like—that a dealership staffer may try to sell after you've completed your price negotiations, but before you sign the purchase agreement. All of these extras may sound appealing, but they are either unnecessary or the dealership will charge an exorbitant price for them.

One big money maker that CONSUMER REPORTS buyers see a lot is VIN etching, in which the dealership etches the car's vehicle identification number (VIN) on the window, supposedly to deter thieves. The salesperson may give you a convincing line about how it could reduce your insurance payment, but you'll pay dearly for the service. Some dealerships don't even give you a choice. For instance, two CONSUMER REPORTS staff members found window-etching charges up to $200 listed in the contracts when they went to sign the final deal on their cars, but they hadn't asked for it. In one case, the dealership had already etched the windows. In both cases, the charges were removed once the staffers refused to pay them.

**How to respond:** We recommend you decline these extras as early in the negotiations as possible. Rustproofing, for example, is no longer necessary for today's far more corrosion-resistant cars. In fact, according to CONSUMER REPORTS reliability information, rust is no longer a major problem for today's vehicles.

If you're asked if you want paint sealant or fabric protection, tell the salesperson, "No, thanks," and make an auto-parts store or a supermarket one of the first stops in your new car to pick up a good-quality wax and spray-on fabric protectant for a few bucks.

Some states do require dealerships to offer VIN etching to their customers, but none require you to buy it, despite what a salesperson might imply. If you decide you want it, you can buy a kit to etch your windows yourself for less than $25.

If you find any extras to which you didn't agree added to your contract, simply put a line through the items and deduct their cost from the total.

# 0 Down, 0 Interest, 0 Payments for 1 Year

Sure the deal looks great. But when the year is up, you find out you owe all of the monthly payments you've delayed—sometimes plus retroactive interest. You end up owing much more than the sticker price on a vehicle that is now a used car.

In some cases, the contract states that the buyer owes the dealership X number of monthly payments at a high interest rate, then must refinance the balance of the loan. That's the deal an insurance-claims assistant in Austin, Texas, signed for a Mitsubishi Montero in 2002. She thought she was paying $31,000, but when the 0-0-0 time was up, a 9.9 percent interest rate kicked in, requiring her to pay $677 per month for five years, or a total of $40,591 for the car. She couldn't refinance at a lower rate because the loan was for much more than the $16,800 that the depreciated vehicle was then worth.

**How to respond:** Don't fall for this gimmick. A 0-0-0 deal costs more in the long run than a conventional loan.

## The Stealth or Mandatory Credit Check

When you first sit down at the salesperson's desk, he may begin to fill out a form, asking for your name, address, phone number, and other details about the kind of vehicle and options you want. He may want to know about the car you currently drive and whether you are interested in trading it in—just basic data for their records, he may tell you. But your antenna should go up if he goes on to ask you for the ID number on your driver's license, date of birth, Social Security number, and similar sensitive personal identifiers. With these data, the dealership's business office can immediately run a credit check and obtain information that can put you at a significant disadvantage.

Another scenario is that a salesperson may tell you that the dealership must run a credit check on you, whether you're financing through the dealership or not.

With a credit check, the dealership can learn whether a history of bad credit makes you someone they wouldn't be willing to work with at all. The staff may also discover what other car dealerships you may be working with and use that information to gain a bargaining edge.

Generally, multiple inquiries concerning auto financing within a 45-day period are treated as a single inquiry and will not lower your score. If you shop for financing repeatedly, however, or are also applying for other credit, your score may drop.

**How to respond:** It is reasonable for the salesperson to ask for information that makes it possible to contact you during the course of your negotiations, but to ask for personal identification numbers of any kind is out of bounds.

If you're paying cash, have other financing, or are just taking a test drive, car dealerships may obtain a credit report only with your written consent, according to a 1998 opinion letter to a car-dealer association by Federal Trade Commission staff. Credit reports may be obtained without a customer's express permission only if the customer is initiating the purchase or lease of a car and wants dealer financing or is writing a personal check for the vehicle, the letter states.

If you have already arranged financing elsewhere or plan to pay cash, tell salespeople the moment you walk in that you do not authorize them to run credit checks on you. Do not give them your Social Security number or your driver's license. If a dealership requests your license for a test drive, you can show it but do not allow a copy to be made. Before you sign any papers, insist that the ongoing credit-check authorization clause be stricken from the document and then read it to make sure it was done before you sign.

# The False Credit Score

Dealerships can make a lot of money on financing because they get a cut of the financing charge you pay. Yet 0 percent and other low-interest financing deals that have been popular in recent years cuts into this potential profit.

Because only customers with the best credit scores typically qualify for these special low-interest deals, some unscrupulous staffers will stoop to lying about a customer's credit score, forcing him to pay a higher rate—and more finance charge—than he should.

Here's how it works: The dealership checks your credit score, telling you it is lower than it really is. (The higher the score, the better your credit.) Alas, you don't qualify for the low-interest car loan that drew you to the dealership in the first place. Therefore, you'll have to pay a higher rate.

One car buyer that a CR reporter talked to checked his credit score before car shopping. His average score from the three major credit bureaus was 750. Generally, scores above 700 are considered excellent. Yet the consumer said he was told by a salesperson that his credit score was too low to qualify for the 0 percent financing offer he had seen on TV. How low was his score? The salesman said he didn't want to say because it would embarrass him in front of his wife and son, who were with him. The salesperson told the customer that the only way he could sell him the car was through a lease or for $2,200 more than a competing price that the customer had gotten from an Internet car-buying site.

**How to respond:** Know your credit score before you shop for a car loan. (See Chapter 10 for more information about credit scores.) Also call the dealership before you go in to see if you qualify for a special interest rate. A salesperson will have less motivation to lie about your credit score if it means you won't even come to the showroom. If you suspect they may be in error, call a second dealership.

All states have laws that protect consumers from deceptive and unfair practices. A representative from the Iowa attorney general's office told us, "If you can prove it was done, it would be illegal." If a dealership staffer says your credit score is lower than you know it is, buy your car elsewhere and report the deceptive dealership to your state attorney general's office.

# 13

# Size Up the Dealerships

**Now is the time you've been waiting for.** You've narrowed down your selection of models to the ones that best fit your needs and means. You've decided on the features and options you want, have checked out the appropriate vehicles at the dealership, and have taken them for thorough test drives. On the financial side, you know what the insurance premiums will be on the models you like. If appropriate, you've compared financing or leasing terms, and have a good idea of the value of your current car. You're now ready for the final step: negotiating a great deal and taking delivery of your new vehicle.

The dealership experience, however, is what many people feel is the most stressful part of the car-buying process. As we've said before, buying a new car can be more like a game of high-stakes poker—with its bluffs, calls, and folds—than a straightforward commercial transaction. If you use a methodical, step-by-step approach and don't let your emotions rule the day, you can maintain control of the process and avoid being manipulated or confused by the dealership staff.

The balance of this book will show you how to play a winning hand by introducing you to the strategies CONSUMER REPORTS has learned while buying more than 60 vehicles a year for testing. In this section, we will walk you through the process of selecting a dealer, bargaining for the best overall purchase terms, and completing the transaction without fraying your nerves. In this chapter, we will give you an initial lay of the land by covering:

- The best time to buy
- The different types of dealerships and other car-buying outlets
- How to select dealerships
- How dealerships make their money
- Who's who in the dealership
- How to find dealerships that have the vehicle you want

## The Best Time To Buy

It used to be that bargain hunters waited for midsummer to start their shopping because that's when dealers were eager to clear inventories in time for September's new-model introductions. This is still the right time for many cars, but now increasing numbers of new models are being introduced throughout the year, and so the discount season is year-round.

Depending on the brand, salespeople face monthly or quarterly sales quotas, through which they get financial incentives for selling a certain number of vehicles. That means that during the last week of the month or quarter, particularly on the last weekend, some salespeople are hungry to make a deal. How they respond to that hunger can vary, though. Many times, the salesperson will negotiate a fair price quickly, without the usual rigmarole. Other times, the pressure to "sell, sell, sell" brings out the worst in a salesperson. He or she will roll out the hard-sell tactics and may want to spend time only with customers who will help make their quota and meet their goals. And that is not the same as meeting your goals.

Historically, the months of November, December, and January are the slowest sales months at new-car dealerships. Car buyers have more leverage then because dealers want to clear out inventory but relatively few people are coming to the showroom. Those who follow sales trends point out that one good time to look for bargains is still the period between the last week in November and the last week in December. This is when most shoppers are distracted by the holidays, and it's also the last chance dealers have to make a good showing for the calendar year. One auto analyst we talked to calls the last week of December "death valley" because so few people come in.

Some also say that you might try the month of March because the fiscal year for several automakers ends on March 31, and they tend to pile on incentives and discounts then. As a rule, avoid the month of April. That's generally been one of the most crowded selling periods since millions of car shoppers receive tax refunds that they use to help buy their next car. Historically, discounts have been sparsest in April.

## Keep an eye on sales incentives

While keeping an eye on the calendar may give you some advantage, it's probably more important to stay on top of any sales incentives being offered on the models you're considering. These days any car that isn't selling fast enough starts gathering incentives, such as rebates and/or special low-interest financing deals, to lure customers into the showroom—sometimes even shortly after it's introduced. These offers can save you hundreds or thousands of dollars.

Sales incentives are often heavily promoted in ads and TV commercials. You can also learn about current ones through other sources. Consumer Reports' New Car Price Reports and the online Consumer Reports' New Car Buying Kit list all national and regional incentives (see Appendix C).

Several car-buying Web sites (see Appendix A) also typically list incentives. Or you can call the dealership. If incentives are being offered, try to take advantage of them, but don't be overly influenced. This should not be your primary reason for choosing a vehicle.

Incentives are offered only for a specific period of time, so it's important to find out when they expire and what the terms are. Any buyer will qualify for a cash rebate, but as we've said before, only people with high credit scores will qualify for many low-interest financing offers. Also, see if incentives are being offered on other models you're considering and, if so, compare the terms.

You can accelerate your car-buying schedule to take advantage of an incentive, but we don't recommend that you rush right into the dealership if that means skipping important steps in the decision-making process. That's a recipe for buyer's remorse. Keep in mind that many vehicles that have had incentives in the past will likely have similar ones again in the future. For more information about sales incentives, see Chapter 7.

Also, keep your eye on the auto ads in your local newspapers for any seasonal sales events or inventory closeouts that are being offered.

Regardless of the best prognostication, however, the best time to buy is still a moving target. If you need or want a new car, go out and negotiate a good deal when you're ready—for many models, the time is always right.

## Should you buy last year's leftovers?

Another way to drive a bargain is to buy a "leftover," a vehicle from the last model year that is still unsold—for instance, buying a 2005 model after the 2006 replacement has arrived in the showroom. Logically, a leftover should be priced like a one-year-old, low-mileage used car, perhaps 25 percent less than its initial sticker price. That's because as soon as you buy it, it has accumulated a year's worth of depreciation almost regardless of the miles on the odometer. If you want to trade in that vehicle two years from now, it will be appraised as a three-year-old.

For that reason, leftovers aren't such a good deal if you plan to sell or trade in the car after a couple of years. But if you plan to drive it for five years or more, or until it wears out, you can save quite a bit of money. On the downside, you may find a very limited selection—cars with few options or too many.

The last cars to be sold from any model year's inventory are probably the least desirable ones, but they'll have the best prices. Once again, if all you want is transportation, last year's models at a substantial discount are the way to go. If you shop for a leftover, start your bargaining at the current price of a one-year-old model. Those prices can be found at any of the used-car-pricing Web sites listed in Appendix A.

## How Dealerships Make Their Money

Don't feel sorry for a salesperson who pleads that the dealership won't make any money when you press for a good price on a vehicle. A dealership has more ways to earn profits on a new-car transaction than a minivan has cup holders, and everyone on the sales staff is in on the game. Profits are earned on the front end of the deal, when the car is sold, and on the back end, through the financing and after-sale options and service. Here are the many places where dealer profits are parked:

**Purchase price of the new car:** The biggest payday for new-car salespeople comes when a customer purchases a vehicle at MSRP because they can earn a hefty cut of the fully marked-up price. On a deal that nets the dealer a gross profit of some $3,000 for a car with an MSRP of $25,000, a sales rep can pocket what in the trade is reverently called a "pounder"—a $1,000 commission. Even when a car is sold at just a hair above the dealer-invoice price, the dealership can still make money, thanks to sales incentives offered by the manufacturer and other built-in payments, such as holdbacks. You should base your target price on what the dealer really paid for the vehicle, as described in Chapter 7, including the holdback and any dealer incentives.

## Do high-volume dealerships have an edge?

High-volume dealerships offer some advantages over smaller ones. First, they are likely to have a greater selection of trim levels and option packages, so there's a better chance that you will find the exact configuration you're looking for. You may also be able to get a lower price at a high-volume dealership, because it may be willing to take less profit on a particular vehicle in order to achieve its higher sales goals. High sales quotas give a dealership certain competitive advantages, such as volume discounts or the opportunity to order more of the hottest models.

Selling techniques at a high-volume dealership, however, can be as aggressive as its prices. The dealership staff can operate like a well-oiled machine to try to get back on financing, extras, and the trade-in any savings they give you on the vehicle's price.

**Trade-in:** Often there are bigger profits for the dealer who buys your old car in trade than there is in selling you a new car. The trade-in price you are offered is its lowball wholesale value. The dealer can often sell it off his used-car lot at a much higher price (see Chapter 8 for more on used-car pricing). If he opts to cash out right away, he can pocket a quick profit by selling it at auction to another used-car dealer.

**Financing:** Most dealerships work with a number of lenders and leasing companies in addition to the captive finance arm of the manufacturer who made the vehicle you're buying. When you arrange financing through one of the companies it represents, the dealership typically collects a fee for placing the loan and a small percentage of the earnings on the deal for the life of the transaction. The salesperson and the finance-and-insurance manager each pocket a commission for selling you the financing package.

**Options and extras:** There's profit in any optional equipment you add to the vehicle, from a pricey audio or navigation system to floor mats or a cargo net for the trunk. Dealers profit handsomely, too, from so-called "packs"—the extras added by the dealership, including rust proofing, fabric protection, "predelivery inspection" charges, pinstripes, and paint sealant. For cars in high demand, they also add on what is often called "ADM," or additional dealer markup, which is pure profit for the dealer. Dealerships also pocket commissions when they sell such insurance products as credit life insurance and disability insurance and extended warranties. If you have not requested any of those items, simply put a line through them on the invoice and inform the salesperson you will not be paying for things you didn't request.

**Service:** Dealerships also make money by selling parts at full markup and charging top-dollar hourly rates for mechanics' labor every time you bring your car in for repairs or scheduled maintenance.

The bottom line is that even if you succeed in getting a price that's only a little over what the dealer paid, there are still several other areas of profit he can take advantage of. Similarly, for every buyer who gets a great deal, there are numerous others who provide the dealership with a hefty profit.

# Who's Who in the Dealership

Before you set out to visit dealerships, consider the cast of characters you're likely to meet at them. Each has a specialized role in the car-buying process. By knowing their roles and what to expect from them, you can be better prepared and more comfortable when you visit the showroom.

## The salesperson

This is the person who will likely greet you when you first set foot on the dealership's lot or with whom you talk when you call the dealership for pricing or vehicle information. The ideal salesperson will be well informed about the dealership's product line, a good listener, responsive to your comments and questions, and will have your best interests in mind throughout the dealership visit. Unfortunately, the ideal salesperson can be hard to find, so it's up to you to look out for your best interests.

Salespeople typically depend heavily on their sales commissions rather than on a salary or hourly pay. Most dealerships pay commissions to their sales people on a sliding scale, with the biggest percentage payouts made on sales that generate the greatest profit margin. In other words, the more profit the dealership makes on a vehicle, the higher the salesperson's commission becomes. You can see, therefore, that he or she can have a strong incentive to get you to pay top dollar for a vehicle.

You might reasonably think that it is the salesperson who holds the keys to your new car. In fact, salespeople can have little influence over the final terms of the deal you negotiate. In most dealerships, salespeople must meet strict monthly sales quotas in order to keep their jobs. Not surprisingly, turnover is high, and as a result, you can expect to find a lot of "green peas" (as inexperienced new salespeople are known in the trade) on the typical dealer's lot.

The pressure of sales quotas could make a salesperson, especially an inexperienced one, eager to cut a deal quickly, even if the profit is slim. That's partially why salespeople are seldom authorized to approve the terms of a sale.

## The closer

If the initial salesperson can't wrap up a deal quickly or at a comfortably profitable price, a closer might be brought in to help out. This is usually one of the dealership's most experienced senior salespeople, and is often used to help a "green pea" sales rep complete the transaction. It is the closer's job to fine-tune a deal that you and the initial salesperson have begun to shape. The closer is skilled at overcoming a buyer's resistance, although he may do this by creating the illusion that the terms are being sweetened while at the same time protecting, or even enhancing, the dealership's profits.

For example, a closer might demonstrate how you can lower the monthly cost of the car you want to buy while carefully neglecting to mention that the length of the loan or lease that will be used to finance the deal will be lengthened. Or he may disarmingly try to get you to agree to split the difference between your last offer and the price the dealership will accept.

Closers generally have more latitude than less-seasoned salespeople to commit the dealership on price. When you meet the closer, stick to your game plan and keep both hands on your wallet.

## The Internet sales manager

As more people have turned to the Internet to shop for cars, dealerships have responded by designating a sales employee to be an Internet sales manager. This person often provides the initial price quotes to Internet customers, conducts the e-mail follow-up, and brings the transaction to completion when the Web shopper stops by for the final negotiations.

## The general manager

The dealership's chief honcho, the general manager (GM) may stop by the salesperson's desk for a friendly meet-and-greet appearance at some point during your showroom visit. He wields his real authority out of sight in a private office, which can overlook the sales floor. The GM oversees the showroom action, and it is he who has ultimate authority to commit the dealership to the terms of a deal. When the salesperson disappears for long periods, the GM is typically the person with which he is conferring.

## The finance and insurance manager

You may never meet him, but the "F&I guy" may have more influence on what you pay for your vehicle than any other showroom employee. It is the finance-and-insurance manager who determines what credit terms you will be offered and draws up the loan or lease contract, making him, in effect, the architect of the profits on the deal you and the salesperson negotiated.

In addition to structuring the financial terms with the all-important interest rate or lease money factor and term of the loan or lease, the finance-and-insurance officer sells extended warranty programs, arranges gap insurance on leases, and adds extras to the vehicle preparation that can run to hundreds of dollars. The financial products procedures generated by the F&I department can add more than 25 percent to a dealership's total revenue. If you relax and let down your guard when dealing with the F&I guy, you risk blowing what might otherwise be a great deal.

### The service manager

A friendly, smooth-functioning service department can make a big difference in how satisfied you will be with your new vehicle.

While you're at the dealership, have the salesperson introduce you to the service manager. Ask him how much the dealership charges per hour for labor, and about the availability of loaners and other dealer courtesies, such as shuttle rides to mass transit when you bring your car in for scheduled checkups or repairs.

Keep in mind, however, that you can have your car serviced at any of the brand's dealerships; it doesn't have to be the one from which you bought the vehicle. Any mechanic certified by the manufacturer whose vehicle you purchase is authorized to do warranty repairs, and any competent garage or service station can handle routine maintenance. (See Chapter 18 for more information about vehicle servicing.)

## Selecting Your Dealerships

You can often get the best deal by pitting dealerships against each other in a bidding war. If possible, plan to get quotes from at least three dealerships for each car on your short list. For instance, if you're interested in buying a Honda Accord, contact three Honda dealerships that have the exact trim level and option configuration you're looking for. If you're also interested in, say, a Ford Focus, contact several Ford dealers to hammer out the lowest price you can get on that model.

Recommendations from friends and families are still a good way to select which dealerships you want to work with. Alternately, you can pick out dealerships from traditional sources such as the local Yellow Pages or by using the Internet. Many car-buying Web sites allow you to get quotes from dealerships by e-mail. These usually aren't the rock-bottom price you could get through smart negotiating, but they can provide a starting point to see how dealerships compare (see Appendix A).

The key is to find out which dealerships have the exact vehicle configuration you're looking for, as discussed in the next section.

## Reach beyond your home territory

If you live in an area where dealers are few and far between, you may want to consider making a special trip to a more competitive major urban center where you can scout out the offerings of several dealerships. Even if you do live in a major metropolitan area, you might also think about incorporating a car-shopping expedition into an upcoming business trip or a visit to another city, where local competition among dealers may be more intense.

To find the location of dealerships, all manufacturer Web sites include dealer-locator tools. After you enter your ZIP code, you'll get a list of all of the brand's dealerships in your area, along with their addresses, phone numbers, e-mail links, directions, and often maps and the distance in miles from your area.

For out-of-town searches, you could enter a center-city ZIP code in the metro area you plan to visit and request the names and contact information for all relevant dealerships.

## Check the Better Business Bureau

You also might want to check the Better Business Bureau to see if there have been any customer complaints about specific dealerships. Individual reports on dealerships can be found on the Bureau's Web site (*http://search.bbb.org/dealersearch.html*) by entering a ZIP code and a mile radius in which you want to search. The report provides general information about the dealership, registers how many complaints have been filed against the dealer over the past one to three years, and reports whether the issues were satisfactorily resolved.

Some Web sites, such as dealerrater.com, provide feedback on dealerships, but there's really no way of knowing who is submitting this feedback, or where it comes from.

# Find Out Who Has Your Vehicle

Through your research and test drive, you settled on the best model, trim level, and options for your needs and budget. Now you need to determine which dealerships have (or can get) the exact vehicle configuration you want. If it's a popular configuration, you shouldn't have any problems. But if it's a configuration that most dealerships don't carry, you may have to look at other alternatives. Ideally, you want to find several dealerships from which you can get competing prices.

The quickest way to do this is to call or e-mail the dealerships. In many cases, you can also visit dealership or automaker Web sites and search the inventories of nearby dealerships to see if they have what you want. But you can't always count on these inventories being up to date. So you should double-check by phone or e-mail anyway to make sure what you find in their inventory listings is still in stock.

Be clear about the trim level you prefer and the exact options in which you're interested, and ask for the vehicle's sticker price to confirm that it matches what you calculated when you figured your target price (see

Chapter 7). If there is a significant difference in price, double-check the trim and options point by point. Sometimes, if a dealership doesn't have the exact configuration you want, a salesperson may still act as if it does while quoting you the price for a different trim or set of options.

If the configuration is right, but you find the sticker prices at various dealerships are consistently different from what you calculated, you may have to redefine your configuration. Perhaps an option you wanted is only available as part of a package, raising the price to more than you had expected. Or a feature may be available only with a higher trim level than you had anticipated.

You also may find that few dealerships carry the configuraton you want. In this case, you have several alternatives:

- Work only with the few dealerships that have the version you want. This may mean traveling farther than you anticipated, and perhaps having fewer dealerships to work with when gathering bids.
- Work with dealerships that can get the vehicle from another dealership. Keep in mind, though that you won't be able to see the vehicle you're buying before you complete the deal. And the dealership staff may not bargain as aggressively on a vehicle that's not on their lot.
- Change your expectations to a configuration that's more widely available. You may decide to drop some features, or accept a higher price to make sure you get all the features you want, even if it means getting some you don't really need.
- Special-order the vehicle from the factory, if possible. (See Chapter 4 for the pros and cons of this option.)

If you're flexible about how the vehicle is outfitted or its color, it'll be easier to locate dealerships. But be sure you calculate a new target price for any other versions you're considering. If a vehicle comes with optional features that you're willing to include but are not on your list of "must haves," increase your target price to include these options. It's best to use the dealer-invoice price for these options and mark it up about 4 percent. Of course, if the car lacks a feature you hoped to have but can live without, drop your target price by the appropriate amount.

# Get Initial Prices

While you're on the phone or e-mailing with each dealership, you can begin inquiring about their initial prices. Make several points clear: Tell each that you're calling several dealerships, that you've have done your pricing research, that you know what the dealer paid for the vehicle, and that you're ready to buy from the dealership that gives you the lowest price.

Try to get at least three prices for any vehicle you're considering. Make sure that the prices are an apples-to-apples comparison; if not, you need to know exactly how the vehicles differ.

Getting initial prices by phone imposes a time limit on the discussion and allows you to keep an arm's length from the salesperson, so you begin to size up him or her without getting sucked into the sales tactics.

A salesperson may be reluctant to discuss price over the phone, urging you to come to the showroom to get the best deal. And he may be right. You may not get the dealership's rock-bottom price this way. But it can show you what an easily obtainable price will be for the car and can give you insight into how aggressive—or obnoxious—a particular salesperson will be when you get deeper into negotiating.

It also signals to the salespeople that you are intent on getting the best price, so if you show up at their showrooms, they will already know that you've been talking price with competing dealerships.

You can check these prices against any quotes that you got through car-buying Web sites to see how competitive they are. You can also see how they compare with your target price.

By knowing how much the dealer paid for the vehicle, you know how much lower the dealership could go.

# Make Appointments

Once you've identified the dealerships you'll visit, call ahead to schedule an appointment to speak with a salesperson. There are many advantages to prearranging your visit time:

- **More flexibility, less hassle.** You can arrive at the dealership ahead of time, scout out what's on the lot, and take a peek in the service area. If another salesperson offers to help, you can simply say you have a scheduled appointment with one of the other salespeople, whom you'll be meeting shortly.

- **You're in charge.** You can also arrange for the all-important initial negotiations to get started on your terms. When you schedule your visit, make it clear that you have no more than one hour. Putting a limit on your visit sends the message that you do not expect to be kept waiting for someone to help you. It will also help avoid having to endure the kind of delays salespeople are prone to use to keep you in the showroom and wear down your resistance.

- **Comfort and convenience.** Prearranging your appointments will allow you to synchronize your visits to several dealerships at a pace that you find comfortable. You should aim to start with any dealership that has an advertised promotion on deals completed by a certain date. Making that dealership an early stop ensures that you'll have time to take advantage of a special deal. If a manufacturer rebate or low-interest financing is in effect, make sure you allow yourself time to complete the buying process before the sales incentive expires. Waiting until the last day an incentive is valid puts unnecessary pressure on you.

Whom should you ask to see? If you previously visited one of the dealerships on your list for a test drive and were satisfied with the salesperson who helped you on that visit, by all means, ask for that person again. Doing so sends a signal that you are someone who goes out of your way to be considerate and expects the collaboration to be reciprocated. Likewise, if you've been in contact with a sales representative via e-mail or by telephone when collecting information on prices and vehicles in inventory, schedule a time when that salesperson will be in the showroom.

## Familiarity Breeds Comfort

Knowing how a dealership works, who the players are, and what to expect once you're in the showroom can make you more comfortable with the car-buying process. Car buyers typically find that after visiting a few dealerships, the process becomes easier, there is less intimidation, and they are better able to handle the various sales tactics they encounter. This is why, aside from getting competing bids, it's good to visit several dealerships and work with different salespeople before you finally buy.

## Dealership Visit Tool Kit

Here's what you should have in your car-shopping tool kit when you head off for your dealer visits:

—— A sheet that shows the exact configuration, including trim level and options, that you're looking for

—— Consumer Reports' New Car Price Report or other printout that shows any current sales incentives

—— Your target price for the configuration you want (see Chapter 7), backed up by the CR Wholesale Price (from a New Car Price Report), if applicable, and any other competitive prices that you've gathered (such as from Internet sales sites or other dealerships)

—— Printouts that show the standard features and options for all trim levels (also included in CR's New Car Price Reports)

—— Notes from your test drives

—— Printouts of e-mails from dealers who responded to your online price quote requests

—— Dealer advertisements for current time-sensitive special offers or limited-availability models

—— Estimates of what your trade-in is worth

—— Calculator

—— Pad of paper or notebook and pen or pencil

—— Cell phone for private calls you may want to make from the dealer's lot

—— Two sets of keys for your current car (one for the dealer to use for a trade-in inspection; the spare is in case the dealer "misplaces" the first set and you want to leave)

## Worksheet: The Dealership Visit (copy for each visit)

Dealership name          _____

Date of visit            _____

Salesperson              _____

Phone number             _____

Vehicle model/trim line  _____

Vehicle stock number/Vehicle Identification Number

                    _____

Options packages         _____

Monroney (sticker) price _____

Price quoted             _____

Your target price        _____

Follow-up notes

_____

_____

_____

_____

# 14

# Pros & Cons of Buying Online

**The Internet has made researching** your car purchase easier than ever. A 2004 survey conducted by CONSUMER REPORTS shows that most new- and used-car buyers now turn to the Web to gather auto information prior to buying. In addition, more and more consumers are going through car-buying Web sites even to make their purchase. Market researchers who track Web trends at Jupiter Research forecast that nearly 13 percent of all car sales—about 7.8 million vehicles—will result from Internet leads by 2006.

Throughout this book we tell you where to turn to find information on the Internet. In this chapter, we take a look at the advantages and disadvantages of using a car-buying Web site.

In general, car-buying Web sites allow you to specify the model, trim level, and options you're interested in and to get price quotes for that specific vehicle from dealerships in your area. Each site is contracted with a network of dealerships. Typically, when you ask for a price quote online, your information is forwarded to appropriate dealerships close to your ZIP code who will then contact you with what they feel is a competitive price.

There are some obvious advantages to this system, as well as some not-so-obvious disadvantages. For starters, the price quotes are free to consumers and there's no obligation to buy, so it's an easy way to get a sense of what the price might be for the vehicle configuration you want.

On the other hand, the quote you get may not be the lowest price. Even if you get quotes through different Web sites, they may be contracted with the same dealerships in your area, and therefore they're not very competitive. Of course, you will still need to go to the dealership to wrap up the details face to face, so you will still have to confront many of the same negotiating pressures when discussing a trade-in, financing, options, dealer extras, and so on.

Using these Web sites effectively requires organization, diligence—and a healthy dose of skepticism. In this chapter, we'll be examining more in-depth the pros and cons of using these sites, and we'll discuss:

- How car-buying Web sites work as intermediaries between you and the car dealers
- How the virtual "showroom" levels the playing field for consumers
- The limits of how far you can go on a virtual vehicle shopping trip
- A 10-step strategy for organizing an online shopping expedition to optimize your chances of getting the vehicle you want at a price you're willing to pay

## Welcome to the Virtual Showroom

There are about 30 Web sites through which you can buy a new or used vehicle (see Appendix A). Because they operate differently, we'll talk about new and used-car sites separately.

**New-car Web sites:** Most new-car sites use a similar process to provide you with a price quote. You input the make and model of the vehicle you're interested in and enter your ZIP code. You then need to specify the trim level, color, and any options you want. In some cases, you'll be asked when you plan to buy and how you intend to finance the vehicle, but this information is typically optional.

You also enter your name, address, phone number, and e-mail address where you want the information sent. Your request is then routed to one or more dealerships in the site's affiliated dealer network. Usually you can expect to receive a quick e-mail confirmation that your request has been received, followed within a day or two by a price quote. As we said, you will still have to go to the dealership to complete the purchase and pick up the car.

There are exceptions to this process. For instance, in addition to providing conventional price quotes from affiliated dealerships, CarsDirect also offers no-haggle prices that have been previously negotiated with contracted dealerships. If you select this option, instead of getting price quotes from local dealerships, you will be assigned a "CarsDirect specialist" who will find the vehicle you want from inventory in the CarsDirect dealership network at the price quoted on the Web site and will arrange for you to pick up the car at the dealership.

The site includes a "low-price guarantee" that states if, within three days after purchasing the vehicle, you find a lower price for the same vehicle identically equipped, CarsDirect.com will refund the difference between the price you paid and the advertised or other dealer's price or, at the company's discretion, buy the vehicle back.

This system further streamlines the car-buying process, but, as is typical with no-haggle prices, with a little serious negotiating as described in Chapter 15, you can probably do better on your own.

Some dealership sites allow customers to bid on a vehicle by entering a price you'd be willing to pay. Naming your own price may seem like an appealing way to cut to the chase, but there is little to be gained—and much bargaining leverage to be lost—by letting a dealer know what you'd be willing to pay before you've actually visited the showroom and seen the car.

**Used-car Web sites:** Sites that sell used cars are essentially the electronic equivalent of a newspaper's classified ad section, except that they list vehicles nationwide. Sellers buy placements on the Web sites and buyers can search the sites for vehicles in which they're interested.

Typically, you're asked to enter the make and model you're interested in, your price range, and the region (usually based on your ZIP code) where you'd like to shop. You then get a list of vehicles that fit your buying criteria, along with the sellers' e-mail addresses or phone numbers. When you zero in on a vehicle that interests you, the Web sites usually present photos supplied by the seller and provide more detail about the vehicle's condition and how it is equipped than could fit in the most generous newspaper classified. If you like what you see or have questions you'd like to have the owner answer, you are able to e-mail the seller from a link on the vehicle's description screen.

Because many sellers are car dealers, most of these specialized sites offer direct links to the dealerships' Web sites. Many services also let you place a classified ad for selling your old car, either free or for a small fee.

One important quality that differentiates used-car Web sites is their depth of inventory and search features. Autobytel, for instance, lets you search all used vehicles in its database or focus only on certified pre-owned vehicles, which are backed by a warranty. The site also lets you sign up to receive e-mail notifications when the make and model vehicles that interest you are added to Autobytel's inventory.

Online auctions (eBay Motors is by far the largest) are another route. The auction system is a little different from standard dickering over price. Once you make a bid, it's considered a contract and you are obligated to complete the purchase if you win. While that means you can snap up a bargain, it also means that you can't get out of the deal unless the seller has made some serious misrepresentation. And it could mean you won't be able to inspect the car before you agree to buy it. However, there are vehicle inspection services available.

If you plan to buy a car you see advertised online, limit the search to the area within which you're willing to travel to inspect a vehicle. No matter how much of the transaction you conduct by phone or e-mail, it's important that you still inspect the vehicle in person and take it for a test drive. For more information on inspecting a used car, see Chapter 6.

One problem we've noticed with online classified-ad-type offerings is the freshness of the information. If sellers don't constantly update their Web offerings as vehicles get sold, the sites grow stale and inaccurate. That can make locating even common models a challenge. Always call before visiting any seller, whether a dealership or a private party, to make sure the vehicle you're looking for is still in stock.

When shopping for a used car online, you may see offers to check out a vehicle's history in order to see if there are any hidden problems. These links take you to Web sites for Carfax or AutoCheck.com, where you can obtain a vehicle history report for a fee. These reports can be helpful in tipping you off to certain problems, such as an odometer rollback, salvage title, or other unseen problems, but don't assume that a clean history report is a guarantee that there are no hidden problems. These reports are only as good as the database information they're drawn from, and this may be incomplete.

## Advantages of Buying Online

Here are some of the many ways that shopping for a new car online can work to your advantage:

- **Save time and energy.** Initiating the buying process at a keyboard in the comfort of your own home rather than on the dealer's turf lets you travel at Web speed to consult online with dealerships about price and vehicle availability. You can identify dealers that have the specific make and model you want in stock and compare prices from many more dealerships than you could easily cover by physically traveling from lot to lot.

- **Preserve your identity.** Everyone is equal on the Internet. Studies have found that groups of consumers, notably women, minorities, and young adults, are routinely subjected to condescension and discrimination in the auto-buying process, and often end up paying higher prices when they venture onto dealers' lots. Communicating with dealers via online car shopping sites allows you to keep to a minimum the amount of personal information you are obligated to share. Most of the car-buying sites require only that you provide your name, an e-mail address, and a phone number so dealers in their network can respond to your request. The dealers don't have to know whether you are young or old, short or tall, male or female, or an English speaker; nor do they have to know the color of your skin.

- **Extend your reach.** If you live in a rural community or a small town where dealerships are few and competition is scarce, you can use online shopping sites to test the market in other areas, collecting dealers' bids and vetting their responses. Do this by entering the ZIP code of another area when requesting price quotes rather than your area. Armed with names of dealer sales representatives selling real vehicles at known prices, you can schedule a productive car-buying trip instead of settling only for the few local choices or setting out blindly on a pressure-packed, expensive journey with uncertain prospects.

- **Narrow your choices.** Dealership price quotes can tell you a lot about which vehicle configurations are readily available and which will be harder to find. If you get a lot of quotes for a different configuration than what you entered, this could be a signal that your configuration will be hard to locate, making it difficult to generate competing bids.

- **Size up the salespeople.** The dealership staffer who responds to your online price-quote request will probably be the dealership's specially des-ignated Internet sales manager, and this person will play a big role in deter-mining the quality of your vehicle purchase experience. By judging the quality of information they send, you will be able to determine whether the dealership is one from which you would be interested in buying a car. After sending a request for a price quote, it's reasonable to expect a time-ly, complete, and courteous response from the dealership. Ideally, the information it provides will describe the vehicle or vehicles that match your specifications, itemizing any options that affect the ultimate cost. It will also provide a precise—and competitive—offering price, indicating any surcharges, such as destination or document-processing fees, that will enter into the final calculation of what you can expect to pay. Vague invi-tations to stop in to chat or, worse, unsolicited phone calls bugging you to schedule a test drive are good indicators of dealerships to avoid.

- **Compare prices.** Getting price quotes from a range of car-buying sites is a good way to see what dealerships are trying to get for a specific vehi-cle and size up how aggressive dealerships will be. Keep in mind that these quotes may not be the lowest price you can get. You can always negotiate further either in the dealership or by e-mail. See Chapter 15 for negotiating techniques.

## Speed Bumps in the Online Lane

Your new-car shopping trip might begin online, but it cannot end there. There are several basic steps that cannot be completed by shopping for a vehicle via the Internet.

- **Closing the deal.** State franchise laws designed to protect local car deal-ers bar you from actually completing a vehicle purchase via the Internet. As intriguing and helpful as cyber-shopping can be, you will still have to complete your vehicle purchase face to face with a salesperson.
- **Getting the vehicle you want.** Online shopping is still a blunt instru-

ment. Despite your best efforts to describe as precisely as possible the vehicle model, trim line, and options you are seeking when requesting a dealer's online bid, you cannot be sure until you visit the showroom and inspect the vehicle against the dealership's paperwork that your quote actually covers the car you want.

- **Paying the lowest price.** As we mentioned, shopping online is a good way to size up the asking prices for different vehicles, but you can find out how much you'll actually pay only by visiting car dealerships and working out the price with a salesperson. Even if a dealership has a car that matches your preferences, the online price quote is valid only for the specific vehicle in stock and remains in effect only as long as it remains unsold, until a purchase agreement is signed, and only when you hand over a deposit.

# 10 Smart Steps to Buying Your Car Online

Anyone who has ever mounted a Web-based fact-finding mission knows only too well that what begins as a simple search for answers to reasonably straightforward questions can quickly lead into a tangle of contradictory sources and information cul-de-sacs. Like any Internet research project, online car shopping can easily drown you in a sea of data unless you take care to plan strategically. The following step-by-step guide will help you steer an efficient path to the information you need to make a smart buy online.

### Step 1: Know your choices before you log on for bids

Whether you buy online or not, it's critical that you do your homework before you contact dealerships. You should narrow your choices, identify the vehicles that are right for you in terms of needs and price, and determine which features and options you want before getting prices.

Follow the advice in chapters 1 through 4 to make sure you know exactly the vehicle you want.

Just as you wouldn't think of sitting down at a salesperson's desk to negotiate a deal until you knew whether you were in the market for, say, an SUV or a sports car, you shouldn't waste time soliciting online price quotes until you're clear on what you want.

## Step 2: Be precise about the vehicle you want

The request you submit should specify as nearly as possible the precise configuration of the vehicle you want—that's the way to ensure the price quotes you get provide you information you can act on. Give as much detail about the vehicle as the site allows, and if you have questions that can influence the response, use the comments box that many car-buying sites offer to bring your special requests to the dealerships' attention.

If you are still undecided in your preference between two or more models, there is nothing to stop you from soliciting price quotes for each. To make the most informed price-to-feature comparison, be sure you're comparing apples to apples. Try to be as clear and detailed as you can in how you describe the vehicles you want to compare, and try to equip them as similarly as possible.

You may end up discovering that your choices are limited if the vehicle you inquire about is loaded with premium options, since dealers try to stock vehicles configured in a way that make them likeliest to sell quickly. For more information about features and options, see Chapter 4.

## Step 3: Protect your privacy

When you venture online to shop for a car, you will be required to share personal information that will circulate from the online shopping sites to their affiliated dealerships and beyond for as long as the recipients of your information find it useful. Long after your new car ends up in a recycling center, your name, address, phone number, and e-mail contact may reside in commercial databases to resurface as junk mail and spam for years to come.

You will want to be conscious of how much information about you is gathered in the online car-buying process. Of course, you should take time to read privacy policies of any Web site you use. Confine the amount of information you share about yourself to the minimum required.

Many of the shopping sites do not insist on having your home address, and some will allow you to use initials instead of a full first name—an option that may appeal especially to women sensitive to possible gender discrimination. When your online car-buying venture ends, take steps to remove your name from e-mail lists.

More strenuous efforts to safeguard your privacy may be warranted. If your employer permits, you may want to provide an office or business phone number, or consider signing up for a free Hotmail or Yahoo! e-mail account exclusively for this purpose. Segregating all of your e-mail exchanges with dealerships in a separate account has the added advantage of making it easier for you to track their responses and follow-ups. When your online vehicle search ends, you can abandon the account. If you don't log on, Hotmail becomes inactive after 30 days, with all folders deleted. In another 90 days, it's discontinued. Yahoo! becomes inactive if you don't log on for more than four months.

## Step 4: Optimize your coverage

The true power of cybershopping for a car comes from your ability to contact and solicit prices from several dealerships with a minimum of travel and inconvenience. To tap that potential, you will want to get your request out to as many different dealerships that sell the vehicle you want as possible. Keep in mind that online price-service sites frequently share a common corporate parent or are affiliated in partnerships that serve identical dealership networks (see page 287).

To get the breadth of dealer coverage you want, choose one Web site from a few of the big online shopping "families." Add to this the site of each manufacturer whose vehicle you are considering in order to pick up the local dealer-franchisees that are not affiliated with the price quote Web sites.

Because vehicle trim levels and dealership inventories and pricing vary based on local competition, you also may want to extend your geographic reach, using the same group of Web sites to test what dealers are prepared to offer in two or more different markets. As we mentioned, this is easily accomplished by submitting separate requests using ZIP codes in each of the markets you want to explore.

## Step 5: Plan a realistic schedule you can live with

The process of shopping for a car online is supposed to work to your convenience. Still, while soliciting an online car price is as simple as sending an e-mail, it is easy to underestimate how long it will take to assemble all of the information you need to make an informed buying decision and to act on it. When you fill out the online bid request forms, some sites will ask how soon you anticipate completing your purchase—typically, within 48 hours, a week, or 30 days. The seeming urgency on the part of the site operators is to discourage idle inquiries and to ensure that dealerships get motivated, serious leads.

You want to convey that you're ready to deal and that you'll respond to competitive offers in a timely way, but setting too short a time frame can put you under pressure to make rushed decisions. Too long a time frame, however, can cause you to lose a potentially attractive buying opportunity on vehicles that may currently be in dealers' inventories.

How much time do you need? The interval from the time you submit your request on the shopping site until you get a dealer response should be no more than 24 to 48 hours, but the process only begins there. The initial information you get from the dealerships may be incomplete in many respects. For one thing, a dealership may have based its quote on a vehicle that differs significantly from the one you had in mind, including options like a moon roof or leather upholstery you didn't want, for example, or having a manual transmission instead of the automatic you asked for. Or the price you receive may have omitted important details like destination charges or a rebate that may be in effect.

You will need time—perhaps several days—to submit your follow-up questions and get a satisfactory reply. Finally, after vetting all of the information you collect and weighing which price quotes most closely match what your research revealed to be a competitive offer, you will want to arrange showroom visits to see the vehicles on which the quotes were based and begin talking with salespeople.

## Step 6: Preserve your flexibility on financing and trade-in

Many car-buying Web sites will ask how you are thinking of paying for your new vehicle and how you plan to dispose of your old one. If you do tip your hand about these key aspects of the car-buying process, you could put yourself at a disadvantage later on when the real negotiations heat up. If you indicate that you are leaning toward leasing the vehicle or are open to financing through a loan, for example, a dealer will use that information to structure a deal that emphasizes what appear to be low monthly payments but have you paying more than you would if you purchased the vehicle for cash. However you ultimately decide to finance your car acquisition, you should preserve your bargaining leeway by indicating, for purposes of requesting a price quote, that you intend to be a cash buyer.

Likewise there's no advantage in letting the dealerships—or the operators of the online sites who are also often in the business of selling used cars—know what you are planning to do with your old car. No dealership can give you an accurate appraisal of what your car is worth in trade until it's inspected. Introducing the trade-in issue at this stage can only confuse and complicate your mission to get the lowest price for the new vehicle you want.

## Step 7: Have the dealership communicate by e-mail

Soon after you hit the "submit" button on your online price-quote requests, you can usually expect dealership responses to start pouring in with a flood of figures, vehicle descriptions, names and phone numbers of salespeople, and limited-time offers—some of them more detailed and complete than others. The challenge of keeping good records on what the dealerships have to offer is compounded with the traffic generated by responses for every additional Web site you consult and for each vehicle make, model, and trim line you are considering.

Be sure to save copies of each of the dealership e-mails you receive in a special folder in your e-mail account that you create specifically for this purpose. Storing each e-mail as it comes in ensures that you will have an electronic document you can print out to show salespeople when it's time to visit the showrooms.

## Step 8: Follow up to fill in missing information and fire up the competition

Having gathered and sorted through all of the dealership offers, you can now use this information as the basis to initiate a qualifying round of negotiation via e-mail to determine which dealership can expect a personal visit from you. The responding dealerships should identify one or more specific vehicles in inventory that closely match the one you're interested in. If they haven't done that in their initial communications with you, ask the dealership if you can be sent a detailed description of the vehicle's exterior and interior color scheme, engine and transmission, and list of any optional equipment. Be sure to ask for the vehicle identification number (VIN). If the salesperson can't supply it, assume the car isn't at the dealership. A general assurance from the dealership that there are plenty of cars like the one you inquired about currently in stock is not a helpful answer.

On the important issue of price, if a dealership neglects to send you a quote for a vehicle you want, let it know that you will be scheduling showroom visits only with dealerships that name a competitive price. If one dealership's offer is higher than another's, you may want to let the higher-cost dealership know, without specifying exactly what the lower-cost dealer offered, that you've seen better prices and that you expect him to come down if he wants to complete a sale.

# Worksheet: Dealership Online Price Quote

| Price-quote site visited | | Date/time bid | |
| Site name and URL | Vehicle requested | request entered | |
|---|---|---|---|
| | | | |
| | | | |
| | | | |
| | | | |
| | | | |

| Dealer's offer | | | | |
| Vehicle ID | MSRP | Invoice | Target price | |
|---|---|---|---|---|
| | | | | |
| | | | | |
| | | | | |
| | | | | |
| | | | | |

| Dealership name | Dealer response<br>Address/phone | Date/time<br>of response | Name of<br>salesperson |
|---|---|---|---|
| | | | |
| | | | |
| | | | |
| | | | |
| | | | |

| Price quoted | Restrictions/<br>limitations | Rate dealer responsiveness<br>1 (fair) to 3 (good) point scale | |
|---|---|---|---|
| | | | |
| | | | |
| | | | |
| | | | |
| | | | |

An initial round of bidding still doesn't lock you into a specific price, and it can give you more insight as to which dealerships will work with you on getting the lowest price. (See Chapter 15 for more information.)

## Step 9: Use a worksheet to track all price quotes from dealerships

In order to help you stay on top of the dealers' responses, we've developed the worksheet on the previous pages to help you organize the key information, prices, and specifics about the vehicles dealerships have offered to sell. This makes it possible for you to compare the terms of all the offers at a glance.

## Step 10: Schedule your showroom visits

By now, you've gone just about as far as the online resources can take you, and it's time to visit the showrooms to finalize the deal. Although the price quotes and the availability of the vehicle that best matches your wishes will be the primary factors in determining which dealerships you visit, you should also consider a dealership's courtesy and responsiveness.

When you call to schedule your appointment, make sure the vehicle you have been discussing via e-mail is still available and ready to be seen. If possible, see if the dealership is willing to send you a copy of the vehicle's invoice with all standard and optional equipment identified (and prices omitted, if they prefer), including the vehicle identification number. Before you head off to the showroom, print out copies of the e-mail exchanges you have had with the dealership and any notes you compiled about the deal. Finally, relax. With all of the ground you've covered online, you are already well ahead in the car-buying game.

For more information about scheduling appointments and preparing for the dealership experience, see Chapter 13.

# Car-Buying Web Sites

Many new-car-buying sites are owned and operated by the same company and share the same dealership network. It's helpful to know this and the approximate number of dealerships with which they are contracted when trying to get competitive price quotes. Sites that sell used cars do not provide price quotes; vehicles are listed by sellers. The following are listed in alphabetical order by network affiliation:

| Company and Web sites | Types of car | No. of dealerships in new-car network | Network affiliation |
|---|---|---|---|
| autobytel.com | new, used | 6,000 | autobytel |
| autosite.com | new, used | 6,000 | autobytel |
| autoweb.com | new, used | 6,000 | autobytel |
| carsmart.com | new, used | 6,000 | autobytel |
| car.com | new, used | 6,000 | autobytel |
| carbargains | new | 21,640* | Any dealer |
| autovantage.com | new, used | 4,000 | AutoUSA Dealer Network |
| autousa.com | new | 4,000 | AutoUSA Dealer Network |
| carsdirect.com | new, used | 3,000+ | CarsDirect |
| autos.com | new, used | 3,000+ | CarsDirect |
| cars.com | new, used | 9,000 | Classified Ventures |
| autotrader.com | new, used | 5,500 | Cobalt/Dealix |
| autos.yahoo.com | new, used | 5,500 | Cobalt/Dealix |
| car-cost.com | new | 5,500 | Cobalt/Dealix |
| invoicedealers.com | new | 5,500 | Cobalt/Dealix |

| Company and Web sites | Types of car | No. of dealerships in new-car network | Network affiliation |
|---|---|---|---|
| dealerscompete youwin.com | new | 5,500 | Cobalt/Dealix |
| womanmotorist.com | new, used | 5,500 | Cobalt/Dealix |
| newcarinsider.com | new | 5,500 | Cobalt/Dealix |
| ebaymotors.com | new, used | NA | eBay |
| edmunds.com | new, used | 21,640* | Edmunds.com |
| kbb.com | new, used | 21,000 | Kelley Blue Book |
| nadaguides.com | new, used | 1,200 | NADA |
| vehix.com | new, used | 1,600 | Vehix.com |

*NADA figure

All sites listed here are free except for carbargains.com, which charges a fee for service.

# 15

# Negotiate the Best Price

**Effective negotiation** is the key to getting the best price on a car. But many people are understandably intimidated by the negotiating process. In our culture, we don't get much practice at wrangling over a marked price. So we can feel uncomfortable when that's expected.

Moreover, auto salespeople are pros who deal with many car buyers each week and have well-established routines for maximizing their dealership's profit on each sale. By contrast, you're likely an amateur at the bargaining game who buys a new vehicle every few years or so.

Still, you don't have to be a good negotiator to get a great deal. You simply have to know how the game is played. As a well-prepared buyer who has done your research and followed the steps in this book, you have the tools and insight to use the car-buying system to your own advantage. There are a few points to remember:

**Ignore the sticker price.** The sticker price is an overinflated figure that's intentionally set high. This gives the dealership's sales staff room to give you a "discount" that will make it seem like you're getting a great price. For confirmation, you need only look at the hundreds or thousands of dollars of cash rebates that some models carry, even shortly after they're introduced. Only models that are in high demand command the full sticker price.

**Work up from what the dealer paid.** By knowing what the dealer paid for the vehicle, you know how much profit margin he has to work with and you can more easily tell if a price you're being quoted is a good one or a token discount. (See Chapter 7 for advice on how to set a target price.)

**Competition is crucial.** Nothing brings a price down faster than having another dealership compete for your business. A common sales tactic is for a salesperson to say that another buyer is interested in the same vehicle you are, with the not-so-subtle suggestion that you had better buy quickly. Well, you can play that game, too, by setting up a bidding war. By contacting different dealerships and gathering competitive prices, you send the message that the dealership better come through with its best price or risk losing your business.

**You have the ultimate control.** You can get up and walk out at any time. The last thing a salesperson wants to see is a promising customer heading for the door. If so, the price will sometimes drop another notch on the spot.

**The pressure is on them to sell you the car.** It's not on you to buy it. You can be as choosy as you want. It's their job to work for the sale.

**Practice, practice, practice.** Another benefit of contacting different dealerships to get competing quotes is that you get more comfortable talking with different salespeople. We've been told over and over by people who were initially put off by the dealership process that the more they worked with different salespeople, the more comfortable they became, and the more clearly they could see various sales tactics being used against them.

In this chapter, we'll show you the techniques that will allow you to wield your bargaining leverage with confidence. We'll cover:

- How to generate competition among dealerships that will work to your advantage
- How to set clear ground rules that let you take command
- How you can extract the best price from each dealership you visit
- How to know when it's time to walk away from a deal that's stalled
- When to discuss your trade-in

# Prepare for Your Dealership Visits

When you show up in a new-car showroom, you can bet that the salesperson knows what he or she wants out of you: the most profitable sale in the shortest possible time. By being prepared with the right information and knowing what to expect from the dealership staff, you can control the process from the time you set foot in the dealership until you drive away in your new vehicle.

When you do sit down with a salesperson, numbers will start flying at a fast and furious pace—prices for the base vehicle, for options and extras, destination charges, and special fees and taxes. The salespeople will be well-equipped with their numbers; you had better be the master of the ones that help you make your case for a better deal.

A good way to stay organized is to keep a separate folder on each model in which you're interested. You should have a sheet of paper that lists the exact model, trim level, engine and transmission configuration, standard features, and options you want, as well as your target price for the configuration you want.

If you've bought a Consumer Reports' New Car Price Report (see Appendix C), keep it handy so you can refer to the list of features (which includes both the retail and dealer-invoice prices), the CR Wholesale Price, and other key information. If not, go to the manufacturers' Web sites (see Appendix A) and print out lists of the standard features and options for each trim level, and highlight the ones you want. While you're there, print out the major specifications for each trim level as well. Having the information for all trim levels will help you make better on-the-spot decisions should the salesperson suggest a different trim level than you had planned on.

Once again, you should have researched your financing options and have a good idea of what competitive interest rates are at the time you want to buy. With a loan preapproval in hand, you will be free to concentrate on extracting the lowest price on the vehicle as a cash buyer and be better able to ignore the salesperson's efforts to have you focus on the monthly payment.

By knowing the duration of the financing and interest rate your lender will charge, you also will have a basis for comparing competitive financial terms a dealer may be able to offer after the price of the vehicle is agreed upon. Of course, if the dealer's financing terms do beat those for which you were preapproved by your own lender, there's nothing to stop you from grabbing the better deal.

Even if you aren't preapproved, it's important to know what terms other lenders are offering. This will help you better assess any special low-interest

## Tuning your attitude for savings

A salesman begins sizing you up as soon as you arrive at the dealership, and the price you pay for a vehicle could be affected by the attitude you present. While trying different buying strategies for a CONSUMER REPORTS article, we found that a shopper's attitude can make a difference in the price paid. An assertive shopper negotiated a price that was $1,800 lower than that negotiated by a more passive shopper (who felt uncomfortable negotiating) for the same vehicle at the same dealership.

When meeting the salesperson, it's important to be friendly and courteous, but also to present yourself as organized, informed, and firm on your objective—getting the vehicle you want at the lowest price.

## What if there aren't competing dealerships?

Some small towns may only have one dealership for any given brand. So, it's hard to generate competing bids from local sources. In this case, contact dealerships in nearby towns to get competing bids. You may find car-buying Web sites (see Appendix A) to be a convenient way of making first contact with these dealerships. Or go to your local library and look them up in the Yellow pages for surrounding areas.

This allows you to assess whether it's worth your while to drive out of your area to buy your new car. And even if it isn't, your local dealership doesn't have to know that.

financing deals the dealership may be offering and allow you to make good on-the-spot decisions, in case you don't qualify for the dealership's lowest rates. For more information on auto financing, see Chapter 10.

## Tips for making the dealership experience go smoothly

Many consumers find the idea of haggling with car dealers distasteful because it can be confrontational and combative. To get the best results, you will want to come across as courteous, knowledgeable, and businesslike. Above all, take your time. There is no need to reply to a question right away. Sit back and think. You should aim to behave like someone who is serious about buying, not a browser. Here are some "dos" and "don'ts" that CONSUMER REPORTS' expert shoppers have found worked best when they set out for their showroom visits:

- **Do bring your partner or another adult with you.** Anyone who will be involved in the purchase decision should be present for the negotiations, even if that person prefers not to take part actively in the discussions. Even if you are the only one involved in the purchase, consider bringing an adult friend along. You may find it helpful to have a second pair of ears to register what the salesperson tells you, and it can be convenient to have someone with you to play the role of the skeptic or to prod you to leave if you're being unnecessarily delayed or the salesperson isn't working toward your best interests.

- **Don't shop when you are tired or hungry.** Buying a car consumes a lot of energy and requires you to be alert. You don't want to try focusing on the details of the deal when you are fatigued, irritable, or thinking about when you will get your next meal.

- **Do dress neatly and comfortably.** Avoid wearing overly casual attire, like a T-shirt, shorts, and beach sandals, or flamboyant accouterments like heavy jewelry and furs that detract from the businesslike purpose of your visits. You want to look like someone who can afford to buy a car but who isn't so rich that you are willing to overpay.

- **Do leave the children at home.** It's a good idea to bring the kids along for your test drives, as advised in Chapter 5. When it comes time to select a car and negotiate a purchase at a dealership, however, leave the children at home. They can be a distraction. You can potentially lose much more money by being rushed into a deal on which you can't fully concentrate than by hiring a babysitter for a few hours.

## Get Your Bearings

Plan to arrive at the dealership ahead of your scheduled appointment. If you want time to browse on your own, you could park on a side street, out of sight of the main entrance, and approach inconspicuously on foot. If you have an appointment with a specific salesperson, be sure to mention this if approached by another.

At first glance, a dealership may look like little more than a showroom and adjoining garage perched in the middle of a parking lot crowded with shiny cars. Look closer and you will see that the dealership's presentation is carefully composed to stimulate your excitement and urge you to buy.

## You need to know

When negotiating a vehicle's price, you've got two arrows in your quill:

- Your target price, based on what the dealer paid for the vehicle
- Competing bids from other local dealerships or car-buying Web sites

The price you finally end up with will likely be somewhere between the two. You can start by showing the salesperson your rock-bottom target price. But don't disclose your competitive bids, which are the upper range of what's acceptable. Otherwise, the salesperson will focus on undercutting that higher figure by a token amount instead of working off of the lower figure.

For example, the CR Wholesale Price for a 2005 Chevy Tahoe LS 4x4 is $30,205. Add a 4 percent to 8 percent markup to that, and that's where you begin your negotiations. Take this price to competing dealerships and tell the salesperson your 4 percent markup figure and tell him or her that you want the lowest markup over that price you can get. Inch up if necessary, but don't go over the lowest competing bid.

Only if the negotiations have stalled, and the salesperson is willing to let you walk out the door, should you show him your lowest competing price, as a way of letting him know that he isn't yet in the ballpark. At that point, the salesperson may concede that he or she can't meet the price or will pay another visit to the dealership's sales manager.

## What's on the lot

Parked in a gleaming row on one side of the showroom entrance will be an array of the dealership's newest and best-selling models; on the other side will be some of the choicest certified pre-owned used cars. The dealer may also put a vehicle that's on special offer on an elevated display—a model-year closeout, perhaps, or a model that features a rebate or low-interest-rate financing.

Off to the sides and behind the showroom will be closely packed phalanxes of vehicles in the dealer's inventory. Ideally, you already know that the dealership has the exact configuration in which you're interested. You could spend a few minutes looking at what's on display for any vehicles that match your requirements. If you find one that you like, note down its vehicle identification number (VIN) from the window sticker.

### Showroom showoffs

Exhibited in the showroom are usually a selection of the dealership's most popular or highest-profile models. These are often loaded with options, accompanied by high-level sticker prices. You may be tempted to spend time exploring these vehicles but you should save your thorough going-over for the vehicle you intend to buy. Different trim levels can have different seats, for instance, so no matter how comfortable the seats are in the showroom car, they may not be the ones you will be living with on a daily basis.

On the other hand, the high sticker prices on these fully loaded models could leave you convinced that the price a salesperson offers you for a more modest vehicle is a great bargain. Enjoy looking, but if you're not in the market for a top-of-the-line model, do not allow yourself to be seduced.

### Getting down to business

Once you've gotten your bearings, it's time to meet the salesperson. You have every right to expect—indeed, to insist—that the salesperson be cordial and professional. He should be courteous, well-informed, and responsive to your questions. It is a clear sign that the chemistry between the two of you is wrong—or that you are being set up for manipulation—if the salesperson comes across as indifferent, patronizing, or inattentive. If so, politely tell him that you'd prefer to work with another salesperson. If you're told that no one else is available, you could simply excuse yourself and leave.

# Negotiate One Thing at a Time

As we've said, the salesperson will likely begin the discussion about price by focusing on the vehicle's MSRP or on your monthly payment. He may even

## Negotiating by phone

As many of CONSUMER REPORTS' regular test-car buyers have found, the telephone can be an effective aid in speeding up the negotiating process. This works best for buyers who have no trade-in and are either paying cash or have financing approved through another source.

The key is to determine the vehicle and exact configuration you want, scout out which dealerships have it in stock, and do a thorough walk-around and test drive of any vehicles you would consider buying before you initiate telephone negotiations.

When you call the dealerships, set the same ground rules you would if you were in the dealership. Tell the salesperson that you know what the dealership paid for the vehicle, have a reasonable target price in mind (use your 4-percent-over-dealer-cost figure), want that price or the lowest markup over that price, intend to buy as soon as possible, are prepared to give him or her your credit-card number for a deposit if you can get the price you want, and, if not, intend to call other dealerships.

Resist pitches for you to come into the dealership to get the best price, and point out that you don't want to spend a lot of time on the phone.

Our buyers often need to call several dealerships and then play one off of the others to get the price as low as possible.

One of the keys to making this work is that the salesperson and dealership staff have so little time invested in this transaction that even if the dealership makes only a marginal profit, it may still be worth it.

Before you hand over your credit-card number, however, it's important that you have the dealership fax the final contract to you so you can review it and make sure everything is correct, including the model, trim, options, and agreed-upon price.

try to disarm you by quoting you a "special" price that's several hundred dollars below the sticker price. But don't fall for the "hundreds off sticker" ploy. Once you allow the conversation to move in that direction, you start playing the dealership's game.

As we described in Chapter 12, don't bite on the question of a monthly payment, either. It's the first step down a slippery slope of being manipulated with numbers and overpaying for your vehicle. Using the monthly payment as the focus, the salesperson will lump the whole process together, including the price for the new vehicle, the trade-in, and financing, if appropriate. This gives him or her too much latitude to give you a "good price" in one area while making up for it in another.

Instead, insist on negotiating one thing at a time. Your first priority is to settle on the lowest price you can get on the new vehicle. Only after you've locked that in should you begin to discuss a trade-in or financing, if necessary.

## Set the ground rules

Rather than get drawn into a discussion on the salesperson's terms, politely explain the following:

- You have carefully researched the vehicle you want and have already taken a test drive.
- You know exactly what trim level and options you want, have researched the price for that configuration and know what the dealership paid for it.
- You have already calculated what you are prepared to pay. Reassure him that your offer will include a fair profit, then give him or her your low-end target price, and say you want the lowest markup over that figure.
- If he or she can meet your target price you'll be ready to buy today; if not, you intend to visit other dealerships.

You will want to come across as friendly and confident, and well-informed but not argumentative. From the outset, you want to prevent the

### New or one-year-old leftover?

The salesperson may suggest another way to lower the price of putting you in the car you want by offering to sell you a nearly identical new vehicle from the previous model year. He might even point out that for the same price as the current year's model the year-earlier vehicle on his lot comes loaded with options that were priced beyond your budget on the car you were originally considering.

You may also discover that there is an attractive manufacturer rebate or other incentive on the previous year's vehicle to help dealers clear out inventory. But consider this option carefully by reviewing the information on previous-year leftovers in Chapter 13.

negotiation from veering off in directions you are not ready to discuss until the matter of a purchase price is settled.

If the salesperson asks about a trade-in, for instance, say that you have investigated various options for selling your old car and that you might be open to a trade-in—but only after you've agreed on the new vehicle's price.

When he or she asks how you'll pay for the vehicle, let him know that you are preapproved for a loan and are prepared to pay in cash, but you may be willing to consider financing through the dealership—provided the rate is competitive and, again, you can come to terms on the purchase price of the new car. Thinking that he has a shot at profiting on the back end of the deal will pique the salesperson's interest, but you will sent a clear message that he'll have to sell you the car you want at a price you like.

Calmly explain that you don't want to waste his time—and yours—in lengthy haggling; and reassure him that if you and he can agree to terms you know to be fair to both of you, he can look forward to making a quick sale and a modest profit. If not, you will move on to another dealership.

Then sit back and wait for him or her to respond.

By now, it should be clear to the salesperson that you know what you're doing. Indeed, he might even be instructed to turn over knowledgeable customers like you to a more senior colleague. If that happens, simply repeat the same ground rules to the next salesperson or manager you meet. But whomever it is that ends up sitting across the desk from you, your clear explanation of what you're looking for will help counteract the diversionary tactics that salespeople often count on to give them the all-important initial bargaining edge. You're in command.

## Money talks

The salesperson's initial reaction is likely to be dismissive, stating flatly that there is no way the sales manager will let him sell you the vehicle at your price. He may even try to tell you that your numbers are wrong. If so, simply show him that your figures for the retail price of the car match those on the window sticker—a sure indication that the underlying invoice figures will also match.

You should mention that you have talked to other dealerships and gathered prices. But don't disclose what they are. If you hold your cards close to the vest, you don't know how low he will go.

Even if he cannot find fault with your numbers, the sales manager may counter your bid with a barrage of objections, pleas, and ploys to get you to raise your offer. Stay calm and smile patiently.

You may be asked to wait while the salesperson goes off to make your case to the sales manager. Since the manager wields the real power to approve deals, you can expect this. But make it clear that you don't have a lot of time to sit around and wait.

You also have some wiggle room. After all, the target price you calculated allowed for a dealer profit of between 4 percent and 8 percent over what the dealer paid for the vehicle (as reflected in the CR Wholesale Price, if you have a Consumer Reports' New Car Price Report). Your initial offer should be at the low end of the range, and you can move up in small increments. If you do raise your bid, you don't want to give the impression that you're simply giving in to pressure. It helps to state a rationale for your flexibility on price by saying, for instance, that you value the fact that his dealership happens to be the one most conveniently located for you, or that you especially like the color of the car he has to sell.

Remind the salesperson that you will be ready to complete the purchase on the spot if he can meet your price. Otherwise, you will have to "think it over." The salesperson will recognize this as a sure sign that, if you leave his showroom, you will be on your way to his competitor's dealership, and he is more likely to relent.

If you see that the salesperson is trying to string you along without real progress, you can excuse yourself at any time and get up to leave. What happens next gives you a clue to how low they will go. Often, the salesperson will try to stop you by telling you that he thinks he can "work something out to make you happy." If he or she simply lets you go, then the most recent price may be close to the dealer's limit.

If the negotiation has stalled at a higher figure than competitive prices you've gathered from dealerships or on the Internet, it may be time to disclose this. Let them know that they're not even in the ballpark. This could motivate another visit to the sales manager for a lower price.

If the dealership gives you a price that's in your target range, you could accept it on the spot, saving yourself more legwork or get it in writing and move on to another dealership in hopes of getting an even lower figure. Keep in mind that if the price is really close to your target, it's not likely to go that much lower somewhere else.

## Know when to walk

If your discussion does stall, remember the ancient Chinese proverb: Of all the stratagems, to know when to quit is the best. Following are occasions when your best bet may be to stage a strategic retreat:

- Quoting a price that is still higher than what you are prepared to pay, the salesperson tells you, "This is as low as I can go." Tell him that you think you have gone as far as you can in this meeting, you will have to think about it at home, and evaluate his best price in light of what other dealerships have quoted.

- The salesperson may try to convince you that the rebate (or low-cost financing) is available only to customers who pay the sticker price. This is not true. Rebates are reimbursed directly by the manufacturer, irrespective of the price you negotiate at the dealership. Don't let the salesperson use rebates against you.

- The salesperson suggests that you come back if another dealership will give you a better price and he'll beat it. Thank him for his time and tell him you are not interested in shuttling back and forth among dealerships. Let him know that you plan to complete the transaction soon, and that once you leave the showroom you may not be coming back.

- If the salesperson makes what he tells you is his take-it-or-leave-it final offer that is "good for today only," you may want to accept only if it satisfies these two conditions: (1) his price meets your target price; and (2) it is a specially featured price for the only vehicle in dealer's stock that matches the model and trim level of the car you intend to buy. Otherwise, don't take this seriously. If the salesperson's price is good today, it should be valid tomorrow if you decide to return.

As you move on to your second and third dealerships, follow the same script you used with dealer number one. And, remember, do not tell one dealer the price another dealer has quoted you. The more you keep them guessing, the more aggressively they will compete for your business.

## Know when to say "yes"

Once you've completed the round of dealer visits, you may have found that one of the dealers is willing to sell you your ideal car at close to your target price. If so, congratulations; it's time to shake hands with the salesperson and proceed to close the deal.

More likely, however, the situation you face will be ambiguous. If so, then you should review the various offers at home in a more relaxed environment.

At this point, you could call back certain dealerships and level with them about the competing prices you've gotten from other dealerships and ask them if they can meet or beat that price. Make it clear that you'd be willing to buy immediately if they can.

If they don't, then you may have to make the call as to whether you want to go with, say, a lower price at a dealership that's farther away or didn't treat you as well or accept a higher price at a dealership that is more convenient or more pleasant to work with. Similarly, if you've been getting quotes on two or three different models, you may have to decide whether a lower price is worth giving up something special you want in another vehicle, or paying more to get a vehicle you may be happier with over the long haul.

### What price convenience?

When you're feeling confident and are swept up in the negotiation game, you may be inclined to think that getting the salesperson to agree to your rock-bottom price is the only acceptable outcome. It isn't. Sure, you want to bargain hard for a good price, but don't let the perfect be the enemy of the good. Before you chase the last penny of savings, consider your own convenience and peace of mind. Do you feel more comfortable working with one dealership over another? Might it be worth your while to pay a little more to end up with a car you'll be happier driving? Provided you've satisfied yourself that the slightly more expensive deal is still a fair one, there's no harm in paying a little extra if it buys you some peace of mind.

## Time to Talk Trade-in?

As we've said, only after you agree on a price for the new car should you turn your attention to the trade-in. In Chapter 8 we showed you how to assess the value of your current car. If you shopped it around to other dealerships, you also know what you can easily get for it at another dealership. Armed with this information, there's no reason why the dealership shouldn't give you its full wholesale value in trade-in allowance.

Tell the salesperson that you simply want what you know it's worth. You should also have the figures to back this up, along with printouts from several pricing sources. This diffuses any attempt on his part to pull out a used-car pricing book with which he can "prove" that your figures are too high.

To lowball you on the trade-in, the salesperson may again try to stall the negotiations and wear you down with frequent visits to the sales manager. You can minimize this by indicating upfront that the new-car deal isn't final unless you get a good allowance on your trade-in. "Deal killer" is the term that salespeople don't want to hear.

Remember, if the trade-in negotiations become too burdensome and you're not willing to pull out of the new-car deal, you can always take the car elsewhere or sell it yourself, which will likely reap you a higher price anyway. If, however, you're dependent on the trade-in to make the down payment you want, these alternatives will mean that you'll have to sell your current car before you can sign the contract for your new one.

## Completing the Purchase

Well done! You've found the right vehicle and negotiated a great price. You're in the home stretch, but your work isn't finished yet. Until you drive off the dealership's lot with your new vehicle, you still have room to improve the terms of your deal, and the dealership has not yet exhausted its opportunities to profit at your expense. We'll warn you about the traps that await you while closing the deal in Chapter 16. Then, in Chapter 17 we'll alert you to things to watch for when you pick up your new car.

# 16

# Close the Deal

**The finish line is in sight.** You have navigated your way through the price negotiations with the salesperson, settled on a final price for the new vehicle, and, if appropriate, you got a fair allowance for your trade-in. Your work isn't done yet, however. Before you can slide behind the wheel of your new car, you will have to finalize the paperwork and dodge the dealership's last-minute attempts to squeeze more profit out of you.

All the effort you put into the negotiations may have left you feeling drained. After settling on the price, you may also feel that you're over the hump and it's just a matter of signing a few papers before you're done. The dealership's staff, however, knows that they can use your fatigue to their advantage, and they may try to get you to agree to costly back-end terms and extras or to overlook a disadvantageous clause slipped into the contract.

So you need to stay sharp. Take a breather outside if you have to, grab a cup of coffee, and have your calculator at the ready. The final phase will require a lot of attention to detail. It's time to focus on:

- What to look for on the purchase or lease agreement
- Which fees you must pay, which ones you should question, and which ones you should refuse
- What you need to know about financing charges, extended warranties, and dealer extras you may be pressured to buy

# The Purchase and Lease Agreements

Now that the formalities of bargaining over the price of the vehicle have been completed, the salesperson you worked with will be ready to hand you off to the finance and insurance manager, who will draw up the paperwork. Despite a title that conjures up a sedate banker or meek insurance agent, the finance and insurance manager (more familiarly known as the "F&I guy") is usually a former salesperson who's graduated to another—often very profitable—selling role. It's his or her job to get you to pay dubious fees that fatten the dealer's bottom line and to buy overpriced options and insurance products you don't need. Before turning to these questionable extras, however, let's discuss the basic information that should appear in a purchase or lease agreement.

### Double check the purchase agreement

Have the salesperson give you a detailed bill of sale describing the vehicle you will purchase. If, in the course of your negotiations, you got the dealership to agree to special terms, make sure to have them added to the contract and have them initialed by the sales manager. Did they promise you free oil changes for the first 50,000 miles? The use of a loaner car when you bring your new vehicle in for servicing? A free set of floor mats, perhaps? If it isn't in writing, the dealership is under no obligation to honor it.

What should be in the purchase agreement? In addition to the vehicle identification number (VIN), the purchase agreement should clearly identify the car's year, make, model, and trim line. It should also specify the purchase price you and the salesperson agreed to, the destination charge, any optional equipment that's listed on the window sticker, and any dealer-installed accessories you agreed to purchase (but no others). Finally, make sure the agreement indicates the odometer reading, a factor that will be important in determining the length of coverage for the vehicle under the factory warranty or the allowable mileage for which you will be charged under a lease contract.

If you intend to finance the vehicle through the dealership, the bill of sale should indicate the annual percentage rate (APR) of the loan, the number of monthly payments to pay the loan off, and the total payments you will make over the life of the loan. Terms of the manufacturer's warranty should be spelled out, along with any restrictions affecting the deal that may appear in the invoice's fine print. Finally, the purchase agreement should also include the dealership name and address, the sales manager's name and signature confirming that the dealership stands behind the transaction, and a mutually agreed upon date when you will take delivery (see Chapter 17 for more information on picking up the vehicle).

Take as much time as you need to read through the contract carefully and to confirm that the information it contains has been recorded accurately. Check the VIN number printed on the sales agreement against the one on the vehicle to see that each letter and number appears in proper sequence. The VIN is stamped on a small plate located where the dashboard and windshield meet, in front of the driver's position.

Speak up if you spot any discrepancy or omission on the contract. Every space on the agreement should be filled in with the applicable number or, if none is called for, with a zero or an indication that the information requested is not applicable (n/a).

It cannot be emphasized too strongly that what may appear to be a small oversight can have big consequences. Don't be afraid to ask about anything you don't understand or to question anything that strikes you as problematic. And don't feel foolish or worry about the F&I manager thinking you're an overly fussy customer. It's your hard-earned money, and you need to be sure everything is acceptable before signing the agreement. If you let an issue that confuses you slide by at this point, you run the risk of living with a costly problem for as long as you own the car.

## Lock in a lease agreement

If you're leasing, you should have already read Chapter 11 to become familiar with the terms and conditions of a leasing contract. That said, the leasing agreement is far more complicated than the bill of sale and requires careful scrutiny.

Like a purchase agreement, a leasing contract should specify the vehicle identification number; the car's make, model, and trim line; and any options and accessories. It should also indicate the number of miles showing on the odometer—the starting point for calculating your total mileage allowance over the life of the lease.

Pay close attention to these key financial numbers:

- **Gross capitalized cost.** This figure on the lease agreement will include the vehicle purchase price as well as any items you agree to pay for over the lease term, such as taxes, fees, service contracts, insurance, and any prior credit or lease balance. Make sure the vehicle price is the one you and the salesperson agreed to in your negotiation.
- **Capitalized cost reduction.** This is any credit that should be applied against the capitalized cost. The capitalized cost reduction, for instance, should reflect your cash down payment, any trade-in allowance to which the salesperson and you agreed, and any rebate that's in effect. This is subtracted from the gross capitalized cost to get the "adjusted" or "net" capitalized cost.
- **Residual value.** This is the vehicle's expected value when the lease ends. When this value is subtracted from the adjusted or net capitalized cost,

the balance is the vehicle's total estimated depreciation over the life of the lease for which you will be required to pay.

- **Lease term.** Both the lease start and termination dates should be entered, and the interval between them should equal the total number of months. You should also take time to make sure you understand the terms and conditions laid out in the lease agreement that govern your use of the vehicle while the contract is in effect and what will happen when your lease is up.

- **Money factor.** This financing charge is a decimal figure that is used to compute the interest rate on the portion of the vehicle's value you will be paying for over the lease term. It is the number that will be used to compute your base monthly payment.

- **Itemized list of payments.** This list of payments, due at lease signing, will typically include an acquisition fee, which is a processing charge levied by the leasing company to cover the cost of initiating the lease; state sales tax, calculated on the capitalized cost of the vehicle; your first monthly lease installment payment; license, registration, and title fees; and a refundable security deposit, which you will get back when you return the car at lease end.

- **Allotted miles.** Check to see that the F&I manager has credited you with the full allotment of allowable miles provided with the lease. Should you exceed this allotment, you will typically be charged 10 cents to as high as 25 cents per mile. If you anticipate that there may be a change in your driving patterns that will cause you to put more miles on the odometer than the lease allows, you may want to purchase more miles in advance when they typically cost less. But don't go overboard; any miles you don't use could end up as a windfall for the dealer when you return the car. They probably won't refund the cost unless this is stipulated in your contract.

- **Disposition fee.** If yours is a standard closed-end lease, you will be expected to return the vehicle to the dealer upon the expiration of the contract or to purchase it. If you return the car, you will likely face a disposition fee—a charge of a few hundred dollars you will have to pay the dealer for processing the vehicle's return and eventual resale. This may be automatically deducted from your security deposit.

- **Purchase price.** You will want to be clear about whether the price you would be able to pay to buy the vehicle at lease end will be the residual value used to calculate the capitalized-cost reduction or if it will be the car's actual market value. Dealers and manufacturers are aggressive in setting a high residual value at the inception of a lease in order to keep the lessee's monthly payment competitive, so the difference between the two can be substantial.

- **Wear-and-tear charge.** You will be responsible for the proper maintenance of the vehicle throughout the life of the lease and for returning the vehicle in good condition. Because you could be assessed a charge for excessive wear and tear, you should get a clear explanation of what is meant by "excessive" and see that this description matches what is in the lease contract clause.

- **Early termination fee.** Be clear about any charge or early termination penalty you will face if you return the vehicle before the lease expires. The early termination charge is meant to compensate the dealer for the fact that a car will depreciate more rapidly in the lease's early months than toward the end, a reality that is not reflected in the uniform monthly payments you make throughout the life of the lease. If a job loss or a reduction of the number of drivers in your household forces you to give up the car before the lease ends, you may have to fork over hundreds of dollars. Read the contract carefully so you understand all of your obligations in that circumstance.

## Check the numbers

Whether you buy or lease, check all the numbers on the agreement, and use your calculator to total them up yourself. Confirm that you have been properly credited with the trade-in allowance, rebates, initial deposit, and cash down payment that will partially offset the purchase price or, if leasing, the capitalized cost.

If you are financing the vehicle through the dealer, make sure the right interest rate or money factor was used to compute your monthly payment. The "Documenting the Deal" worksheet in Chapter 11. It provides a side-by-side comparison of the key terms and numbers involved in a purchase and a lease.

Some of the charges you may encounter are clearly warranted, others are questionable, and a few may be entirely unnecessary. The worksheet "Fees Fair and Foul" summarizes the common charges you may encounter and helps you track how much they can add to the cost of your new vehicle. Remember, unless you pay fees and taxes upfront, they're added to the total package and you will pay interest on them. Following is a rundown of the charges you will have to pay and the ones you should challenge:

- **Destination charge.** Set by the manufacturer, this covers the cost to deliver the vehicle from the factory to the dealership's lot. You will need to pay this automaker charge. Some dealers, however, may try to tack on a second delivery fee, including it as an item on a second sticker the dealer pastes on the car near the regular, federally mandated window sticker. If you see a line itemizing an additional "delivery" or "destination" charge, you should object. It's unwarranted, and you should avoid paying it.
- **Title and registration.** The dealer customarily takes care of arranging for the state Department of Motor Vehicles to issue an owner's card in your name and provide temporary tags, passing along fees incurred in the process—typically between 1 percent and 3 percent of the price of the vehicle. You will have to reimburse the dealership for this outlay.

- **Documentation fee.** Sometimes called "conveyance fees," this is supposed to cover the cost of processing the title and registration paperwork. Every convenience has a price, after all. Dealers, though, have been known to load on charges for preparing all the paperwork involved in completing the transaction, so ask what's included before you agree to pay. A reimbursement of $50 or so may be reasonable to cover the title and registration paperwork, but a charge for preparing documents unrelated to registration would be excessive and should be challenged.

- **State sales tax.** You will have to pay sales tax at the rate prevailing in the state where you register the vehicle, and most dealers are equipped to handle registrations in other states, also. However, if you will relocate soon after your purchase or lease, or you are buying the vehicle for someone living in another state, you may have to register the vehicle temporarily in the state where the sale is completed, then reregister in the state of residence before your temporary title expires, usually within 30 days. You can claim a refund for sales tax paid in the state where you purchased by submitting proof that you've reregistered the vehicle and that you've paid tax in the state where permanent tags are issued.

- **Advertising fee.** Manufacturers assess their dealerships with a fee to pay for national advertising that promotes the brand, and they include that charge in the dealer invoice price. Regional dealer associations also levy assessments to dealers to cover local newspaper, radio, and television ads, and it has become increasingly common for dealers to pass along a portion of that expense as a fee of a few hundred dollars or so on each new car sale or lease. This charge should be disclosed and agreed to by you before you find it on the closing paperwork. Some dealers list it on a separate sticker posted in the vehicle's window. If you're hit with an advertising charge out of the blue at the deal closing, challenge it and ask to have it removed.

# Dealer Financing

If the F&I manager is doing his job correctly, he will turn on the charm—and turn up the heat—to get you to buy a host of optional back-end products, a major source of profits for the dealer and commissions for him.

Unless you've made it clear that you have your own financing arranged, one of his goals will be to try to persuade you to finance the purchase or lease through the manufacturer's finance subsidiary or another institution with which the dealership has a relationship.

Dealer-arranged financing may be worth considering if the manufacturer of your new vehicle is offering a subsidized loan or a subvented lease, but you should already be familiar with what terms are available elsewhere so you can make an informed decision. (See Chapter 10 for more information on financing or Chapter 11 for leasing.) Also, be alert for interest-rate bumping, as described in Chapter 12, in which the dealership quotes you a higher rate than you actually qualify for.

Sometimes you have to choose between a special low-interest financing rate and a cash rebate that can be credited toward your down payment (lowering the amount you need to finance). Crunch the numbers both ways to see which option gives you the most benefit. You can use the calculator at *www.consumerreports.org/smartcar* to help decide which is best for you.

Consumers who did not take steps to prearrange financing before they shopped, who are careless in comparing loan and lease terms, or who have problematic credit histories are particularly susceptible to the seductions of the F&I guy.

The dealer will move heaven and earth to get an inattentive or poor-credit car shopper a high-interest-rate loan—no matter what the cost to the hapless borrower. If you find yourself relying on the F&I guy to work out your financing for you and a manufacturer-subsidized deal isn't an option,

# Worksheet: Closing Fees Fair and Foul

| | Fee | What it's about | Amount |
|---|---|---|---|
| **Unavoidable** | Documentation fee | A modest charge of $50 or less for processing documents that establish your title and registration is warranted. Question anything higher than $100. | $ |
| | Gap insurance | A must for leased vehicles. Covers the difference between your payments over the life of the lease and the residual value of the vehicle in case it is stolen or totaled in an accident. | |
| | Title and registration | Let the dealership handle the formalities of establishing you as the new owner of the vehicle and obtaining temporary tags. Expect dealer to pass along what the state charges—typically between 1 percent and 3 percent of vehicle cost—plus the documentation fee. | |
| | Sales tax | Some states calculate tax on the full price of the car, but most figure tax on the difference between the price and the trade-in. | |
| | Destination charge | A standard charge levied to cover shipment of the vehicle. Question any secondary "delivery fee," however, that's listed on the contract. | |
| **Maybe** | Advertising charge | Increasingly common, regional dealer cooperatives assess fees to support promotional efforts. If this charge shows up only at the closing, contest it. You may end up having to pay. | |
| | Extended warranty | Extra coverage for major repairs that may be needed after the manufacturer's warranty expires. It's your call. But if you do buy, we recommend buying coverage backed by the vehicle manufacturer or an established third-party company. You don't have to buy on the spot; take your time to compare contracts. | |
| | Additional dealer markup | Sometimes added to hot-selling models for additional profit. You can contest this, but if the model is in high demand, the dealer may not have any incentive to work with you. | |

| | Fee | What it's about | Amount |
|---|---|---|---|
| **Avoid Paying** | Dealer preparation fee | Most manufacturers pay the dealers to remove the coatings and coverings that protect the vehicle during shipment and to clean up the car for you. There is no justification for you to pay the dealer again for this service. | $ |
| | Credit life insurance | Your survivors will be able to pay off the vehicle if you die before your payments end. Term life insurance is cheaper, but make sure it will pay enough to cover loan payments. | |
| | Disability insurance | Covers your car payments if you are unable to work due to a disabling accident or extended illness. You may already have disability coverage through your employer; if not, you can purchase it more cheaply elsewhere. | |
| | Pinstriping | Expensive tape that a detailing shop can put on for you at a lower price than the dealer can. | |
| | Rustproofing/ undercoating | Today's vehicles are manufactured to withstand corrosive weather and road conditions. You will not need it. | |
| | VIN etching | This is an antitheft measure in which the vehicle identification number is etched into the glass. Some states require that dealers offer it to you, but none require that you buy it. It can be done less expensively elsewhere or even by yourself with a $25 kit. | |
| | Fabric protection | This is just expensive Scotch Guard. Just say "no." | |
| | Paint sealant | It is little more than a vastly overpriced liquid wax you can easily purchase from an auto supply shop for $10 or less. | |
| | Security/anti-theft system | An alarm or theft-recovery device can reduce your car insurance premium, but the savings will be more than offset if you buy it from the dealer. | |
| | Total | | $ |

you can be pretty sure you will be overpaying. This may be a good indication that it's time to rethink whether you can afford to go through with your purchase at this time.

# Extended Warranty

The F&I guy will almost surely try to sell you an extended warranty or service plan for your vehicle that can easily cost more than $1,000. According to a Consumers Union study, for example, Texas consumers paid an average of $1,376 for extended warranties. If it's added into the loan, you will also pay interest on this amount.

An extended warranty kicks in when the manufacturer's basic warranty expires and, depending on the contract you purchase, will pay for some or all of the repairs your vehicle may need. Think of it as an insurance policy against major problems down the road.

Do you need one? Most new cars today come with at least a three-year/36,000-mile bumper-to-bumper factory warranty. Most luxury vehicles have a four-year/48,000-mile warranty. Many vehicles also come with a separate powertrain warranty (for the engine, transmission, and drivetrain) that extends longer than the basic warranty.

Obviously, if you trade in your vehicle every five years or so, or if you lease your new vehicle under a typical 3-year lease with a 12,000-mile-per-year mileage allowance, buying an extended warranty would be a waste of money.

Even if you plan to keep your vehicle longer, we recommend you give careful consideration before signing up for an extended warranty. In general, cars have become much more reliable in recent years. Properly maintained, a vehicle's major components, such as the engine or transmission, should go without a major failure for at least 10 years or 100,000 miles. Many vehicles can reach 200,000 miles without a major breakdown. The chance of needing the coverage of an extended warranty isn't as great as it used to be.

As a general rule, if the model you're buying has an above-average reliability record—earning a very good or excellent CONSUMER REPORTS predicted reliability rating—it's probably not worth spending the money for an extended warranty. If the model has had a below-average record, and you plan to keep the vehicle well past the factory warranty period, it may be worth hedging your bet by buying the coverage. (See Chapter 2 on how to check a vehicle's reliability.)

This is especially so if a model has had problems with drivetrain components or has a lot of advanced electronics systems that could be expensive to repair. There's room for negotiation in the dealer's extended-warranty price, though, so take advantage of it.

On the other hand, you could play the odds by putting $1,500 into an interest-bearing account and using it only if you have a major problem. If you never dip into it, this account will make a nice down payment on your next vehicle.

If you do decide that an extended warranty is for you, don't feel pressured to buy a warranty the same day you buy the vehicle. You can usually buy a plan any time before the basic warranty expires. We suggest sticking to a plan offered by the automaker. Third-party coverage a dealer may offer varies enormously in quality, coverage, and price.

You can also buy coverage directly. So don't let the F&I guy talk you into buying it through the dealership until you've compared coverage and cost elsewhere. The dealer is likely to charge more for a contract than you would pay for equivalent coverage directly from an independent company. Two well-known direct sellers are Warranty Direct (*WarrantyDirect.com*) and 1 Source Auto Warranty (*1SourceAutoWarranty.com*).

Review any service plan carefully to find out what is and isn't covered, who must perform repairs, and how to file a claim. You also should determine if you need to do anything to keep coverage, such as provide proof you properly maintained the vehicle. (It is always a good idea to keep complete and accurate records of any maintenance and repairs on your car.)

## You need to know

**Q.** What is an extended warranty?

**A.** It is a prepaid service contract sold by an auto manufacturer or other company that administers claims for covered repairs. Contracts may be sold for periods ranging from 4 years or 60,000 miles (whichever comes first) to 7 years or 100,000 miles. For a new car, the period of coverage begins from the date you take possession of the vehicle. Thus, a 4-year/60,000-mile warranty extends only 1 year or 24,000 miles beyond the standard 3-year/30,000-mile factory warranty. Naturally, the longer the warranty, the more you will pay. A warranty doesn't let you off the hook for taking care of your car; you must follow the maintenance procedures the manufacturer lays out in your owner's manual. That means you're responsible for regular oil and filter changes and replacing belts and plugs using certified parts. Be sure to keep records documenting that you've had the car serviced on the specified schedule.

**Q.** What does it cover?

**A.** Warranties are typically offered with different levels of coverage. A basic contract may only pay to repair the engine, transmission, and drivetrain, which could be adequate for a no-frills car. A more comprehensive contract could also cover antilock brakes, radiators, turbocharged engines, power windows, and most other components found in today's well-equipped vehicles. Premium coverage will offer bumper-to-bumper protection with no exclusions. Any warranty contract should provide coverage for damage caused by engine overheating and general wear and tear.

**Q.** How are claims paid?

**A.** The policy you purchase should permit you to have repairs made by any Automotive Service Excellence-certified mechanic, not just those authorized by the warranty claims administrator. A good warranty contract will pay the repair shop directly. You should avoid purchasing from a company that requires you to pay the repair shop and then submit a claim. You could be out of pocket for months waiting to be reimbursed or even discover that your claim is rejected for not being covered under your contract.

**Q.** When should I buy?
**A.** You don't have to buy immediately upon taking title to your new car, but don't wait too long. The newer your car is, the less your contract will cost, and most warranty companies will not write contracts for vehicles that are more than 7 years old or have more than 60,000 miles, although some go up to 100,000 miles.

**Q.** How do I choose one?
**A.** The best choice is one that's backed by the vehicle manufacturer. Third-party providers vary greatly in terms of quality and coverage.

**Q.** What else should an extended warranty include?
**A.** The new warranty should allow for a 100 percent refund of the premium within 60 days of your purchase of a the contract if you are not satisfied and have not submitted any claims under the contract. The contract should not require you to pay more than one deductible per repair visit. Many better policies will include reimbursement for towing charges, auto rental if your car is in the shop for a few days, and travel disruption that covers your costs to return home after your car's breakdown. The policy should be transferable when you sell the car—a feature that can be an attractive lure for a prospective buyer.

If you're buying from a dealer, always negotiate the price. And make sure the plan is transferable if you sell the car.

# Insurance

Another pitch you might hear from the F&I guy is for insurance. Here are some of the profitable protections he may offer and how you should respond:

### Gap insurance

This is essential protection if you lease your new vehicle. Gap insurance covers the difference between the payments you will make over the life of the lease and the remaining value of the vehicle in the event that it is stolen or totaled as the result of an accident. Many lease contracts already include it and bundle the premium with your monthly payments; others may charge you for it as part of the down payment due at lease signing. The cost can vary widely, so if it isn't part of your lease contract, shop around. (See Chapter 11 for more information on gap insurance.)

### Credit life insurance

The cost may appear modest, and it guarantees that your survivors will be able to pay off the vehicle if you die before your car payments end. If you have a life insurance policy, you already have enough coverage, and even if you don't, the odds are that you and your heirs will never need this protection. Some dealers may tell customers with poor credit histories that credit life insurance is mandatory. It isn't.

### Disability insurance

This is important coverage for anyone whose dependents rely on his or her earnings to support a household. You may already have disability coverage through your employer; if not, you should be able to purchase it less expensively elsewhere.

# Dealer Extras

Before they let you go, the dealership may also try to get you to buy extra services that are usually overpriced. This can include:

- **Pinstriping.** If you really must have decorative tape to make your new car complete, have a detailing shop do it at a fraction of what a dealership will charge.

- **Rustproofing and undercoating.** Don't bite on this. Today's vehicles are manufactured with good corrosion protection. In fact, according to CONSUMER REPORTS reliability surveys, rust problems have almost vanished in modern vehicles. Standard rust-through warranties for most domestic and imported vehicles run five years or more, and many will cover you for an unlimited number of miles during the warranty period.

- **Fabric protection.** This is the most expensive Scotch Guard you can have sprayed on your upholstery. Instead, spend a few bucks for a can of fabric protector and apply it yourself.

- **Paint sealant.** The dealer may tell you that an application of this clear coating will protect your car's surface for years, but it is little more than a vastly overpriced wax. You can easily purchase a good protectant from any auto parts store and apply it yourself.

- **VIN etching.** This is a service in which the vehicle identification number is etched into the vehicle's windows to deter theft. Some states require that a dealer offer it to you, but none require that you buy it. It's not unusual to find a charge for VIN etching already printed on the purchase agreement, as if it's assumed that you will pay for this service. This has been the case for several vehicles that we've bought for testing. We recommend that you refuse this charge, and if it's printed on the contract, put a line through the entry. Even if you decide you want VIN etching, you can have it done less expensively elsewhere, or even do it yourself with a kit that costs about $25.

- **Security or antitheft system.** The dealer may tell you that an alarm system or theft-recovery device will cut your insurance costs, and this is true. But the discount, which can range from 10 to 30 percent of your comprehensive-insurance premium, may not warrant an expensive dealer-installed system. Check the price of the system versus how much you'll save on your insurance discount. You also might get a sales pitch for LoJack, a system that can help police track and locate your vehicle after it is stolen, and can result in your getting your car back before it can be stripped and sold off for parts. You will spend far less buying from an auto-security specialty shop. Make sure, however, that the alarm or theft-recovery system you buy is authorized for installation on your vehicle. If it is not, you risk voiding your warranty.

# After the Sale

■ CHAPTER 17: What to Watch for When Taking Delivery     **325**
■ CHAPTER 18: Save Money on Vehicle Maintenance     **337**
■ CHAPTER 19: Recalls & Service Problems     **357**

# 17

# What to Watch for When Taking Delivery

**Picking up your new car** is a time to savor. Maybe it's the relief that all the research, number crunching, and haggling is behind you combined with the thrill of driving something new home to show off to friends and family.

Don't let your eagerness, however, distract you from ensuring that all the "i's" are properly dotted and all "t's" are crossed. Careless mistakes and common oversights at this stage can have serious consequences that may be difficult or impossible to undo and could diminish your satisfaction with your new purchase.

In this chapter, we'll walk you through the final steps of taking possession of your new vehicle by explaining:

- How to prepare for your delivery appointment

- What to look for when performing a predelivery inspection

- Potential problems to be alert for in the final paperwork

We've also included a list of items you will need at the closing and a handy delivery checklist to ensure you have covered all the bases.

# Before You Take Delivery

In your excitement at getting your new vehicle, you might be tempted to drive it home immediately after completing your negotiations. Instead, we recommend that you give yourself some breathing space and schedule a time to come back and pick it up on another day. This gives the dealership more time to properly prepare the vehicle and paperwork, reducing the possibility of errors, and gives you time to recover from the negotiating experience and approach the delivery with fresh energy and a rested mind.

A so-called "spot delivery" leaves you vulnerable to last-minute errors in the paperwork, problems missed that a more thorough inspection of the vehicle would reveal, or other potentially costly oversights that could result from your fatigue and excitement or from carelessness on the part of the dealership.

It's better to take a day or more to reflect on the deal you've negotiated, so you don't feel the sharp pangs of buyer's remorse once the novelty has worn off.

Schedule your pick-up appointment during daylight hours, preferably when someone can join you to help with a visual inspection of the vehicle. Most dealerships will give you a list of what you'll need to bring with you when taking delivery. (See our own list later in this chapter.)

If you would like to review the final contract before you return to the dealership, ask the salesperson to send it to you via fax, overnight mail, or e-mail. You should read every paragraph, determine that the vehicle is correctly identified, beginning with its vehicle identification number (VIN), confirm that all terms you agreed to have been properly entered, and check that there are no omissions or blank spaces on lines where information should be entered. As you review the document, note any questions or issues you will want to discuss when you close the deal.

Let the salesperson know that the car should be prepared for your inspection; unless you want to provide free advertising for the dealership, tell him not to affix a decal or license plate frame with the dealership's name on the rear. Ask the salesperson to have the dealership arrange for the Department of Motor Vehicles to issue temporary tags and registration (unless you're transferring old plates) for the car. It's much easier for the dealership to do this for you than to have to fight the crowds at the DMV office yourself, and the convenience is well worth a nominal processing fee.

To forestall any delays or glitches, confirm that the salesperson has your driver's license number, correct address, and other information needed to process the state paperwork. Request that the new tags not be put on the vehicle right away, though. Instead, leave the dealer's tags on the car until after you've taken a final test drive. If the temporary tags issued under your name are on the car, then you are on the hook for any damage if anything happens to the vehicle while you are testing it.

## Make sure you're insured

Before your appointment with the dealer, you will want to call your insurance agent to arrange protection for your new car. The policy you have on your existing car may give you temporary coverage until a new policy can be written, but you should be clear about the extent of your protection and liabilities. For example, if you do not have collision coverage on your old car, put a temporary binder on your new car that will pay for its repair should you be involved in an accident.

You may plan to keep your old car, so you will need additional coverage for your new one. The premium you pay should reflect the fact that you will have two or more vehicles insured by the same underwriter. Make sure, also, that the insurance company is aware of any safety or antitheft equipment on your new vehicle—antilock brakes, electronic stability control, side air bags, or a LoJack theft-recovery system, for instance—that can lower your premium. See Chapter 9 for more information about auto insurance.

## Finalize your financing

If you've been preapproved for a loan, make sure you finalize any arrangements with your bank, credit union, or other financial institution so it can complete the paperwork and issue you a check or arrange a payment transfer to the car dealer's bank. You will have to provide the lender with a basic description of the vehicle and its vehicle identification number. The lender will also need to know the amount of your down payment.

There is key information you need to know, as well, such as the precise dollar amount of your monthly payments. You may also be required to pay loan origination and filing fees when the loan document is signed and notarized. See Chapter 10 for more information on auto financing.

## Prepare to make the down payment

Finally, you will want to make arrangements to pay the balance of the down payment on the new car. Most car dealers will not accept a personal check but will insist on having a certified or bank-issued check.

Your dealer will probably accept payment charged to a credit card, but if you decide to go this route, you must make sure you will not exceed your card's credit limit and commit to pay off the sizeable bill as soon as possible. After negotiating so carefully for a good price on the new car and arranging a favorable rate on your loan, it makes no sense to pay a credit card's revolving-balance finance charges at an annual rate of, say, 18 percent or more on your down payment.

# Delivery Day

Once the big day comes, keep an objective outlook until all the paperwork is completed to your satisfaction, you've completed a thorough inspection of the car, and any problems have been addressed.

The first thing you should do is have the salesperson give you an orientation on the vehicle. In the driver's seat, he or she should familiarize you with the controls, gauges, seat adjustments, and warning lights. Make sure you understand how to operate the headlights, windshield wipers and washers, cruise control, audio system, heating and air-conditioning controls, keyless entry/antitheft system, travel computer, and other common functions.

Have the salesperson demonstrate any advanced mobile electronics systems, such as a GPS navigation system, rear video entertainment system, hands-free phone system, or multifunction control system. Don't hesitate to ask questions. Take advantage of your one-on-one tutorial.

In the trunk or cargo area, have the salesperson show you where the spare tire and jack are stored and explain how they are removed and replaced. Check under the hood and locate the oil dipstick, the coolant canister, the master brake-fluid cylinder, and the container for windshield-washer fluid.

## Do a thorough inspection

Along with your orientation, you should give the vehicle a close inspection. First check to see that the vehicle identification number, located where the windshield and dashboard meet in front of the driver's position, matches the number that appears on the paperwork. If the vehicle has been specially ordered from the factory or was acquired through another dealer, make sure that it matches the specifications you requested. Also make sure that you can find and identify all the features listed on the vehicle's window sticker along with any dealer-installed accessories you may have requested.

The vehicle should be freshly washed and buffed. Moving systematically from front to rear and top to bottom, examine all surfaces of the exterior for any nicks, dings, scrapes, scratches, or dents. Inspect closely to see if the vehicle has been repainted in spots—an indication that damage during shipping has occurred. Check the fit and alignment of seams around doors, roofline, hood, and trunk. They should be straight, level, and evenly spaced. Make notes about any defects you spot.

Check the interior of the trunk to see that the material liner fits properly and has no rips. Examine the wheels to see that they are the proper size and

---

## What you'll need when you pick up the car

---

\_\_\_ A valid driver's license

\_\_\_ Loan documentation

\_\_\_ Certified check for payment of the balance of your initial cash deposit

\_\_\_ Bank check for the balance due on the purchase price

\_\_\_ Notebook, pen, and calculator

\_\_\_ A spouse, companion, or friend to assist you with the inspection

\_\_\_ Copy of the bill of sale or lease (obtained and signed by the dealer representative when the negotiation was completed)

\_\_\_ Ignition and trunk keys (including spares) and ownership papers from your old car, if trading in

\_\_\_ Proof of insurance coverage

\_\_\_ Registration and title of the car you're trading in (if appropriate)

that the tires match, and that any specially ordered oversized wheels or other special wheel treatments are what you asked for. Sometimes dealers will exchange wheels from one car for another; other times, factories have been known to make mistakes.

Turning to the vehicle's interior, inspect the seats carefully for stains, tears, or pulls at the seams. Look at the carpeting in the front, the rear, and under the seats. It, too, should be clean and well-fitting. If you ordered floor mats, they should be in place.

Check the roof liner to see that it is snug at all points where it meets front, side, and rear windows and around the ceiling light and sunroof, if so equipped. Make sure the interior lights work properly in all positions. All vanity lights should work.

Check to see that there is an owner's manual in the glove compartment. Examine the dashboard, center console, and instrument panel to see that fit and finish are free of defects. Knobs, dials, and switches should be secure and function smoothly. Take special note of the mileage reading on the odometer. The car shouldn't have more than 100 miles on it, unless it came from another dealership or was used as a demonstrator or by dealership personnel. If the latter is the case, you will want to bring that to the salesperson's attention, and the price of the vehicle should be reduced to reflect its used status.

If you didn't drive this particular vehicle when you did your prepurchase test drive, do so now as part of your inspection to make sure that everything is functioning properly. See Chapter 5 for advice on performing a thorough test drive.

The salesperson should go through the owner's manual with you and explain any special procedures for the break-in period as well as routine maintenance schedules. He or she should also introduce you to the service manager and show you the service department so you'll be familiar with it when you bring your vehicle in for maintenance or repair.

When you are satisfied that your examination is complete, review your notes and questions with the salesperson. It is essential that you immediately report any defects, discrepancies between what you ordered and what you found on the vehicle, and missing accessories. If you drive off the lot without having spotted a flaw and come back a few days later to report it, the dealership is going to tell you that, sorry, the ding is your doing, and it will be unwilling to fix it for free.

Discuss any repairs or remedies that may be needed with the salesperson. As disappointing as it may be to have to leave the dealer's lot without your new car, you should have any major defect remedied before you take possession, and ensure that the work is done properly before signing the final paperwork.

Make sure the salesperson puts in writing a commitment to complete any work that needs to be done, such as ordering a noncritical part or accessory. Should the delay leave you without transportation because you've already sold your old car, the dealer should be willing to provide a loaner to see you through the interim.

# Completing the Paperwork

After your inspection and orientation, it's time to wade patiently through the documentation that comes with taking delivery of the car. As with all complex transactions, the devil is in the details.

Begin by raising any questions you may have from your earlier reading of the contract that you asked the dealer to send you. If you are presented with a new copy of the contract, scrutinize it carefully to see that it is identical in every respect to the one you read originally.

Read through the financing section line by line if you are financing through the dealer. Ask the salesperson or the dealership's finance representative to clarify anything you don't understand. Get an explanation for any differences or changes in the lease duration or interest rate.

Do not sign a document that contains blanks or indicates that the final arrangements are "subject to loan approval." You run the risk that the terms of your loan can change significantly—to your disadvantage. If you were originally quoted a 5.75 percent interest rate on a standard 48-month car loan where the principal to be financed is $20,000, for example, an increase of one-percentage point on that rate would add about $440 over the life of the loan—the equivalent of nearly one full monthly loan payment at the lower rate. If the dealer doesn't immediately reinstate the terms to which you originally agreed, politely ask for your deposit back and be ready to leave. Usually the dealer will back down and apologize for the mistake.

When you accept delivery of a car being financed through the dealership, make sure there is a coupon payment book or some equally clear understanding of how billing for monthly payments will occur. If the precise amount of monthly payments and arrangements for making them are left vague, even at this delivery date, chances are good that you will hear from the dealership several days after you've taken the car home to learn that the original financing "fell through" but (good news!) the dealership was able to line up new financing for you that will cost you more. Speak now, or your options may be limited.

Next, be sure to inspect the warranty. This should list all applicable coverage, including the standard bumper-to-bumper warranty, as well as any separate warranties for the drive train, emissions systems, audio system, tires, and so on. Look carefully to see that the dealer has entered the current date as the effective start of the warranty time clock. If the vehicle had previously been used as a demonstrator, the dealership may have entered an earlier warranty start date, effectively reducing your protection.

Finally, look over the title and registration to make sure your name is spelled correctly, your address is right, and your driver's license number and the vehicle description are accurate. The license-plate number on the documents should match the plates that will be on the car when you drive off the dealership's lot.

Once you are satisfied that everything is in order, you can sign the contract and any other papers and take possession of your new car.

Congratulations—you've done it! The salesperson should give you two sets of keys, his pledge to help you with any questions or problems you may have about your new car, and a hearty handshake of respect for a customer who negotiated smartly and now will drive a great car.

# New-Car Delivery Checklist

| What to look for | Yes | No | N/A |
|---|---|---|---|
| **Inspect the vehicle** | | | |
| Examine the **exterior** for scratches, scrapes, dings, and dents. Note any disfigurations carefully, and have the dealership repair them before you take possession, or get a written commitment, signed by an authorized manager, describing the work to be done and a date when it will be completed. | | | |
| Confirm that the **vehicle is clean** inside and out. | | | |
| Check to see that a proper **state inspection sticker** is affixed to the windshield. | | | |
| Make sure **headlights, tail lights, parking lights, and turn signals** function properly. | | | |
| Make sure the **alarm system** works properly and can be armed and disarmed easily. | | | |
| There should be plenty of **gas in the tank**. | | | |
| See that the following items are included. <br> ■ Spare tire <br> ■ Jack and tire iron <br> ■ Wheel-lock tool <br> ■ All body trim <br> ■ Gas-tank cap <br> ■ Owner's manual and warranty books | | | |
| Ensure that all **dealer accessories** have been added. <br> ■ Floor mats <br> ■ Trunk cargo net <br> ■ Mud flaps <br> ■ Pinstriping <br> ■ Spoiler <br> ■ Custom radio or speakers <br> ■ Alarm or other security device <br> ■ Other: | | | |

# New-Car Delivery Checklist

| What to look for | Yes | No | N/A |
|---|---|---|---|
| **Inspect the vehicle** | | | |
| The **odometer** should register no more than a few nominal miles of use. If there are more than 100 miles on a vehicle from the dealership's lot, the price should be reduced to reflect the car's used status. | | | |
| **Owner's manual** is in glove compartment | | | |
| **Powered features** should function flawlessly<br>■   Windows<br>■   Locks<br>■   Seat positioning<br>■   Radio/CD/tape/DVD player<br>■   Antenna<br>■   Side-view mirrors<br>■   Heat/air conditioner fan motor and settings<br>■   Sun/moon roof<br>■   Other: | | | |
| **Steering** should be fluid, quiet, and responsive. | | | |
| **Transmission** should shift smoothly at appropriate RPMs. | | | |
| **Ride** should be quiet, smooth, and free of rattles. | | | |
| **Braking** should be responsive and firm at all speeds. | | | |
| **Check the paperwork** | | | |
| Read every clause of the **contract** and question anything you don't understand. | | | |
| The **Vehicle Identification Number (VIN)** on the car should match VIN appearing on the:<br>■ Bill of sale<br>■ Registration certificate/owner's card<br>■ Financing or lease agreement | | | |

# New-Car Delivery Checklist

| Check the paperwork, continued | Yes | No | N/A |
|---|---|---|---|
| Confirm that the **engine size and transmission type** are as ordered and that this information is correctly entered on the contract. | | | |
| **Loan document** should correctly state the: | | | |
| ■ Purchase price you and the dealer negotiated (including any dealer-installed options) | | | |
| ■ State sales tax computed at appropriate prevailing rate | | | |
| ■ Trade-in allowance for your old car | | | |
| ■ Total net payment due | | | |
| ■ Down payment you have made | | | |
| ■ Annual percentage rate of the loan | | | |
| ■ Term of the loan (in months of payments due) | | | |
| ■ Monthly payment | | | |
| There should be no blank spaces | | | |
| **Lease document** should correctly state the: | | | |
| ■ Capitalized cost (purchase price) | | | |
| ■ Trade-in allowance for your old car | | | |
| ■ Residual value at end of lease term | | | |
| ■ Capitalized cost reduction | | | |
| ■ Acquisition cost | | | |
| ■ Initial payment | | | |
| ■ Money factor | | | |
| ■ Term of the lease (in months) | | | |
| ■ Monthly payment | | | |
| There should be no blank spaces | | | |
| Payment book with monthly coupons for loan reimbursement should accurately reflect the number of monthly payments and dates when payments are due. | | | |
| State registration should have your full name, correct address, and proper identification of the vehicle. | | | |
| Warranty certificate is included, all terms are clear, and is dated for the day you take delivery. | | | |

# 18

# Save Money on Vehicle Maintenance

**Properly maintaining your vehicle** is not only the best way to maximize its resale value, but it's also the best way to reinforce your pride of ownership. To keep your car in top shape mechanically, it's important that you have the car serviced regularly, following the service schedule in your vehicle's owner's manual. In fact, if the vehicle is under warranty, you're required to do this to keep the warranty valid. Regular washing will help keep the exterior looking good, while frequent cleaning will do the same for the interior.

With advanced electronic systems controlling most engine operations, a lot of the tune-up and maintenance jobs that were routine a few decades ago are no longer needed. Typically, the only "tune-ups" that modern engines require is to have filters, spark plugs, and fluids replaced on schedule.

While it's important to stay on top of maintenance and repair, many people overspend, wasting money on overly frequent oil changes, using premium gasoline in an engine designed for regular, or being scammed into having needless service done by a dealership or repair shop.

This chapter will cover some of the more common maintenance items with which you should be familiar and show you how to minimize your driving expenses. We'll discuss:

- What you need to know about the care and fueling of your new car
- How to break in your new car properly
- Finding a mechanic you can trust
- The keys to everyday car maintenance
- The importance of good record-keeping

At the end of this chapter, you'll also find handy logs for keeping track of maintenance and fuel consumption.

## Read Your Owner's Manual

Perhaps you've heard the line, "As a last resort, check the owner's manual." This is funny because it's all too true, especially for those of us with a natural instinct to figure out things on our own. Nevertheless, we suggest that soon after bringing your new vehicle home, you take some time to familiarize yourself with its owner's manual. If you bought a used car that has no owner's manual, you should be able to order one through a local dealership.

You don't have to read every page, but you should become familiar enough with how to operate your vehicle that you don't become distracted while you're driving and trying to, say, change seat adjustments, save radio stations, or adjust the climate-control system. You should also check out the recommended maintenance schedule and read any safety warnings. Following are some of the topics with which you should acquaint yourself:

## Grade of fuel

Essentially, the only real difference between grades of gasoline is the octane rating. Typically, regular fuel has an octane rating of 87, mid-grade is 89, and premium is 91 to 93. The rating of each grade is posted on gasoline pumps. The octane rating indicates how resistant the fuel is to knocking or pinging, which is a condition in which fuel burns uncontrollably in the engine's combustion chambers. When severe, this can damage an engine.

The engines in most vehicles are designed to run just fine on regular gasoline. Despite what many people think, using premium fuel in these vehicles will not make the engines run better. It will only cost you more money. For instance, at 20 cents more per gallon, running a Ford Explorer on premium fuel rather than regular could cost you about $200 more per year with no additional benefit.

Premium fuel is recommended for many sports cars and luxury vehicles, which have higher-performance engines. (Because they use a higher compression ratio, they need a higher resistance to knocking.) Even so, modern electronic engine-control systems often allow you to run lower-octane fuel in these engines by adjusting the ignition timing slightly if any knock is detected. This gives up some power potential, but it's likely that most drivers won't notice it.

Check with your dealership's service department to be sure, but as a rule of thumb, if the owner's manual says premium fuel is "recommended," you can typically use regular instead. If the manual says that premium is "required," you should stick with the higher grade.

## Recommended motor oil

The recommended oil weight will vary primarily according to the temperature range in the region where you do most of your driving. An oil's weight, or viscosity, is simply a measure of how easily it flows. Viscosity is designated by an SAE (Society of Automotive Engineers) rating system that ranges from 5 to 50. The higher the number, the thicker or heavier the oil and the slower it flows.

# The black death of sludge

Sludge is a condition in which the engine oil oxidizes and breaks down after prolonged exposure to high temperatures. The baked oil turns gelatinous and can block vital oil passages, which could lead to repairs exceeding $8,000 or even an engine replacement.

While sludge often results from poor upkeep, notably not changing oil at prescribed intervals, some engines appear prone to it, regardless of maintenance and mileage. See the chart below.

The Center for Auto Safety received about 1,300 sludge complaints between 2004 and 2005. The National Highway Traffic Safety Administration received about 900 complaints. All vehicle owners should keep thorough records of their automobile maintenance and repairs and make sure all receipts contain the date, mileage, and vehicle identification number. Those with sludge-prone engines should use an American Petroleum Institute-approved synthetic motor oil or change the oil according to the "extreme use" schedule in the vehicle's manual. Synthetics have a higher tolerance for extreme heat and flow better in cold temperatures. Changing oil on the extreme-use schedule (and saving the records) provides evidence that you tried to protect the engine from sludge.

| Model | Model year | Engine |
| --- | --- | --- |
| Audi A4 | 1997-2004 | 1.8L four-cyl. turbo |
| Chrysler Concorde | 1998-2002 | 2.7L V6 |
| Chrysler Sebring | 1998-2002 | 2.7L V6 |
| Dodge Intrepid | 1998-2002 | 2.7L V6 |
| Dodge Stratus | 1998-2002 | 2.7L V6 |
| Lexus ES300 | 1997-2001 | 3.0L V6 |
| Lexus RX300 | 1999-2001 | 3.0L V6 |
| Saab 9-3 hatchback | 2000-02 | 2.0L four-cyl. turbo |
| Saab 9-3 convertible | 2000-03 | 2.0L four-cyl. turbo |
| Saab 9-3 Viggen | 1999 | 2.3L four-cyl. turbo |
| Saab 9-5 | 1999-2003 | 2.3L four-cyl. turbo |
| Toyota Avalon | 1997-2001 | 3.0L V6 |
| Toyota Camry | 1997-2001 | 2.2L four-cyl. or 3.0L V6 |
| Toyota Camry Solara | 1999-2001 | 2.2L four-cyl. or 3.0L V6 |
| Toyota Celica | 1996-2001 | 2.2L four-cyl. |
| Toyota Highlander | 2001 | 3.0L V6 |
| Toyota Sienna | 1997-2001 | 3.0L V6 |
| Volkswagen Passat | 1997-2004 | 1.8L four-cyl. turbo |

Grades with a W (5W, 10W, 15W, etc.) are appropriate for cold starting in winter temperatures.

A thinner or low-viscosity grade is better for starting an engine in colder temperatures because it flows more easily in these conditions, but a higher viscosity formula is better once the engine has warmed up because it provides a thicker cushion of oil. That's why most recommended oils today are multiviscosity formulas that change according to the temperature. A 10W/40 formula, for instance, has a base viscosity of 10 to provide easy flowing in cold temperatures. As the engine heats up, the oil thickens to a viscosity rating of 40 to provide better lubrication at higher temperatures.

Always use the motor oil grade that's recommended in your owner's manual for your vehicle and climate. For some vehicles, the manufacturer specifies synthetic oil. This is more expensive, but is more resistant to breaking down in high heat and other demanding conditions.

We'll discuss oil changing later in this chapter.

## Dashboard warning lights

There are usually individual warning lights to alert you to critical problems with your vehicle. These typically include low brake fluid or a malfunctioning braking system, engine overheating, or low oil pressure. All modern vehicles also have a "Check Engine" light that warns you of a problem in the engine or emissions-control system. Learn where these warning lights are located on your vehicle's instrument panel and how they display when activated.

## Controls that affect comfort and safety

With the engine running, the transmission in "park" or "neutral," the parking brake on, and the owner's manual open in your lap, become acquainted with instruments that you may want to operate while driving. For example, you should learn how to operate your windshield wiper and washer sys-

## What to do if the "Check Engine" light comes on

All modern vehicles have a built-in diagnostic system that constantly monitors the engine's and emission system's electronic-control system. If a problem is detected, it illuminates a light in the dash that's commonly labeled "Check Engine." What should you do if this happens?

The Check Engine light can represent any of dozens of different problems, ranging from something as minor as a loose fuel-filler cap to something more serious, such as a failing catalytic converter.

If the light is flashing or your car is stalling or misfiring, get service immediately. If, however, the light remains on continually and there isn't any noticeable problem with the vehicle, it's OK to continue to drive it normally for a while. Check that the gas cap is tight. Even if the cap is loose, be aware that the light may take several trips before the light resets. If the light doesn't go off by itself, take your vehicle into the shop within a few days.

Whatever the problem, an illuminated Check Engine light means that the vehicle is emitting excessive pollutants. As a result, there's a good chance you'll fail any state emissions test that you're required to have.

When the light goes on, the system stores a diagnostic code that a mechanic can read to help pinpoint the problem. There are relatively inexpensive devices you can buy to read the code yourself, but unless you know a lot about cars, you're probably better off taking your vehicle to a mechanic.

tem, change settings on your audio system or trip computer, adjust the driver's seat and side view mirrors, and open or close the sunroof. These are not switches you want to have to search for, fumble with, or be distracted by while you're driving and attempting to maneuver in traffic.

Some advanced electronics system, such as a navigation system, multifunction control system, or hands-free phone system can be very distracting to use while driving. Take the necessary time to become familiar with this type of system before you begin driving.

### Child safety-seat positioning

If you'll be using a child safety seat frequently in your car, learn how to properly position and secure it. The National Highway Traffic Safety Administration estimates that about 7 in 10 children may not be adequately protected while in a child car seat. Common problems are loose harness straps securing the child in the seat and loose seatbelts around the seat.

Because installing a child seat can be difficult, you should carefully read both the child-seat and vehicle owner's manuals. Even then, you may find inconsistencies between the two. For installation help, you can search for a certified safety technician at *www.nhtsa.dot.gov.*

All cars manufactured after September 2002 are required to have a universal Lower Anchors and Tethers for Children (LATCH) system that works with specially equipped child seats. It consists of a top tether and two lower attachments in the crease between the backrest and seat cushion. The LATCH system was designed to be easier to use than securing child seats with the car's safety belts. But in our testing we've found that the lower anchors in some cars are positioned too far into the crease, making them difficult to access.

For children who have outgrown a child seat, it's critical that the car's shoulder belt is properly positioned on the shoulder, not across the neck, and the lap belt across their hips, not their abdomen. This may require the use of a booster seat. If the vehicle has adjustable upper safety-belt anchors or belt guides, learn how to use them to position the belts correctly.

# The Break-in Period

During the first 1,000 miles you drive your new car, the moving parts need to settle in to mesh smoothly together, and that can happen only if you drive with restraint. Your owner's manual will explain the specific break-in period requirements of your vehicle, but some common sense rules apply to all new cars:

- Avoid fast starts and stops.
- Do not accelerate rapidly or change gears aggressively.
- Vary your speeds over the full range of highway and city driving, and minimize your use of cruise control.
- With manual transmissions, don't drive in too high a gear so that the engine seems to be lugging. It's better to allow the engine to rev in a lower gear than lug in a higher gear.

Each time you fill up with gasoline during the first thousand miles, check the oil level. Because the engine is new and its moving parts haven't yet been fully lubricated by use, oil consumption can be higher than it will be after it has more miles on it. Thereafter, try to check the oil level every 500 miles up to the first scheduled service.

Likewise, transmission gears, which can be damaged by bare metal-on-metal grinding, have to be broken-in gently. If your vehicle has a manual transmission, the manufacturer may recommend that you shift gears at lower engine speeds than would be appropriate after you've put on more miles. Typically, if it would be normal shifting from first gear to second gear at 25 miles per hour, discipline yourself to shift at 20 mph, instead; from second gear to third gear, shift at 30 mph instead of 40; and so on. Avoid downshifting to slow the vehicle during the break-in period, unless you're descending a long grade and need to use a lower gear to avoid overheating the brakes.

Keeping your car's exterior clean also requires special attention during the break-in period. Hand-wash your car initially. Some manufacturers recommend that you avoid having your car washed at an automated commercial car wash during the first six months you own it, as the paint will not have hardened sufficiently to withstand the harsher detergents and high pressure hoses and scrubbers they use.

# Make Regular Maintenance A Habit

As we've said, sticking to your maintenance schedule is the best way to prevent expensive problems from blindsiding you. In addition, the more you drive your car, the more you'll become attuned to its subtleties and the easier you'll notice small changes. Being aware of these types of things can also help you catch small problems before they become major ones.

You can perform many common maintenance tasks yourself, which will save you money and keep you in better touch with your vehicle's condition. The most basic ones are covered in your owner's manual. If you're mechanically inclined and want to tackle more advanced tasks, such as changing brake pads or spark plugs, you can order a service manual for your vehicle from the dealership.

There are several key areas that should get your priority attention.

## Tires: They're more than "black and round"

A vehicle's tires play a crucial role in a car's safety. As the only parts of the car that physically touch the ground, they are one of the key factors affecting a vehicle's handling, braking, ride comfort, and traction. In addition, underinflated tires cost you more money at the pump. Underinflated tires can also build up excess heat, which can lead to tire failure.

Proper attention to the care of your tires will cost you nothing more than the price of a decent tire-pressure gauge and a few minutes of your time each month. We recommend getting a good tire gauge with a digital readout, available at auto parts stores. Pencil-type gauges that we've tested were just as accurate as the digital models but were a little harder to read.

Get into the habit of checking your tire pressure at least once a month. You will find the recommended air pressure printed on a placard or label usually located in the driver's-side door jamb or on the inside of the glovebox lid. Check your owner's manual for the location on your vehicle.

Check the tire pressure when tires are cold, before you start driving. As

## Shop around for maintenance

You might expect that the price for, say, a 30,000-mile service procedure on a specific model would cost about the same from one dealership to the next. But you'd be wrong.

For a report we did in 2002, a CONSUMER REPORTS reporter called 36 dealerships and auto-repair shops in Houston, San Francisco, and Syracuse, N.Y., asking for a price for a 30,000-mile checkup for a 2000 Honda Accord or a 60,000-mile checkup for a 1998 Ford Explorer. Service quotes for the Accord ranged from $125 to $527; prices for the Explorer, $143 to $650. Even within the same city, the difference amounted to hundreds of dollars.

In 2005, we got an even wider range when a reporter called seven Nissan dealerships in one area on Long Island, N.Y., and asked for a price for the 60,000-mile service on a 2000 Nissan Pathfinder. The quotes ranged from $269 to $1,078—a difference of more than $800.

Prices vary so much because dealerships often include service items that go well beyond those listed in the owner's manual. A few of the Nissan dealerships even added services that Nissan advises against, such as putting additives in the fuel and oil.

When we called the Nissan dealerships back and asked for only the items that are specified in the owner's manual, the quotes dropped as much as $521.

Before you take your vehicle in for scheduled maintenance, call around for prices and ask that they only include items that are listed in the owner's manual. Anything else should be quoted separately.

Typically, you can also take your vehicle to an independent shop, which is generally less expensive than dealerships, without compromising your warranty. Just be sure to keep all receipts, so you can prove the service was performed on schedule should there be an issue involving a warranty claim.

tires heat up from driving, the pressure may rise 5 psi or more. To easily add air, consider buying a small portable air compressor that runs off of your car's power outlet. It's a lot more convenient than finding a compressor at a gas station.

When you check air pressure, also inspect the tire's tread and sidewalls for cracking, bubbles, or lumps. Ideally, tires should wear evenly across their tread. Underinflated tires have heavier tread wear on the outer and inner edges. Overinflation will be evident when the center of the tread shows excessive wear. Excessive wear on one or another edge of one of the front tires is an indication that the wheels may be out of alignment and need adjustment. Spotty and uneven wear on tire treads may be signs of suspension or tire abnormalities.

Even when properly inflated, the tires on the drive wheels will wear more quickly, which is why vehicle and tire manufacturers recommend that the tires be regularly rotated to lengthen their useful life. Check your owner's manual for the correct interval.

## Oil and filter changes: Keep the lifeblood flowing

Motor oil is literally the lifeblood of your car's engine. Ensuring that your car always runs with an adequate supply of clean oil is an essential prerequisite for problem-free driving.

The oil level should be checked at least once a week, following the directions in your owner's manual. Basically, make sure your car is parked on a level surface and the engine is off. Ideally, the engine should be cold, but if you've been driving, wait a few minutes after you've shut off the engine to allow the oil to settle in the crankcase. Then remove the dipstick, wipe it clean, and reinsert it. The oil level should fall between the minimum and maximum calibration lines (the difference between the two usually being one quart of oil) indicated on the dipstick. Running with low oil will cause excessive wear and internal engine damage. Overfilling can also result in engine damage, as well as oil leaks and overconsumption.

## You need to know

When it comes to maintaining your vehicle, popular misconceptions abound. Among the most common:

**Myth:** Tires should be inflated to the pressure shown on the sidewall.

**Reality:** The tire-pressure figure shown on the tire's sidewall is the maximum pressure. Always use the vehicle manufacturer's recommended pressure, which is determined to provide the best balance of ride, handling, and fuel economy. It's usually printed on a sticker on a doorjamb, the glovebox, or the fuel-filler door. Check your tires against the recommended pressure when your car has been at rest for a while.

**Myth:** If regular-grade fuel is good, premium must be better.

**Reality:** Most vehicles are designed to run just fine on regular-grade (87 octane) fuel. A higher octane number doesn't mean your vehicle will perform better. It just means it's more resistant to engine knocking or pinging. Use the octane grade that's recommended in your vehicle's owner's manual. Filling up with a higher grade is usually a waste of money.

**Myth:** Engine oil should be changed every 3,000 miles.

**Reality:** Although oil companies and quick-lube shops like to promote this idea, it's usually not necessary. Go by the recommended oil-change schedule in your vehicle's owner's manual. Most vehicles driven under normal conditions can go 7,500 miles or more between oil changes. Some models now come with a monitoring system that alerts the driver when the oil needs changing. Depending on driving conditions, these can extend change intervals to 10,000 or 15,000 miles.

**Myth:** You don't have to worry about replacing tires until they're worn down to the minimum tread depth.

**Reality:** If a tire's tread wears to the minimum depth of $1/16$ inch, it should be replaced. But a tire's grip can be compromised well before this mark if you drive in rain, slush, or snow. As the tread wears, it's easier for the tire to hydroplane or lose traction and for the driver to lose control.

When you check the oil level, take note of the color of the oil coating the dipstick. It should be nearly clear light amber. Darker shades indicate that the oil is getting dirty and should be changed.

If you need to add oil, make sure it's the formula specified in your owner's manual (see page 339).

It's important that the oil be changed at the recommended interval in your owner's manual to prevent excessive engine wear. For normal driving conditions, this is typically 7,500 to 10,000 miles. Despite what oil companies and oil-change shops tell you, there's no reason to change your oil every 3,000 miles unless you drive in "severe" conditions, as listed in your manual. This is usually defined as driving in dusty conditions or lots of stop-and-go traffic; extended high-speed driving; running the engine under a heavy load, such as when towing; or doing many successive short trips during which the engine doesn't have time to achieve and maintain its normal operating temperature.

If you add a new quart of oil to your car's engine on a regular basis, don't assume that this takes the place of changing the oil, since changing is still needed to remove contaminants and replenish the additive packages.

Whether you change your car's oil yourself or have a mechanic do it for you, replace the oil filter each time. A clogged filter will impede oil flow, reducing the system's ability to lubricate and protect the engine.

If you change the oil yourself, you must dispose of it properly. You can find resources based on your ZIP code at *www.earth911.org*.

## Drive belt: It keeps things moving

The drive belt performs heavy-duty work connecting your engine's crankshaft, generator, air conditioning compressor, and power steering pump—a big load for a serpentine stretch of reinforced rubber to carry. You will want to rely on a mechanic to replace or adjust the drive belt, but regular inspection by you can head off potential problems before the belt breaks unexpectedly, possibly leading to engine failure or a major breakdown.

# Tips for cutting the cost of driving

How you drive your car will have a big impact on your cost of ownership. Following are common-sense habits that will save you money. For more tips, see "You need to know" on page 348.

- Have maintenance performed according to the schedule in the owner's manual. A poorly maintained engine can cut gas mileage by 10 percent to 20 percent. And neglecting maintenance can lead to costly problems down the road. Still, when you take your vehicle in for maintenance, make sure you're only paying for the items that are specified in the owner's manual (see "Shop around for maintenance" on page 346).

- Avoid rapid starts and stops, if you can. Driving smoothly and steadily makes the best use of your fuel. Smooth acceleration, cornering, and braking will also extend the life of the engine, transmission, brakes, and tires.

- An engine runs most inefficiently when it's cold. It not only uses more fuel but also creates the most exhaust emissions and suffers the most wear. Avoid many short, separate trips—and unnecessary cold starts—by combining as many errands as possible into one trip.

- Keep tires properly inflated. Low tire pressure increases fuel consumption and can shorten tire life. If you use winter tires, remove them after the snow threat has passed; they wear more quickly than all-season tires.

- Run the air conditioner only when you need it. The A/C compressor adds load to the engine, increasing fuel consumption.

- At highway speeds, more than 50 percent of engine power goes to overcoming aerodynamic drag. Try not to add to the drag by carrying things on top of your vehicle. A loaded roof rack can decrease a car's fuel efficiency by 5 percent. Even driving with an empty ski rack wastes gas.

- You'll save fuel by not letting the engine run at idle any longer than necessary. After starting the car in the morning, begin driving right away; don't let it sit and "warm up" for several minutes. An engine actually warms up faster while driving.

While the engine is cold, carefully inspect the belt along its edges and undersides for signs of wear. Look for cracks, missing sections of the drive ribs, signs of pilling (when the rubber wears off and creates deposits on the adjacent drive pulley), or glazing caused by deposits of oil, grease, or other engine fluids that can lead to belt slippage. These danger signs indicate that a belt may need to be replaced or that a belt-driven component may be failing.

Belt tension should be checked and adjusted on a regular basis. With the engine shut off, test belt tension by pressing a section of the belt in an accessible spot between components. A belt's tension is correct if it has between ½ inch to 1 inch of play. A belt that is too tight adds load to engine bearings, causing them to wear out more quickly. If you hear a squealing sound when the engine is running, the drive belt is probably too loose and is slipping. This can shorten the belt's life and cause the components to which it is attached to work less efficiently. If you spot a defect, have your mechanic take a look at it at the earliest opportunity.

## Cooling system: Taking the heat off

Proper maintenance of your car's cooling system helps protect the engine from overheating. It's particularly important during the initial break-in period because the coolant level may drop as the coolant fills air pockets in the engine and cooling system.

The coolant level should be checked at least once a month, and more frequently during the summer. Some models have a sensor to warn of low coolant level. You can easily see the coolant level inside the translucent coolant expansion tank located within the engine compartment. The coolant should be between the minimum and maximum levels embossed into the tank's side. If it's below the minimum level, add a 50/50 mix of water and the type of antifreeze specified in your owner's manual. You can also buy a premixed 50/50 blend in auto parts stores. After filling the tank, run the engine until it is hot, then check the coolant level again.

Do not remove the radiator cap when the engine is hot, as coolant can spill over, scalding you. When checking the coolant level, also examine the condition of the hoses that run from the coolant expansion tank and the radiator for cracking or softness that can lead to leaks.

## Paint: How to keep that "new car" look

Keeping your car clean is more than an aesthetic choice; it's essential for preserving the new-car finish and maximizing resale value. Don't wait for a layer of crud to accumulate on the exterior before washing. Dead bugs, bird droppings, and chemicals from the atmosphere all leach acids that can strip away wax and eventually eat into your car's paint. If left too long, they can cause damage that requires sanding and repainting the area to correct.

Wash off dead bugs, bird droppings, and tree-sap mist as soon as possible. Other than this, a weekly car wash will keep the finish in its best shape.

If you do your own car washes, use a dedicated car-wash product, which is milder than household cleaning agents or dishwashing detergent. Apply the suds with a large, soft natural sponge or a lamb's-wool mitt.

Grease, rubber, and road-tar deposits often accumulate around the wheel wells and along the lower edge of the body. These can be stubborn to remove and may require a stronger product, such as a bug-and-tar remover. Use a soft, nonabrasive cloth to remove these deposits, as they can quickly blacken your sponge. Use a separate sponge to clean the wheels and tires, which may be coated with sand, brake dust, and other debris that could mar the car's finish. Mild soap and water may work here; if not, a dedicated wheel cleaner may be required. Be sure the cleaner is compatible with the type of finish on the wheels. A strong formula intended for mag wheels, for instance, can damage the clear coat that's used on the wheels that come on today's cars. To be on the safe side, choose a cleaner that's labeled as safe for use on all wheels.

Rinse all surfaces with water before you begin washing to remove loose dirt and debris that could cause scratching. Work the car-wash solution into a lather with plenty of suds that provide lots of lubrication on the paint surface. And rinse the sponge often. Using a separate bucket to rinse the sponge keeps dirt from getting mixed into the sudsy wash water.

Don't move the sponge in circles. This can create light but noticeable scratches called swirl marks. Instead, move the sponge lengthwise across the hood and other body panels. And don't continue using a sponge that has dropped on the ground without thoroughly rinsing it out. The sponge can pick up dirt particles that can scratch the paint.

If you live in the snowbelt, be sure to wash inside the wheel wells and under the car to clean away any road salt.

Don't let the car air dry, and don't expect a drive around the block to do an effective drying job. Either will leave watermarks, which are the minerals left after evaporation. In addition, don't use an abrasive towel or other material that can leave hairline scratches in the paint. Instead, use a chamois (natural or synthetic) or soft terry towels. It's best to blot the water up instead of dragging the towel or chamois over the paint.

Keep the car's painted surfaces protected with regular waxing using any low-abrasive wax or protectant that's labeled "safe for clearcoats."

You should also have deep scratches and stone chips in the paint repaired as quickly as possible, as they can result in rusting. Buy a bottle of touch-up paint from your dealership and keep it handy. More extensive damage may need the attention of a body shop, but don't neglect it or you risk more lasting damage that can significantly reduce your car's value.

# Where to Go for Maintenance and Repairs

Before you consider where to take your vehicle for maintenance and repair, you need to understand the difference between the two. Routine maintenance items are those listed in your vehicle's owner's manual as part of the model's service schedule. They are intended to keep your vehicle in top operating condition. Repairs are service that needs to be performed to fix a problem. Where you take your vehicle may depend on what needs to be done.

**Scheduled maintenance** can be performed at any dealership; you don't have to go to the one where you bought the vehicle. Likewise, you can take your vehicle to an independent auto-repair shop or franchise, which are typically less expensive than dealerships. Federal law gives you the right to service your vehicle wherever you like without affecting your warranty coverage. (Depending on the contract, lessees may be required to have all service performed at a dealership.)

Mechanics in your dealership's service department are specifically trained and certified in all aspects of your model's service needs, and the shop will be equipped with all of the necessary diagnostic equipment. Because maintenance items are fairly basic, however, any professional auto shop should be able to perform the necessary tasks.

Wherever you go for service, make sure they have access to the manufacturer's latest technical service bulletins (TSBs), which are basically instructions on how to fix common problems with a particular model. Often, an automaker will do TSB repairs for free, but you'll have to go to a dealership to get the work done. For more on TSBs and other service issues, see Chapter 19.

**Repairs** can range from basic tasks such as a brake job or auto-body repair to complicated service such as overhauling a transmission or diagnosing an electronics system problem. Go to a dealership if your car is covered by the original warranty and you want the manufacturer to pay for the fix. Use a dealership, too, if your car has been recalled or is the subject of a "service campaign" in which the automaker offers to correct a defect. If you have an extended warranty, you'll need to check the terms to see who must perform covered repairs.

If the vehicle is out of warranty, the type of problem may determine where you take it for repair. A reputable independent shop should be able to handle most common repairs. Shops that specialize in your vehicle's brand are more likely to have the proper training, equipment, and up-to-date information. A good technician will let you know when a problem warrants a trip to the dealership or a speciality shop.

If you're experiencing a problem with a system that's exclusive to your model or automaker—especially electronics, such as a navigation or multi-function control system—consider taking the vehicle to a dealership. You also need to take it to a dealership to have a safety recall work performed.

# Keep Records of Maintenance and Repair

As long as you own a vehicle, and especially during the warranty period, you should keep all records and receipts of maintenance and repair work. Complete documentation should include the type of work done, the dates the work was performed, the mileage on the odometer when it was completed, who did the work, and what you paid for the parts and service.

A detailed maintenance log could be critical if you have a dispute with the manufacturer over a covered warranty repair. It's also documentation of repeat problems that could mean there was an undetected manufacturing defect that could lead to more costly repairs later on and, if left unaddressed, could potentially haunt you for as long as you own the car. A sample maintenance log appears on the next page.

Having a log and receipts will also provide a complete service record that will confirm that you faithfully completed all scheduled service and attended to replacement of parts, such as tires, mufflers, shock absorbers, and batteries, which wear out over time. This can be helpful when you decide to sell your car, and can easily show that it has a proven service history.

## Maintenance log

| Date | Odometer reading | Service or repair completed | Parts replaced | Where work was done | Total paid |
|------|------------------|-----------------------------|----------------|---------------------|------------|
|      |                  |                             |                |                     |            |
|      |                  |                             |                |                     |            |
|      |                  |                             |                |                     |            |
|      |                  |                             |                |                     |            |
|      |                  |                             |                |                     |            |
|      |                  |                             |                |                     |            |
|      |                  |                             |                |                     |            |
|      |                  |                             |                |                     |            |
|      |                  |                             |                |                     |            |
|      |                  |                             |                |                     |            |
|      |                  |                             |                |                     |            |
|      |                  |                             |                |                     |            |

## Fuel consumption

| Date | Odometer reading | Miles driven since last refill | Fuel purchased | | Miles per gallon (miles driven divided by gallons purchased) |
|------|------------------|--------------------------------|----------------|----------------|-------------------------------------------------------------|
|      |                  |                                | Number of gallons | Cost per gallon |                                                         |
|      |                  |                                |                |                |                                                             |
|      |                  |                                |                |                |                                                             |
|      |                  |                                |                |                |                                                             |
|      |                  |                                |                |                |                                                             |
|      |                  |                                |                |                |                                                             |
|      |                  |                                |                |                |                                                             |
|      |                  |                                |                |                |                                                             |
|      |                  |                                |                |                |                                                             |
|      |                  |                                |                |                |                                                             |
|      |                  |                                |                |                |                                                             |
|      |                  |                                |                |                |                                                             |

# 19

# Recalls & Service Problems

**Your automobile** is probably the most complex piece of machinery you own. Things can and will go wrong, despite your best efforts to maintain it.

Most auto repairs can be serviced relatively quickly with few unexpected problems. Sometimes, however, a problem can arise that requires special attention. Some problems that affect the vehicle's safety, for instance, require that the automaker issue a recall. For the safety of your passengers and yourself, it's important that you respond to these promptly and that you take the car to the dealership to have it fixed within an appropriate amount of time (usually specified in the recall notice).

Often, a model will have a reoccurring problem that causes the manufacturer to issue a technical service bulletin (TSB). This instructs dealerships on how to correct the problem. Unlike recalls,

TSBs aren't announced to the general public, so many car owners don't know they exist. Being aware of TSBs related to your model, however, can help you get problems repaired efficiently and, in some cases, give you more leverage in getting a problem fixed for free even after your factory warranty has expired.

Sometimes you may encounter a problem that can't be fixed to your satisfaction or a vehicle that suffers from an ongoing array of problems. In these cases, you may need outside help to get the trouble resolved or to get reimbursement for service that didn't do the job.

In this chapter, we review all three of these scenarios, including:

- How to find out about the little-known TSBs, sometimes called "secret warranties" or "hidden recalls"

- What you need to know about safety recalls and how to learn about the safety-related vehicle defects that lead to them

- The remedies available to you under federal and state lemon laws to replace a defective vehicle that cannot be repaired

# Technical Service Bulletins

After a model is released, the auto manufacturer carefully tracks problems related to it. If it sees that different dealerships are reporting a similar problem, it may issue a technical service bulletin, commonly called a TSB, to all of the service departments in its dealership network. Essentially, a TSB includes detailed instructions on how to correct the problem and may specify any special tools or parts needed for the procedure.

TSBs are issued on virtually all vehicles, even the most reliable. Through the middle of 2005, for example, the popular 2002 Toyota Camry, which has been consistently reliable in our subscriber surveys, had 79 TSBs released. Many include diagnostic guidelines, but others cover repairs or adjustments needed on everything from an engine heat indicator light to a balky gas cap. Included in these are no fewer than seven different fixes to the driver-side, passenger-side, and side-curtain air bags.

In most states, manufacturers are under no legal obligation to disclose TSBs to customers, because the problems are not safety-related nor do they seriously compromise performance. The exceptions are California, Connecticut, Virginia, and Wisconsin, where dealerships are required to tell you about TSBs. In any case, TSBs are so common that you should make it your business to know about those that affect your new vehicle from the outset and continue to track them throughout the time you own the car.

If your vehicle has a problem that's covered by a TSB, the related repairs will be performed free during your factory warranty period, with the manufacturer picking up the tab. If you don't know a TSB exists, you may never be aware that such service work has been performed. That's why TSBs are sometimes called "hidden recalls" or "secret warranties."

After the warranty period, you are required to pay for the repair. As a result, you'll want to have any necessary TSB-related service taken care of before your warranty expires.

Even after the warranty period, it helps to know about TSBs. A TSB verifies the fact that a certain problem is common to your model. As such, it can help you build a case to have the automaker perform the repair for free or at least give you a partial price break.

TSBs can also be handy in helping a mechanic isolate a specific problem with your vehicle, by telling them exactly what the trouble is and how to fix it. If your vehicle is exhibiting a symptom that matches that described in a TSB, simply point this out to the mechanic or service writer. It can help eliminate time wasted on unnecessary testing and diagnosis.

If you take your vehicle to an independent repair shop, make sure it has access to TSBs for your vehicle and ask them to check for any new ones when you take your car in for servicing. If the car is out of warranty and you are willing to pay for the repair, your regular shop will likely be able to do the work. However, to have a TSB repair performed for free, it must be done by a dealership.

**Sources of help.** Fortunately, information about TSBs is publicly available to consumers, though you have to do a bit of digging to get all the details you will need to act on them. You can search for TSBs at the National Highway Traffic Safety Administration (NHTSA) Web site (*www-odi.nhtsa.dot.gov/cars/problems/tsb/tsbsearch.cfm*). There you can read a summary of each TSB, which is often enough information for a vehicle owner who is taking the car to a professional repair shop. TSBs are also summarized for all makes and models built since 1981 on Edmunds' Web site (*www.edmunds.com/maintenance/vehicle.do*).

Complete TSBs can be purchased on a subscription basis from ALL-DATA, a provider of diagnostic, repair, and estimating information to automotive professionals, at *www.alldata.com/recalls/index.html*. However, the subscription costs $25 per vehicle and you likely won't need the complete TSB unless you intend to do the repairs yourself.

Consult these or other resources where TSB information is available before service visits, and write down the reference number for any TSBs that apply to your car. If you are mechanically inclined and have a well-equipped tool kit, you may be able to handle many of the fixes on your own.

## Safety Recalls

In 2003, close to 32,000 occupants of passenger vehicles were killed and an additional 2,650,000 were injured. While many factors contribute to this, defects in vehicle safety resulting from flawed designs, malfunctioning parts, or manufacturing shortcomings are ones that are avoidable. Federal law entrusts NHTSA with the responsibility for establishing and, in cooperation with auto manufacturers, for monitoring vehicle safety standards.

When necessary, NHTSA is authorized to intervene by ordering manufacturers to recall and remediate vehicles with known defects. Since NHTSA's establishment in the mid-1960s, more than 300 million vehicles of all types have been recalled—some by government mandate, though many voluntarily by the manufacturers themselves.

## How recalls are determined

Unlike TSBs, there is nothing secret or optional about recalls because fundamental issues of a vehicle's safety are involved in their issuance. Problems that can lead to a recall include design or manufacturing flaws affecting critical components or systems that don't meet federal standards or pose a risk to the safe operation of the vehicle.

Thus, faulty wheel and steering components, a defective fuel system prone to stalling or leaks, and wiring that shorts out are all regarded as unacceptable threats to passenger safety. So, too, is defective safety equipment such as air bags that don't deploy properly, malfunctioning seat-belt retractors, and seats or seatbacks that break in normal use. Tires that are prone to sudden blowouts or tread separation also fall under NHTSA purview and are subject to recall orders.

Newly released or redesigned vehicles may be especially prone to recalls as their manufacturers uncover design flaws that emerge only as early buyers encounter problems. Even the priciest and most highly engineered luxury models are subject to dangerous defects that lead to voluntary manufacturer-released recalls.

For example, shortly after BMW began selling its new luxury 7 Series sedans, its engineers discovered a defective engine management control unit affecting more than 6,500 cars manufactured over a three-month period in mid-2004. The consequences of a failure of this critically important part are severe, leading to engine stalling, the loss of power steering, and the failure of power-assisted brakes.

Safety-impairing defects in vehicles that have been on the road for several years are less likely to be discovered by the manufacturer and are more commonly the result of NHTSA investigations into driver complaints and analyses of accident records. If it determines that a problem warrants a recall, the NHTSA requires the manufacturer to determine how many vehicles are afflicted with the problem, develop a plan to repair them, and notify their owners.

## Recall complications

The law stipulates that all recall-related service is to be done at the expense of the manufacturer and that the owner should bear none of the cost. That information must also appear in the recall notice you receive. The manufacturer has three legal options for addressing the problem that led to the recall. The vehicle can be repaired; it can be replaced with a similar vehicle; or it can be repurchased at its fair market value determined by its age and mileage.

Recall procedures look straightforward, but you can face situations that frustrate your efforts to get prompt, reliable relief. Manufacturers can challenge an NHTSA recall request, tying up the resolution of a problem until a drawn-out negotiation or a court battle determines whether the recall is warranted. However, in the meantime, a manufacturer may be required to notify customers of the recall request.

If you do have a problem that is subject to an unresolved recall, you will have to pay for the service on your own. If the outcome of the challenge ultimately is decided in your favor, NHSTA requires that owners be reimbursed for repairs made as of the beginning of NHTSA's engineering analysis of the alleged defect or one year prior to the manufacturer's defect notice, whichever is earlier. You'll need to document the repair, so be sure to hold on to all service receipts. You'll also need to file your claim within 10 days of being notified that the recall is in effect.

In any case you should not delay in having the necessary repair work done if you are concerned about a problem that may result in a collision. Driving a vehicle in which you feel safe should be your first priority.

Owners of older vehicles, too, may find that they are ineligible for reimbursement when a recall for a problem with their car is ordered. In order to be eligible, a vehicle cannot be more than 10 years old on the date the defect or non-compliance is determined. The age is calculated from the sale date to the first purchaser. If, for example, a defect is found in 2005 and a recall is ordered, only cars purchased new in 1996 through 2005 are eligible. As frustrating as this exclusion may be, you shouldn't postpone having the necessary work done.

## How to find out about recalls

Whether a recall is initiated by the manufacturer or the result of a NHTSA investigation, once the recall order is given, the manufacturer is required to notify all registered owners and purchasers by first-class mail. The notification will describe the problem and explain its potential safety risk. You must be told how you may get the defect repaired, when service will be available, and how much time will be required to complete the work on your car.

Despite the law's built-in safeguards to ensure that all affected owners are notified, oversights do occur and state DMV records can contain errors. With the value and operating safety of your car on the line, you may not want to passively wait until the manufacturer contacts you. Regularly log on to the NHTSA Web site to see if your car has an outstanding recall.

**Sources of help.** The NHTSA Web site (*www-odi.nhtsa.dot.gov /cars/problems/recalls/recallsearch.cfm*) allows you to enter the make, model, and year of your vehicle to search its database of recall orders. You can also find out if your car is subject to a recall campaign by calling the U.S. Department of Transportation toll-free Auto Safety Hotline (888-327-4236). The Edmunds Web site (*www.edmunds.com/maintenance/vehicle.do*) provides recall information through a searchable database for all vehicle makes and models. Finally, you can ask the service manager at the dealership to run a computer check on your car's VIN to see if a recall order has been issued.

# Lemons, Lemon Laws, and Lemon Aid

A lemon is a vehicle that continues to have a defect that substantially impairs its use, value, or safety after a reasonable number of attempts to repair it. Lemon laws vary from state to state but typically require the consumer to attempt to obtain repairs a minimum number of times and provide written notice to the dealer or manufacturer before pursuing a claim. Some states require fewer repair attempts when the defect is safety-related.

## Your legal protections

If you are convinced that your car is a lemon, you do have an abundance of laws on your side when you try to seek amends. A 1975 federal statute, the Magnuson-Moss Warranty Act, gives the buyer of any product costing more than $25, and that comes with a written warranty, the right to sue for redress and have attorney's fees covered also. The laws of all fifty states specify that the manufacturer of a defective new vehicle must provide repair or replacement when a substantial defect cannot be fixed in four tries, a safety defect that could cause death or serious injury within two tries, or the auto is out of service for 30 days, within the first 12,000 to 18,000 miles or 12 to 24 months. (Only about half of all states allow plaintiffs to recoup legal fees.) But with those legal rights come obligations on you to build your case breakdown by breakdown through documentation, correspondence, arbitration, and, if circumstances require, legal action.

## Document, document, document!

Keeping complete maintenance and repair records is a good idea for any car, but if you suspect your vehicle may be a lemon, a thorough documentary record of its history of repair attempts will be essential if you are going to have any chance of recovery. The paper trail you keep should demonstrate not only the unsuccessful efforts to repair a recurring problem but the routine oil changes, periodic check-ups, and other service visits that prove you held up your end of the bargain to take good care of the vehicle. If you have a problem that persists, write down its symptoms and carefully record the situations when it occurs. When you take your car in for servicing, be sure to describe the problem as precisely as you can to the service manager or mechanic who writes up your work order. If this is a repeat visit for correction of a problem that has reappeared, make sure you describe it exactly as you had before, and check that the work order records the problem just as you described it.

Precision on this point is essential; if there is any difference in how a defect is described, the dealership and manufacturer will justifiably be able to claim that they were not asked to repair a previously unaddressed flaw. For example, if your car experiences a recurring difficulty starting when cold and the dealership's mechanic simply writes "starter problem" on the work order, he may not be able to duplicate the symptom, and your documentary record will not reflect your original description.

When you bring your vehicle in for repair, note in your repair log the date, the odometer reading, and what you asked to be done in your maintenance log. When you pick the car up after the work is done, complete the incident entry by noting the date the work was completed, the description of the work done as it appears on the invoice, the invoice number, and what you paid for the job. (The sample repair log on page 368 provides a template you can use.)

In addition to a master record, ask for and keep all receipts for work you have done—even if it is for a warranty repair for which there is no charge. And, of course, test the vehicle carefully as soon as you bring it home to confirm that the problem was fixed. If the defect reappears, schedule another visit to the shop right away. Remember, the clock is running on your warranty or the state lemon law, and you don't want to have to be burdened with an unreliable vehicle any longer than absolutely necessary.

If you think that your vehicle has an irreparable glitch, expand your record-keeping. If your car ends up stranded on a highway shoulder on a wintry evening, for example, write down the date and time of the event, how long you had to wait for help to arrive, and how much you had to pay to have your car towed and/or for transportation home. Your ability to document the misery and cost you suffered as a result of your car's faults will prove helpful if you must later wage a legal fight for restitution.

## Time to talk

If after your first repeat visit to the service department, your car's problem hasn't been solved, you should have a candid discussion with the service manager about what the dealership intends to do to correct the defect. Review the steps that were taken to rectify the situation and let him know that you are aware that state law requires the dealership to fix the problem or make amends. Ask him to describe and put in writing the follow-up steps the dealership plans to take.

You may also want to take your vehicle to another mechanic for a diagnosis. Bring your repair log and other documentation with you so the new service shop can quickly be brought up to speed on the situation. You may have to pay for the second opinion, so get an estimate before any work is done. If you get a different diagnosis, discuss the new findings with the original mechanic.

If progress is still slow, it's time to move up the chain of command. The manufacturer's district manager may have the authority to approve additional repairs, reimburse you for your expenses, or buy back the vehicle. If he cannot or will not help, contact the manufacturer's customer service department and inquire about the company's procedures for filing a formal complaint.

Your letter to the manufacturer should be accompanied by copies (not originals) of your maintenance log and invoices demonstrating your efforts to have the problem repaired. It should also include descriptions of any inconvenience and expense caused by your car's breakdowns and a statement of your loss of confidence in its reliability and safety. Send the letter by certified mail, return receipt requested.

## Mediation

If you purchased or leased your car from a franchised dealer, you may be eligible for—or required to resort to—an arbitration procedure to resolve your complaint. This can be a perfectly satisfactory shortcut to a cost-effective resolution of your dispute. Many cases are handled by the Automotive Consumer Action Program (AUTOCAP), a group sponsored by auto dealers that has consumer representatives comprising at least half of its arbitration panels.

There are several good reasons you may wish to go this route. For one, in mediation you do not have to be represented by an attorney, sparing you legal bills. For another, the outcome of an arbitrator's ruling is not legally binding on you. If you don't like the result, you can still take the manufacturer to court. Whether you purchased a new car or a used one, an arbitration panel that decides on your behalf can require the automaker to reimburse you for your costs, buy back the vehicle, or both.

## Legal action

Ultimately, you may have to take the final step of resorting to the courts. Because the financial damages involved in the resolution of a new-car lemon law case can be substantial, you may not be able to resolve your case in a small claims court, where limits on damages are commonly capped at about $5,000 or less in most states. For a used-car claim, however, small claims court may be an ideal solution. Check with the court clerk on damage caps and filing procedures in your state.

Disputes involving larger damage claims must go to a higher court. This can be a complicated and very expensive undertaking, requiring the assistance of an attorney experienced in the litigation of lemon-law cases in your state. The initial consultation with the attorney should be free, and the laws in many states enable consumers to recover legal fees if their case prevails. Before you take this step, you will want to be sure that your paperwork is in order, that the record is airtight, and that you have the stomach

# Worksheet: Documenting Repeat Problems

| Repair Log | | | Vehicle Make & Model: | |
|---|---|---|---|---|
| **Date** | | **Odometer Reading** | **Repair Shop** | **Description of problem** (as indicated on work order) |
| **In** | **Out** | | | |
| | | | | |
| | | | | |
| | | | | |
| | | | | |
| | | | | |
| | | | | |
| | | | | |
| | | | | |
| | | | | |
| | | | | |
| | | | | |
| | | | | |
| | | | | |
| | | | | |
| | | | | |
| | | | | |
| | | | | |
| | | | | |
| | | | | |
| | | | | |
| | | | | |
| | | | | |
| | | | | |
| | | | | |
| | | | | |
| | | | | |

| Purchase Date: | Vehicle Identification Number: | |
|---|---|---|
| **Work Done** (as indicated on invoice) | **Work order/ Invoice number** | **Amount paid** |
| | | |
| | | |
| | | |
| | | |
| | | |
| | | |
| | | |
| | | |
| | | |
| | | |
| | | |
| | | |
| | | |
| | | |
| | | |
| | | |
| | | |
| | | |
| | | |
| | | |
| | | |
| | | |
| | | |
| | | |
| | | |
| | | |
| | | |
| | | |
| | | |
| | | |
| | | |
| | | |
| | | |

for a fight. As justifiably upset and abused as you may feel, you will want to have exhausted all other avenues before heading to court. Whatever the outcome, a lawsuit over a car that you found to be a lemon is sure to leave a sour taste in your mouth.

**Sources of help.** The best way to avoid buying a lemon is to check its pedigree before you purchase. For new and used cars, check CONSUMER REPORTS reliability ratings (see Appendix C). For advice on checking the history of used cars, see Chapter 6.

Web sites can provide answers about basic questions on lemon laws and guidance on what the state statutes require to make a lemon law claim. The Center for Auto Safety, a nonprofit consumer advocacy group, has a summary and complete text of each states law and a list of legal experts at its Web site, *www.autosafety.org.* On the site for the National Association of Consumer Advocates, *www.naca.net,* you can search the NACA member database for lawyers with lemon-law expertise.

# Appendices

■ APPENDIX A: Online Resources      **373**
■ APPENDIX B: Same Cars, Different Names      **375**
■ APPENDIX C: Car-Buying Resources from Consumer Reports      **379**

# Appendix A: Online Resources

## Major research sites

It's easy to research all aspects of buying a vehicle in just a few hours on the Internet. To help, we've put together this list of some of the major providers of auto information and services. While CONSUMER REPORTS has not rated and does not endorse sites listed here, they're included for you convenience. All Web addresses begin with "www."

For CONSUMER REPORTS' in-depth online resources, see Appendix C.

### BUYING INFORMATION

#### New- and Used-Car Buying & Selling

| | |
|---|---|
| Auto Trader | autotrader.com |
| Autobytel | autobytel.com |
| AutoVantage | autovantage.com |
| Autoweb | autoweb.com |
| CarBargains | checkbook.org |
| Car.com | car.com |
| Cars.com | cars.com |
| CarsDirect | carsdirect.com |
| Dealernet | dealernet.com |
| eBay | ebaymotors.com |
| Imotors | imotors.com |
| InvoiceDealers | invoicedealers.com |
| MSN Autos | autos.msn.com |
| Usedcars.com | usedcars.com |
| Vehix.com | vehix.com |

### Pricing: New & Used Cars

| | |
|---|---|
| AutoSite | autosite.com |
| Edmunds | edmunds.com |
| Intellichoice | intellichoice.com |
| Kelley Blue Book | kbb.com |
| National Automobile Dealer Association | nadaguides.com |
| VMR (used cars only) | vmrintl.com |

### Vehicle Reviews & Comparisons

| | |
|---|---|
| AutoWeek | autoweek.com |
| Automobile | automobilemag.com |
| Car and Driver | caranddriver.com |
| Epinions | epinions.com |
| J.D. Power | jdpower.com |
| Motor Trend | motortrend.com |
| MSN Autos | autos.msn.com |
| New Car Test Drive | nctd.com |
| Road & Track | roadandtrack.com |

## FINANCIAL INFORMATION

### Auto Loan Rates & Lenders

| | |
|---|---|
| Bank Rate Monitor | bankrate.com |
| Capital One Auto Finance | capitaloneautofinance.com |
| E-Loan | eloan.com |
| LendingTree | lendingtree.com |
| VirtualBank | virtualbank.com |

### Credit Reports

| | |
|---|---|
| Equifax | equifax.com |
| Experian | experian.com |
| FICO | myfico.com |
| My Credit | mycreditfile.com |
| Trans Union | transunion.com |

### Leasing Deals & Information

| | |
|---|---|
| Automotive Lease Guide | alg.com |
| Federal Reserve Board | federalreserve.gov/pubs/leasing |
| Intellichoice | intellichoice.com |
| LeaseSource | leasesource.com |

### Maintenance/Ownership Costs

| | |
|---|---|
| Dent Doctor Rx | dentdoctorusa.com |
| Dent Pro | dentpro.com |
| Ding King Dent Repair Tool | dingking.tv |
| Dent Out Paintless Dent Repair | dentout.net |
| Intellichoice | intellichoice.com |
| Edmunds | edmunds.com |

## CONSUMER INFORMATION

### Consumer Issues

| | |
|---|---|
| Edmunds | edmunds.com/maintenance/vehicle.do |
| Alldata | alldata.com/recalls |
| Consumers Union of U.S. | consumersunion.org |
| Consumer Web Watch | consumerwebwatch.org |
| National Association of Consumer Advocates | naca.net |
| Office of Defects Investigation | odi.nhtsa.dot.gov |

### Fuel Economy/Emissions

| | |
|---|---|
| AMES Award | amesaward.com |
| DOE/EPA fuel-economy estimates | fueleconomy.gov |
| EPA Green Vehicle Guide | epa.gov/greenvehicles |

### Safety/Crash Results

| | |
|---|---|
| Insurance Institute for Highway Safety | hwysafety.org |
| National Highway Traffic Safety Administration | nhtsa.dot.gov |
| NHTSA crash tests/ rollover ratings | safercar.gov |

### Vehicle History Reports

| | |
|---|---|
| Carfax | carfax.com |
| Experian | autocheck.com |

## AUTOMAKERS

These sites are best for checking retail prices, features, options, and specifications. Some let you check dealer inventories.

| | |
|---|---|
| Acura | acura.com |
| Audi | audiusa.com |
| BMW | bmwusa.com |
| Buick | buick.com |
| Cadillac | cadillac.com |
| Chevrolet | chevrolet.com |
| Chrysler | chrysler.com |
| Dodge | dodge.com |
| Ford | fordvehicles.com |
| GMC | gmc.com |
| Honda | hondacars.com |
| Hummer | hummer.com |
| Hyundai | hyundaiusa.com |
| Infiniti | infiniti.com |
| Isuzu | isuzu.com |
| Jaguar | jaguar.com/us |
| Jeep | jeep.com |
| Kia | kia.com |
| Land Rover | landrover.com |
| Lexus | lexus.com |
| Lincoln | lincolnvehicles.com |
| Lotus | lotuscars.com |
| Mazda | mazdausa.com |
| Mercedes-Benz | mbusa.com |
| Mercury | mercuryvehicles.com |
| Mini | miniusa.com |
| Mitsubishi | mitsubishicars.com |
| Nissan | nissanusa.com |
| Pontiac | pontiac.com |
| Porsche | us.porsche.com |
| Saab | saabusa.com |
| Saturn | saturn.com |
| Scion | scion.com |
| Subaru | subaru.com |
| Suzuki | suzukiauto.com |
| Toyota | toyota.com |
| Volkswagen | vw.com |
| Volvo | volvocars.com |

# Appendix B: Same Cars, Different Names

## A Car By Any Other Name ...

Let's say you're very interested in the Ford Explorer sport-utility vehicle. Knowing that the Lincoln Aviator and Mercury Mountaineer are essentially the same vehicle, except for the name and styling details, can open up a lot more possibilities for you in terms of the number of vehicles you can look at in your area and the number of dealers you can pit against each other to get the lowest price.

These three models are an example of what we call "twins," "triplets," or "quadruplets," depending on the number of related models. By producing these, automakers can use one basic model to fill a slot in the lineups of several brands.

Another trend that has gained momentum in recent years is to use one platform—essentially the drivetrain and undercarriage (suspension, brakes, axles, and so on)—as a basis for different models. While models that share platforms aren't as similar as true twins, they often have similar driving characteristics and can be a reasonable alternative.

To help you keep track of related models, we've put together the following list:

## Direct twins

| | |
|---|---|
| Acura MDX | Honda Pilot |
| Buick Terraza | Chevrolet Uplander, Pontiac Montana SV6, Saturn Relay |
| Chevrolet Astro | GMC Safari |
| Chevrolet Avalanche | Cadillac Escalade EXT |
| Chevrolet Colorado | GMC Canyon |
| Chevrolet Silverado | GMC Sierra |
| Chevrolet Tahoe | Cadillac Escalade, GMC Yukon |
| Chevrolet TrailBlazer | Buick Rainier, GMC Envoy, Isuzu Ascender, Saab 9-7X |
| Chrysler Town & Country | Dodge Caravan/Grand Caravan |
| Chrysler Sebring | Dodge Stratus |
| Ford Crown Victoria | Mercury Grand Marquis |
| Ford Escape | Mazda Tribute, Mercury Mariner |
| Ford Explorer | Lincoln Aviator, Mercury Mountaineer |
| Ford Expedition | Lincoln Navigator |
| Ford Freestar | Mercury Monterey |
| Ford Five Hundred | Mercury Montego |
| Ford Ranger | Mazda B-Series |
| Ford Taurus | Mercury Sable |
| GMC Yukon XL | Chevrolet Suburban, Cadillac Escalade ESV |
| Nissan Armada | Infiniti QX56 |
| Pontiac Vibe | Toyota Matrix |
| Saab 9-2X | Subaru Impreza |

# Similar platform

| | |
|---|---|
| Acura RSX | Honda Civic |
| Acura TL | Honda Accord |
| Audi A4 | Volkswagen Passat |
| Audi TT | Volkswagen New Beetle, Volkswagen Golf |
| BMW 3 Series | BMW X3 |
| BMW 5 Series | BMW 6 Series |
| Buick LaCrosse | Chevrolet Impala, Pontiac Grand Prix |
| Buick Rendezvous | Pontiac Aztek |
| Cadillac SRX | Cadillac CTS, STS |
| Chevrolet Corvette | Cadillac XLR |
| Chevrolet Equinox | Saturn Vue |
| Chrysler 300 | Dodge Magnum |
| Dodge Durango | Dodge Dakota |
| Ford Explorer Sport Trac | Ford Ranger, Mazda B-Series |
| Ford Five Hundred | Ford Freestyle |
| Honda Element | Honda CR-V |
| Hummer H2 | Chevrolet Tahoe, GMC Yukon |
| Hyundai Elantra | Hyundai Tucson, Kia Sportage, Kia Spectra |
| Hyundai XG350 | Kia Amanti |
| Infiniti FX | Infiniti G35 |
| Infiniti G35 | Nissan 350Z |
| Lexus ES330 | Toyota Camry |
| Lexus GX470 | Toyota 4Runner |
| Lexus LX470 | Toyota Land Cruiser |
| Lexus RX330/400h | Toyota Highlander, Sienna |
| Lincoln LS | Ford Thunderbird, Jaguar S-Type |
| Mazda3 | Volvo S40/V50 |
| Mitsubishi Lancer | Mitsubishi Outlander |
| Mitsubishi Galant | Mitsubishi Eclipse, Endeavor |

| | |
|---|---|
| Nissan Armada | Nissan Titan |
| Nissan Altima | Nissan Maxima, Quest |
| Nissan Frontier | Nissan Xterra |
| Pontiac G6 | Chevrolet Malibu |
| Scion xA | Scion xB |
| Toyota Camry | Toyota Camry Solara, Lexus ES330 |
| Toyota Sequoia | Toyota Tundra |
| Volkswagen Touareg | Porsche Cayenne |

# Appendix C: Other Car-Buying Resources from CONSUMER REPORTS

**There are numerous sources** of auto information today, in print and online. But just as there's a wide range of quality in the vehicles you can buy, there's also a wide range of quality in the information you get.

When buying a car, more people turn to CONSUMER REPORTS than to any other publication. That's because CR, which is published by the nonprofit Consumers Union, holds a unique place in the world of auto information. Unlike other publications that review cars, CR accepts no advertising, and we buy our test vehicles anonymously from dealerships rather than borrowing pre-prepped vehicles from manufacturers. That means the cars we test are in the same condition as the cars you buy. It also means we don't have to pull punches in our ratings, reviews, and safety information to avoid upsetting a manufacturer or advertiser.

In addition, CR has the most comprehensive auto-test program of any U.S. publication or Web site. Each CR-tested vehicle is is evaluated for months and driven for thousands of miles. Other reviewers typically drive vehicles for one or two weeks, or less. Our comprehensive reliability information is based on hundreds of thousands of responses from our annual subscriber surveys and we are the only publication that maintains a list of recommended vehicles. This list, along with our easy-to-reference list of the overall ranking of all tested vehicles is continually updated in our auto publications and on our Web site, ConsumerReports.org.

All this adds up to ratings and advice that you can trust to be thorough and unbiased. In short, we'll tell you what others won't.

## Where to find CONSUMER REPORTS auto information

CONSUMER REPORTS publishes automotive ratings, reviews, and advice in a number of different publications and on ConsumerReports.org. Publications with automotive information include the following:

**CONSUMER REPORTS magazine.** Every issue of CONSUMER REPORTS, except the April Annual Auto Issue, includes head-to-head tests of several competitive vehicles, ranging from sedans to sports cars to SUVs. Each report includes full test results and a summary of each vehicle's driving performance and overall highs and lows. You'll also find regular features on important automotive issues, first looks at new models, and tests of tires and popular aftermarket auto products.

**CONSUMER REPORTS' Annual Auto Issue.** Every year, the April issue of the magazine is devoted entirely to cars. It includes summary reviews of all available models, complete ratings of all of our tested vehicles, comprehensive reliability and safety information, a guide to the best and worst used cars, and updates on the latest automotive issues that affect consumers.

**CONSUMER REPORTS' autumn "What's new in cars" issue.** The October issue of CONSUMER REPORTS includes a special automotive section that looks at what's new in the auto market for the upcoming model year. It also includes other timely articles on trends and products.

**CONSUMER REPORTS car publications.** CR also publishes a series of special automotive publications and buying guides that are available at newsstands and bookstores. These provide a convenient way to check the latest ratings and other key information on the vehicles you're considering.

For new-car buyers, the series includes:

- New Car Buying Guide
- Complete Pricing & Ratings Guide
- New Car Preview
- New Car Ratings & Reviews
- Best & Worst New Cars

Each new-car publication includes summary reviews, key specifications, and a rundown of safety features and crash tests for all current models, as well as up-to-date ratings on tested vehicles and detailed reliability charts for most models.

For used-car buyers, the series includes:

- Used Car Buying Guide
- Used Car Reviews

Each used-car publication includes a summary review of all major 1- to 8-year-old models, as well as detailed reliability ratings, average price ranges for each model year, available safety features, and crash-test results.

## How CONSUMER REPORTS can help you online

CONSUMER REPORTS has provided an online companion Web site to this book at *www.ConsumerReports.org/smartcar*. The companion site contains links to CR's main Web site, where you can find a wide array of other free auto information on topics ranging from our list of Top Picks or best-in-class vehicles to safety updates.

Because Consumers Union doesn't accept advertising, Consumer

Reports.org is primarily a subscription site. Site subscribers can access all of CR's up-to-date ratings on vehicle performance, comfort and convenience, reliability, owner satisfaction, safety features, crash-test results, and more, which can be vital in choosing the right vehicle for your needs and lifestyle. You'll also be able to read the full road-test reports on all of CR's tested vehicles and use interactive tables that let you easily compare the test results, dimensions, and cargo capacity of different vehicles.

Subscribers also have the full run of CONSUMER REPORTS' online information. This includes feature articles on timely consumer issues, test results and ratings on products ranging from tires and batteries to digital cameras and lawn mowers, and a wealth of buying advice on everything from auto maintenance and aftermarket auto products to personal finance and health and fitness. Subscriptions are available on an annual ($26) or monthly ($4.95) basis. Subscribers to CONSUMER REPORTS magazine get a special discount price of $19 a year.

## CONSUMER REPORTS premium car-buying services

To further help car buyers, CR offers several for-pay services that can help you, whether you're just starting the buying process or ready to cinch your best deal. For more detailed information go to *www.ConsumerReports.org /carbuying.*

### For new-car buyers:

**New Car Price Reports.** Available for any current model, these reports are designed to help you get the best deal by giving you all the pricing information you should know before you negotiate. Each report includes retail and dealer-invoice prices for each trim level and option. It shows you any available consumer rebates or unadvertised dealer incentives or discounts. You'll get the CR Wholesale Price, which goes beyond the dealer-invoice price to give you a good starting point for your price negotiations. The CR Wholesale Price is the dealer-invoice price minus the holdback and any sales incentives that are currently available, which gives you a close approximation of what the dealer paid for a vehicle.

Each report includes alternative models that CR recommends and key safety information, including crash-test results. New Car Price Reports cost $12 ($10 for each additional model) and can be ordered online or by calling 800-422-1079. Reports can be mailed, faxed, or viewed online.

**New Car Buying Kit.** This interactive online service gives you a number of valuable CONSUMER REPORTS car-buying tools and services all in one place. The kit helps you select, research, and compare models, and gives you the same key pricing information described above. A three-month subscription ($39) allows you to:

- Get unlimited New Car Price Reports online
- Use a sophisticated interactive selector that uses CR's ratings to help you pinpoint vehicles that meet your personal priorities
- Consult CR's in-depth, behind-the-scenes technical reports on all tested cars
- Do side-by-side model comparisons of test results, ratings, specifications, and more

## For used-car buyers:

**Used Car Price Reports.** These reports help you assess the value of any 1- to 8-year-old used car, which is critical information, whether you're buying, trading in, or selling one yourself. Each report includes the retail and wholesale values for the base model, plus step-by-step information for determining the value of a specific vehicle by factoring in the mileage, options, and condition.

Each report also includes CR's reliability ratings in 14 different areas. Used Car Price Reports cost $10 and can be ordered online or by calling 800-422-1079. Reports can be mailed, faxed, or viewed online.

**Used Car Buying Kit.** This online subscription service will help you research and price a used car. A three-month subscription ($24) allows you to:

- Get unlimited Used Car Price Reports online
- Get a list of vehicles that meet your personal priorities by using our interactive selector
- Read original road-test reports from our comprehensive test program.
- Do side-by-side model comparisons of test results, ratings, specifications, and more

The book you hold in your hands is just the beginning of how CONSUMER REPORTS can help you buy your next car. The expert advice and in-depth information in these pages will guide you through the buying process and prepare you for the dealership experience. Then, to get the latest ratings, reviews, reliability and safety information, and more, see CR's other auto publications, the Autos area of ConsumerReports.org, or one of CR's helpful car-buying services. They can be a vital aid in helping you choose a vehicle you'll be happy with for years to come.